Challenges
and development

Challenges and development

Adult education research in Nordic countries

Editorial committee

Sigvart Tøsse, Norway. Chief editor
Pia Falkencrone, Denmark
Arja Puurula, Finland
Bosse Bergstedt, Sweden

Tapir Academic Press

© Tapir Academic Press, Trondheim 1999

ISBN 82-519-1546-5

Front-page illustration:
Kjell Nupen: "Meridan"
© Kjell Nupen / BONO 1999

Printed by Tapir
Binding: Grafisk Produksjonsservice AS

Secretariat:
Bodil Blom and Margit Lea Myklebust,
Norwegian Institute of Adult Education

Tapir Academic Press
N–7005 TRONDHEIM

Tel.: + 47 73 59 32 10
Fax: + 47 73 59 32 04
Email: tapir.forlag@tapir.ntnu.no
http://www.tapir.no

PREFACE

The present book is a continuation of the series *Social Changes and Adult Education Research* first published in 1992, and subsequently in 1993, 1994, 1995 and 1997. The 1998 yearbook is entitled *Corporate and non-formal learning*, with the subtitle *Adult Education Research in Nordic Countries*. The aim of the book is to present the most recent, on-going research into adult education in the Nordic countries to an international audience.

The yearbook is a joint enterprise by educational institutions in Denmark, Finland, Norway and Sweden, with one person from each country constituting the editorial staff. The editors have been responsible for the selection of articles from their respective countries. All are new articles which have not previously been published outside the Nordic countries. Although the yearbook cannot give a complete picture of the research being carried out in these countries, it nonetheless represents current trends of research and areas of interest in the field of adult education research.

The editorial committee.

INTRODUCTION

Sigvart Tøsse

The selection of articles presented in this Nordic yearbook of adult education research in the Nordic countries confirm that the current trend of research is towards studies of learning processes and opportunities in working life, labour market training and human resource development. More recently the studies of the ageing workforce have been added to this vocational trend. A relatively new theme represented here is the relationship between entrepreneurship and education. The book also concerns the development of adult education in general, offer a critical discussion of forms knowledge and a conceptual approach to mapping political education. A common aspect is that the contributions address problems in adult education, development and future challenges, which reflect the present ambivalence, uncertainty and feeling of being in a period of transition. The following is intended to give a short presentation.

Per-Erik Ellström is revisiting some of the issues, problems and arguments that were put forward in the studies of the Swedish Labour Market Training in the late 1980s. On the bases of these studies he makes a distinguishing between two cultural orientation, labelled the school culture and factory culture, which differ in a number of respects, e.g. with respect to teaching goals and content, teacher roles, and communication style. He explains the marginal position of the Swedish LMT-system from the mid 1940s to the early 1990s in terms of those two, partly inconsistent, institutional environments, the world of work and the world of education respectively. Ellström concludes that the cultural factors and the professional orientation have been very important determinants of teaching practice within LMT and he claim that this teaching culture is closely related to a scholastic type of paradigm.

One of the researchers in the Danish project Working Life, Learning Processes, and Democratization *Steen Høyrup* analyzes the experiences of implementing The Danish Confederation and Trade Unions' vision of "The Developing Work", which is intended to benefit both the individual worker and the firms. A focus on the workplace as a learning environment requires however a clarification and redefinition of the concept of learning. The first part of the article is accordingly devoted to an outline of the Concept of Learning and reflections concerning different spheres of learning. In the second part Høyrup discusses what kind of learning is a necessary precondition for employees' functioning in production groups (teams) and describes what characterize teams as learning environments. Results and experiences from the research project give basic knowledge to this discussion.

A great challenge facing the labour market is the ageing labour force and the effect of human resource management policies as a means of combating the pull and push factors of early exit. *Erika Löfström* and *Maarit Pitkänen* have studied 100 small and medium size enterprises in Finland and explored attitudes towards ageing workers and suggestions of training areas for the older ones. Attitudes are overall positive, but significant differences were found between age groups and between managers and older workers. Special training programmes and other measures especially designed for the ageing are found rare, partly due to the unawareness of the ageing in general. The authors question however if it is necessary to design programmes only for older workers as the effects of such programmes in small or medium size companies are not proved to fill existing gaps between generations, rather it could possible create or strengthen antagonism.

The contribution of *Jukka Tuomisto* is a critical analysis of learning opportunities in working life. Against the dominant individualistic emphasis in international discussions of lifelong learning and the mantra of 'self-directiveness', Tuomisto is particularly focused on the role of social structures in developing lifelong learning. Structures examined are the labour market system, production relationships, development of means of production, structure of workforce, and nature of work. The author is however not defending structural factors against individual psychological factors but argue for the need of interaction of social structures and the development of learning opportunities. This relationship is discussed on the macro, meso, and micro level.

Entrepreneurship is a relatively new theme in educational discourses and as *Paula Kyrö* states entrepreneurship and education do not share a common scientific knowledge base. It is nevertheless interesting to relate these two fields of science to each other and Paula Kyrö highlights some of the essential features of entrepreneurship from the traditional to the postmodern area. In her article entrepreneurship and education search for each other is approached from a historical and cultural perspective. Like narratives it comprises past and present and she suggest that in the present post-modern transition learning theories have started to value those qualities involved in entrepreneurship. The validity of this will however depend on our actions. Thus, what entrepreneurship can give to education will be seen in the future, Kyrö concludes.

Ove Korsgaard claims there has been a shift from an old phenomenon of educating adults to adult education, which around 1970 in Denmark became related to the concept of lifelong learning. This also implied a shift from education to development. Korsgaard presents Professor K. Grue-Sørensen as a critic to new trend and adjoining concepts of adult pedagogy and contrasts him with professor Johan Fjord Jensen who propagated "the gospel of adult age". Fjord Jensen was deeply influenced by the humanistic growth psychology and saw a decisive difference between educating young people and educating adults. Fjord Jensen – as the author himself – is however sceptical to the latest trend back to an education which partly consists of training and instruction. According to Fjord Jensen all adult education is not proper education.

On the basis of the history of ideas *Bernt Gustavsson* is focusing on three forms of knowledge. His trisection of knowledge, originating from Platos' and Aristotle's episteme, techne and phronesis, are scientific knowledge, practical professional knowledge, and ethical-political knowledge. These three forms of knowledge are still existing and are much disputed in philosophical and scientific literature. The aim of the article is to describe what characterizes these three forms, from what traditions they have sprung, and to compare them with the purpose to demonstrate how they relate to each other. The critical difference, Gustavsson says, is that the theoretical conception of knowledge, characterized as abstract and universal, is supplemented by two practical forms of knowledge which are contextual and situational.

Arild Mikkelsen, is concerned about the possibilities to sustain the ideals of Popular Enlightenment in the future of a globalized world. The Nordic movement of popular education and enlightenment has both been a counter-cultural force and an integrated and vital element in the development of the national. Mikkelsen asks the question whether the movement should fight to retain the influence it once had, or resign and preserve its tradition in a museum. Making references to different writers such as Habermas, Lasch, Giddens, and Bauman Mikkelsen discusses solutions and possibilities. Drawing from the best of them he concludes that the Nordic tradition has a potential in a globalized world. Against those who argue to build shelters against the blowing wind of globalization Mikkelsen proposes to build windmills for the utilization of the wind.

The point of departure of *Petri Salo* and *Juha Suoranta* is the discoursive practices which are an integral part of the hegemonic struggle of adult education. From a discussion of three moments of the history of adult education they move on to a forth, the movement of life politics, which they predict to be the trend of the future. Life politics is however challenged and counteracted by the present vocabulary of education as a vehicle for economic efficiency and growth. The authors taking a critical-constructionist stance, examine the possibilities of a new scheme of adult education practice with a particular focus on improving people's welfare and empowerment. Admitting that ambivalence according at present a basic experience, as Beck says, they argue for the productions of new meanings and the creation of active, collectively oriented solutions. There is a need of being more conscious about the choices of life and the challenge of adult education is to strengthen our general reflexive capacity in life.

The concluding article of *Sigvart Tøsse* is a conceptual approach to analyzing political education. The foundations of political education are first discussed. The main arguments for political education derive from the obligations of democracy, pedagogical imperatives and the Marxist theory. Second the article is concerned with how the practice of political education should be described and analyzed. One conceptual approach is to analyze this education in terms of aims, content, methods, arenas, clientele, and effects. The concept comprises also several and interrelated dimensions which provide the researcher with the additional approach of analyzing the value dimension, information dimension, inquiry dimension, and participation dimension. In the theory and practice of political education we may also distinguish different positions and approaches. Four of them discussed in the article is the liberal position, the community approach, the radical and Marxist criticism, and the position of Freire. Finely the article discusses the difference between political education and other related concepts such as education for citizenship, civic education, and political literacy.

Content

PREFACE --- i
INTRODUCTION -- vii

Working life challenges and learning processes

BETWEEN WORK AND EDUCATION: ON THE CULTURAL SHAPING OF VOCATIONAL EDUCATION AND TRAINING (VET)
Per-Erik Ellström --- 1

THE PRODUCTION GROUP AS A LEARNING ENVIRONMENT - ILLUSTRATED BY A CASE AND VARIOUS ASPECTS OF THE CONCEPT OF LEARNING
Steen Höyrup -- 23

AGEING WORKERS, HRM AND TRAINING IN SMEs
Erika Löfström and Maarit Pitkänen -- 41

ENTREPRENEURSHIP AND EDUCATION SEARCH FOR EACH OTHER IN THE POSTMODERN TRANSITION
Paula Kyrö --- 69

SOCIAL STRUCTURE AND LIFELONG LEARNING
Critical analysis of learning opportunities in working life
Jukka Toumisto -- 99

Adult education development and lifelong learning

EDUCATION OF ADULTS VERSUS ADULT EDUCATION
Ove Korsgaard --- 121

POPULAR ENLIGHTENMENT - PRESERVED IN MUSEUMS OR STILL ON DUTY?
Arild Mikkelsen -- 135

THE FOUR MOMENTS OF ADULT EDUCATION: FROM MORAL ECONOMY TO LIFE POLITICS
Petri Salo and Juha Suoranta -- 149

Forms of knowledge

THREE FORMS OF KNOWLEDGE
Bernt Gustavsson -- 169

Political education

POLITICAL EDUCATION: A CONCEPTUAL APPROACH
Sigvart Tøsse --- 187

Contributors -- 209

BETWEEN WORK AND EDUCATION: ON THE CULTURAL SHAPING OF VOCATIONAL EDUCATION AND TRAINING (VET)

Per-Erik Ellström

Introduction

In the late 1980s and early 1990s the present author and co-workers (e.g. Ellström & Svedin, 1989; Ellström, Davidsson & Rönnqvist, 1990; Ellström, 1992) carried out a series of studies concerning the restructuring of the Swedish Labour Market Training (LMT) that took place in 1986, and the consequences of this with respect to LMT as a "learning environment" (see also Ellström, 1999 b). On the basis of these studies, it was possible to distinguish between two cultural orientations that were shown to shape the content and practices of the teaching. These two teaching cultures were labelled the school culture and the factory culture, respectively. It also proved possible to distinguish between these two cultures in terms of teaching goals and content, teaching practices, teacher roles and communication style.

The purpose of this paper is to revisit some of the issues, problems and arguments that were put forward in this series of studies of Swedish Labour Market Training in the late 1980s, and to explore their implications for our present understanding of: (a) the role of institutional and cultural factors as driving forces for the restructuration of vocational education and training (VET) systems; (b) the importance and role of cultural factors in the shaping of teacher roles, teaching content and practices; and (c) different cultures and paradigms of teaching in relation to a dynamic labour market with changing competence requirements.

If these ideas are also of some relevance to other VET-systems, there are some quite strong implications not only for the strategies and practices of educational reform within this field, but also for the relations between VET and the labour market, particularly, the role of VET in the formation of occupational competencies for a dynamic labour market.

Theoretical Perspective

Much of the research, and also the policy debate concerning the relations between VET and the labour market, seems to be strongly influenced by a technological-functional view of education (for an overview and critical perspectives on research within this field, see Nijhof & Brandsma, 1999). According to this view (see e.g. Collins, 1979), the VET-system is assumed to be able to provide - in a more or less unproblematic way - the qualifications required by the labour market. If the qualification requirements are expected to change in certain ways, it is assumed that the VET-system is able to adapt to these changes, thereby providing a competent work force with qualifications which correspond to the new requirements of the labour market. Thus, there is a strong belief in the possibility that the VET-system can be shaped in accordance with changes in the labour market through policy decisions, i.e. the VET-system is seen as a malleable tool in the hands of policy makers.

Contrary to this view, there is, however, considerable empirical evidence and theoretical arguments to the effect that the educational system has a relative autonomy both in relation to the state and in relation to the labour market (e.g. Dale, 1982; 1997; Carnoy & Levin, 1985). Furthermore, as indicated by a number of organizational studies, particularly studies undertaken within a neo-institutional perspective, educational organizations are only to a limited extent rational instruments for achieving stated goals. Rather, there is ample evidence that organizational structures and processes, including educational practices, to a large extent emerge as the result of conflicts and compromises between different interests and ideologies, or as the more or less unintended products of contextual constraints and possibilities, and culturally determined rules of appropriateness or obligation (March and Olsen, 1989; Meyer and Rowan, 1977; Meyer and Scott, 1983; Scott, 1987; 1991; 1995).

Consistent with the latter perspective, the present paper argues that VET-systems, their content and educational practices, are not primarily the results of deliberate decisions on the part of policy makers, but rather the more or less unintended results of cultural and institutional processes with dynamics of their own. An important mechanism behind this process of cultural shaping is the normative pressure on teachers and other professionals to act in conformity with different ideologies and cultural assumptions (cf. DiMaggio & Powell, 1983; Scott, 1991; 1995; Swidler, 1986). An important consequence of this thesis is, of course, a considerable scepticism concerning the possibility of controlling and changing teaching content and practices through centrally defined policies.

Swedish Labour Market Training in a Historical Perspective - From Governmental Agency to State Owned Company

Labour market training (LMT) has traditionally been one of the most important measures for implementing Swedish labour market policy, and, thereby, also overall economic policy (Dahlberg and Tuijnman, 1991; Ellström, 1999 b; Ellström and Svedin, 1989). In its modern form, labour market training dates from the middle of the 1940s when a new governmental agency (Royal Board of Vocational Education and Training, in Swedish abbreviation: KÖY) was established and became responsible for all vocational education and training, including courses for unemployed people. Until then VET had been a part of the National Board of Education. This new agency was explicitly established in order to underline and strengthen the relations between VET and the labour market, but also in order to mark the special character of VET as distinct from other fields of education, and its need for a closer relation to the development of the labour market (Marklund, 1982; Murray, 1988). The volumes of labour market training were, however, quite low during the 40s and most of the 50s. It was not until the late 50s that the training volume started to expand (Ellström & Svedin, 1989).

From the mid 1960s the governmental agency (KÖY) responsible for VET, including labour market training, was formally integrated within the National Board of Education (NBE) in an effort to create a comprehensive system of VET and general education. However, with respect to labour market training, the integration was only partial. Formally, the labour market training became jointly governed by two central agencies: the NBE and the central labour market agency called the National Labour Market Board (NLMB). The latter had the fiscal responsibility and the overall responsibility for LMT as a labour market policy measure. More specifically, this meant that the NLMB was responsible for determining the scope, vocational orientation, and location of the training. This authority was also responsible for the recruitment of trainees, decisions on training grants, and providing assistance in finding employment for trainees on completion of their training. Thus, while the NLMB was the commissioning authority, the NBE had the operative responsibility for executing the training courses. This responsibility included the administrative, educational, technical, and financial management of the training courses arranged at the 50 or 50 local LMT-Centres all over the country (Ellström & Svedin, 1989).

This administrative system, with two governmental agencies jointly responsible for the labour market training, remained until the restructuration of the LMT in 1986 (Ellström, 1999 b; Ellström & Svedin, 1989). This meant that the formerly strong organizational link to the educational system was broken. As in the 1940s the LMT-system was separated from the system of general education. The new LMT-system that was established through this restructuration had a separate board - the National Board of Labour Market Training - with, at least formally, only limited powers (the duties of the Board comprised only supervisory functions with respect to the quality of the training and its economic results, decisions on syllabi, and developmental work). The new organization was strongly decentralized, and organized as a group of 24 commissioned authorities (one in each county). Each of these regional authorities was supposed to cover its costs by selling training courses to the labour market authorities, other authorities, and firms competing on equal terms with other providers of training on the market. The general idea behind this restructuring may be characterized by threGe keywords: decentralization, flexibility and market-orientation. Thus, after the reform in 1986 most of the formal organizational bonds to the educational sector were broken (for a detailed analysis of this restructuring and the history of labour market training, see Ellström and Svedin, 1989).

In spite of all the efforts invested in the 1986 reform, a new major restructuring was initiated again at the beginning of the 1990s. In 1992 labour market training was transformed into a state owned company (AMU Gruppen AB). This was officially done as an effort to further strengthen the relations between LMT and the labour market, and to continue the process of decentralization and increased market-orientation. After 1992 there have been a number of restructuring measures and reductions in personnel, educational programmes, and premises (during 1997 the goal was to reduce the personnel by 40 per cent). Today the company is organized into four so-called business areas focused on: (a) advanced vocational training within different occupational areas; (b) programmes for business development in large companies and organizations; (c) development of basic vocational qualifications to increase individuals' chances of employment; and (d) training of people with functional handicaps in order to increase their opportunities to find worthwhile work (Annual Report, AMU Gruppen AB, 1997).

In sum, then, the Swedish Labour Market Training (LMT) system has, during the last 50 years, been the object of at least four major restructurings. An important focus in all these has been the relations between the LMT-system, the labour market and the general educational system. It is one of the main theses of this paper: (i) that the LMT-system historically has had a marginal position between two institutional environments, in the text below identified as the world of work and the world of education, respectively; (ii) that this marginal position created a number of latent contradictions within the LMT-system; (ii) contradictions which, taken together, became an important driving force behind the different restructurings of the LMT-system from the mid 1940s up to recent changes during the 1990s.

On the Marginal Position of Labour Market Training: Between the Worlds of Work and Education

As indicated above, Swedish Labour Market Training (LMT) has historically been a part of two policy sectors: on the one hand, and primarily, the labour market policy sector; and on the other, the educational policy sector. Although the reform in 1986 changed the formal organization and in part the means of financing LMT, its double role as part of two policy sectors did not change. Thus, also after the 1986 reform LMT was supposed to be guided by two sets of goals as decided by the Parliament (Government Bill 1984/85:59), i.e. both the goals of labour market policy, emphasizing economic stabilization and growth, and the goals of the adult education policy, emphasizing education as a way to increase the participation of adults in cultural, social, and political life (the so-called democracy goal), and, of course, as a way to meet individual demands for further and continuing education. Furthermore, in contrast to the mainly reactive role of LMT emphasized by labour market policy, the adult education goals express a more proactive role, stating that LMT should educate adults for a variety of tasks, and, thereby, "contribute to changes of the working life" (Government Bill 1984/85:59, p. 7).

Now, as already mentioned, the main argument of this paper is that these two policy sectors represent two partly inconsistent institutional environments, called the world of work and the world of education, respectively, and that these inconsistencies are mirrored in the content and teaching practices within LMT (see Figure 1 below). As defined here, the notion of institutional environment refers to socially constructed and institutionalized beliefs, ideologies, and norms to which individual organizations must conform if they are to receive support and legitimacy from their environments (DiMaggio and Powell, 1983; Meyer and Rowan, 1977; Meyer and Scott, 1983).

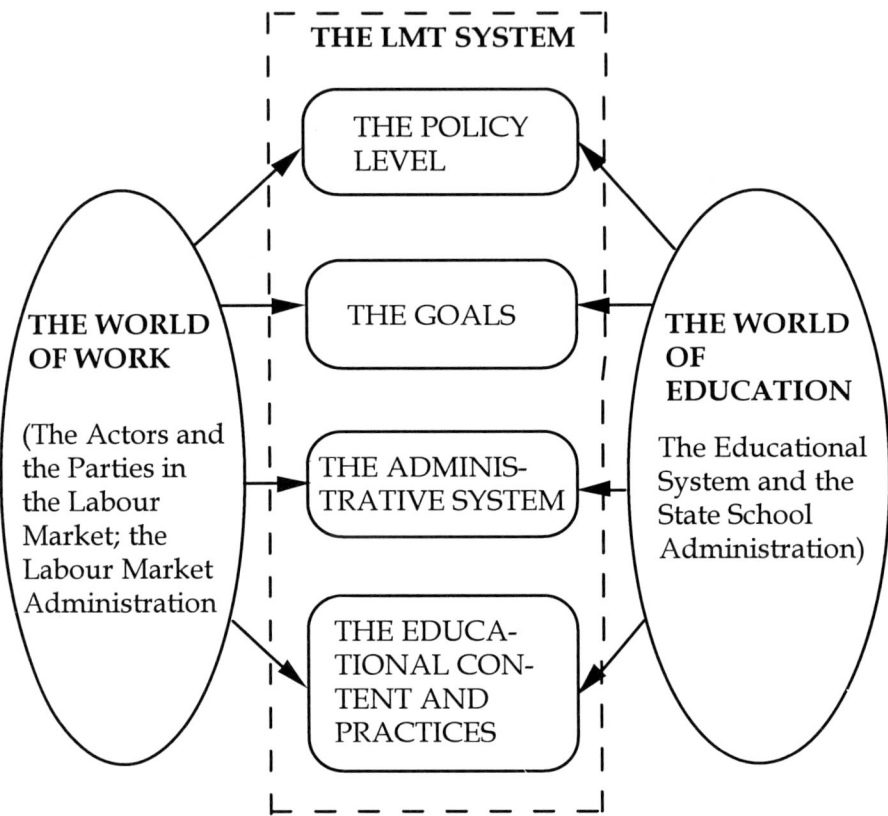

Figure 1: The Model of Analysis.

The worlds of work and education are conceived of as two social spheres or fields that, in the words of DiMaggio and Powell (1983), constitute recognized areas of institutional life. More specifically, the world of work is assumed to comprise the different collective actors in the labour market, that is, firms and agencies, the organized interests of the supply and the demand side of the labour market (i.e. unions and employer associations), and the state labour market administration. The world of education is, at least seemingly, more homogeneous. This world is assumed to comprise the educational system and the state school administration.

As indicated above, it is assumed that the worlds of work and education place different and, at least partly, inconsistent demands on LMT. More specifically, it is assumed that these two societal spheres represent different *institutional logics*, and, thereby, different norms and belief systems concerning the characteristics of a modern, rational, effective etc. labour market training. What, then, are assumed to be the main differences between these two institutional environments? A fundamental difference seems to be related to their primary social function. Following an influential tradition in the sociology of education (Bernstein, 1977; Lundgren, 1984; Carnoy & Levin, 1985), a distinction is usually made between productive and reproductive functions and processes in society. In terms of this distinction, the worlds of work and education may be equated with *the social sphere of economic and cultural production* and the sphere of *economic and cultural reproduction*, respectively. At least with respect to the world of work, this way of characterizing its social function is complicated by the fact that this sphere, as defined here, comprises also the parties of the labour market and the state labour market administration. However, on both theoretical and empirical grounds (Offe, 1985; Rothstein, 1986) it may be argued that these organizations are subordinated to the social function of production.

Now, this difference with respect to primary social function between the worlds of education and work may be expected to imply a number of differences with respect to basic norms and belief systems concerning the functions, the content, and practices of vocational education and training (VET). One example of such a difference is the traditional emphasis on values of democracy, justice, and equality within the world of education, and, in line with this orientation an emphasis on the distributional goals of education. This is in contrast to the traditional emphasis within the world of work on values of productivity and economic growth, and on the role of VET as an instrument for promoting these values. In the Swedish policy debate concerning the content and goals of labour market training and other forms of VET, these basic differences in values have been mirrored, among other things in the issue of specialized vocational training oriented towards a specific occupation versus more general vocational training oriented toward a broader occupational area, but also in discussions concerning the emphasis on general subjects (e.g. language, maths) versus vocational subjects in labour market training.

What relative influence, then, have the worlds of education and work, respectively, had on the policy and practice of labour market training? Using the metaphor of a magnetic field with two opposite poles corresponding to the work and education, respectively, it is assumed that these opposite poles represent forces that tend to attract and move the system in two different directions. As shown by Ellström and Svedin (1989), the two spheres had, at least until the reform in 1986, varying degrees of influence at different levels/subsystems of the LMT-system (see Table 1 below).

Table 1: An Analysis of the Relative Influence of the Worlds of Work and Education on the Labour Market Training System.

Level/Subsystem of LMT	The Relative Influence of:	
	the World of Work	the World of Education
The Policy Level	Strong	Weak
The Goals	Strong	Weak
The Administrative System	Weak	Strong
The Teaching Content and Practices	Weak	Strong

As is clear from Table 1, the influence of the world of work relative to the world of education has traditionally been very strong at the policy level. This is fairly obvious and mirrors the fact that LMT is primarily a measure of labour market policy, and only secondary an educational policy measure. However, if one looks at the operational levels, i.e. the levels of administration and teaching, the relative influence of the two worlds has been almost reversed. Up to the reform in 1986, the administrative system at the central, regional, and local levels was heavily controlled by the formerly National Board of Education (NBE), and, thereby, by the world of education. The influence of the world of education was strong also at the level of teaching, that is, with respect to the content and methods of training. In contrast, the world of work had only a relatively weak and indirect influence both on the administration of LMT and on the actual content and methods of teaching.

According to this analysis, there was, at least until the 1986 reform, a split or a decoupling (Meyer and Rowan, 1977) between the policy level and the operational levels, or between what Lindensjö and Lundgren (1986) call the area of policy formulation and the area of policy realization. Thus, while LMT at the policy level was clearly influenced by the world of work, it may, at the operational levels (the levels of administration and teaching), be more aptly described as serving the interests and policies of the educational world. In this perspective, the reorganization in 1986 and perhaps also the reorganization in 1992, may be analysed as an attempt to handle the asymmetry in influence between the two worlds, and also as an attempt to tighten the loose couplings between the policy level and the operational levels of the LMT-system.

Challenges and development

However, in order to understand more clearly the tensions within the LMT-system as a driving force for the different restructurings it is necessary to introduce another dimension in the analysis. This dimension concerns the degree of centralization and decentralization of the LMT-system. If we cross this latter dimension with the dimension discussed above, i.e. between the worlds of work and education, it is possible to construct the scheme of analysis shown in Figure 2.

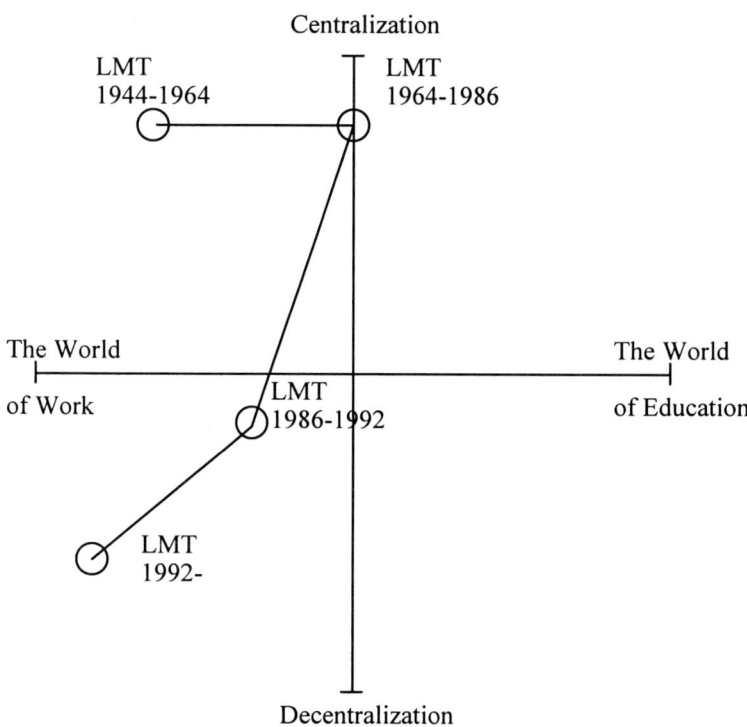

Figure 2: The Different Restructurings of the Swedish Labour Market Training.

As is clear from Figure 2, the different restructurings of the LMT-system may be understood as a movement from a strong formal degree of centralization to an increasing degree of decentralization during the 1980s and 1990s. Before the reorganization in 1986, most decisions concerning the administrative, educational, technical and financial management of the education and training all over the country were made centrally within the National Board of Education (NBE). Thus, the bureau within NBE responsible for LMT was a kind of large scale "principle's office". In this perspective the reorganization in

1986 meant a considerable decentralization to the regional level, but also to the level of the local training centre.

In the other dimension the restructurings may be understood as a movement from a strong influence of the world of work during the period mid 40s to mid 60s to a stronger influence from the world of education during the expansive period of the 60s, 70s and early 80s. After that period of time the links to the world of education were broken almost completely, first with the establishment of a separate Board of Labour Market Training in 1986, and later through the establishment of LMT as a state owned company in 1992.

Institutional Environments, Teaching Cultures and the Content and Practices of Teaching

A basic thesis within neo-institutional theory of organizations (see e.g. Scott, 1995; Thomas et al, 1987), is that organizational structures, processes, and cultures are structured by and tend to become isomorphic with their institutional environments. The underlying idea is that the ability of an organization to conform to its institutional environment is an important precondition for its legitimacy, for its ability to attract resources, and, ultimately, for its survival. Furthermore, it is assumed that organizations facing *inconsistent* institutional environments tend to develop structures, processes, and cultures that are isomorphic to these inconsistencies in their institutional environment (Brunsson, 1989; DiMaggio and Powell, 1983; Meyer and Rowan, 1977; Meyer and Scott, 1983).

Applying this neo-institutional thesis to the analysis of Swedish Labour Market Training (LMT) as given in the preceding sections, it may be asked to what extent the marginal position of LMT between the world of work and education, respectively, is mirrored in the teaching culture, and the content and practices of teaching within labour market training. Although we do not have longitudinal data on these aspects of the LMT-system, there are data from the late 1980s, when a follow-up study of the 1986 reform was carried out.

This study, which is reported in Ellström, Davidson, and Rönnqvist (1990), was carried out as an analysis of the learning environment of nine schools (LMT Centres) in three counties. The purpose of this study was to describe and analyse the teaching process within LMT, and the extent to which the teaching processes was shaped by contextual factors at a societal and an organizational level. Thus, the purpose was to study if and how teaching processes at the micro level, i.e. at the level of the classroom, were related to, and possibly explained by, contextual factors at a meso or a macro level. The data were collected through: (a) questionnaires to administrators, teachers, and trainees; (b) structured interviews with administrators and teachers; and (c) systematic observation of the teaching in three subjects at three of the schools.

In support of the neo-institutional thesis mentioned above, two teaching cultures were identified, labelled the *factory culture* and the *school culture* (Ellström et al., 1990; cf. Berner, 1989). The two teaching cultures that were identified, were assumed to have their roots at an institutional level, i.e. in the the world of work and education, respectively (these and a number of other differences between the two cultures of teaching are summarized in Table 2 below).

The two cultures were shown to be characterized by, among other things, different views of teaching and the role of the teacher. A teacher belonging to the factory culture tended to view the school as a factory, the teaching as a production process, and his own role as analogous to that of a factory foreman. He also tended to identify himself with the values and social patterns of his "old" occupation. In contrast, a teacher belonging to the school culture was more likely to have cut the emotional bonds to his "old" occupation, and had instead adopted a traditional teacher role (cf. Lortie, 1975), and an identification with the school system and the teacher training.

Differences with respect to the teachers' object of identification, i.e. the "old" occupation versus the school system, were shown to be mirrored in several ways in the daily teaching (Ellström, Davidson, and Rönnqvist, 1990). Thus, teachers belonging to the factory culture tended to use individualized teaching methods to a greater extent than teachers belonging to the school culture, while the latter tended to prefer lecturing methods. With respect to goals, teachers belonging to the school culture placed greater emphasis on the importance of LMT as a means of achieving broad skill development and social equality, while teachers belonging to the factory culture tended to emphasize goals related to the needs of the labor market or the work place.

A third difference concerned teaching practices. Teachers belonging to the factory culture tended to rely on an action-oriented mode, characterized by a focus on practical activities and the manual skills of the trainees in handling tools and machinery. These teachers used little abstract reasoning and explanation in their communication with the trainees. In contrast, teachers belonging to the school culture relied more strongly on a subject-oriented mode of teaching, putting greater emphasis on conceptual-theoretical matters. They also tended to use a more explicit and elaborated way of communicating with the trainees.

Although no direct data are available concerning differences in the view of knowledge between the two cultures within LMT, the results presented by Berner (1989) showed that teachers belonging to what we called a factory culture tended to favour the learning of manual skills and practical, rule-based knowledge ("knowing-how"), while teachers belonging to a school culture tended to emphasize theoretical (propositional) knowledge ("knowing-that"). Thus, while the school culture seems to be built on a logic of education emphasizing abstract reasoning and the manipulation of words and other symbols, the factory culture is built on a logic of production which emphasizes the practical handling of machinery and concrete materials.

Table 2: Two Types of VET Culture Within the Swedish Labour Market Training.

Dominant:	Two Types of VET Culture:	
	A School Culture	A Factory Culture
* Institutional roots/ identification object	the world of education: the school system, the teacher training	the world of work: the "old" occupation
* Teaching goals	broad skill development, social equality	specialized skill development related to "the needs of the labour market"
* View of knowledge	conceptual theoretical knowledge ("knowing-that")	rule-based, manual- practical skills ("knowing-how")
* Teaching practices	a subject-oriented mode of teaching based on lectures in a classroom setting	an action-oriented, individualized mode of teaching - "the assembly line principle"
* Communication style	abstract, explicit	concrete, implicit
* Teacher role	lecturer	"factory foreman"

How, then, can we explain why teachers developed an identification with one or the other of these two teaching cultures? An interesting finding related to this question, was the considerable homogeneity in the observed patterns of belief and practices between different schools and counties. Considering these results, observed differences between teachers with respect to "cultural orientation" were interpreted as depending primarily on differences in their background and socialization to the teacher role. In fact, it was possible to show that vocational teachers who were not certified by a school of education were more likely to become socialized to a factory culture, than their colleagues who had acquired a teacher certification (Ellström et al., 1990). Thus, whether or not the teachers had completed a teacher training course and had received certification as a vocational teacher proved to be the most important determinant of their cultural orientation.

By implication, and basically consistent with neo-institutional theory (e.g. DiMaggio & Powell, 1983), it seems as if cultural factors and the professional orientation of the teachers are more important determinants of the teaching practices within LMT than organizational factors related to the individual school. If this is correct, organizational demographics, i.e. the composition of the group of teachers within a VET-system becomes a significant factor that may determine the relative strength of a factory and a school culture, respectively (cf. Pfeffer, 1983). Considering this evidence, it is also reasonable to expect that the professional ideals acquired in teacher education are important factors in the cultural shaping of VET, and perhaps more important than decisions on new VET-policies and curricula.

Teaching Cultures and the Development of Occupational Competence for a Dynamic Labour Market

Although the teaching cultures identified above differ in many respects from each other, they may also both be seen as instances of what we may call a technical-bureaucratic conception of teaching, or what Wackerhausen (1997) calls the scholastic paradigm of Western education, which is characterized by, among other things:

* a focus on propositional knowledge, i.e. knowledge that can be expressed in explicit, propositional form e. g. in a textbook;
* a view of competence as essentially based on declarative knowledge ("knowing-that") and rule-based skills ("knowing-how");

* that has a personal character, i.e. it can only be acquired and possessed by individual persons, and not, for example, by organizations or communities of practice.
* that can effectively be transferred through means of lectures, written instructions, textbooks, articles and other forms of written material.

The scholastic paradigm, specifically in versions like the factory culture described above, appear also to have close affinities with a Tayloristic production concept. This production concept is in glaring contrast to the new ideas of allegedly "high-commitment" and "learning-intensive" production systems that are currently emerging within different sectors of working life. Common to these new production concepts is an emphasis on the need for more flexible and integrated work systems, that try to integrate learning and production, and, by implication, require an upskilling of the work force (see e.g. Pfeffer, 1995; Stern, 1992). To the extent that the actual teaching within a VET-system is characterized by a scholastic and Tayloristic paradigm, this seems to be a serious obstacle to the development of competencies that are required by emerging concepts of production, e.g. an increasing emphasis on cognitive skills, communicative and social skills (cf. Berryman & Bailey, 1992; Nijhof, 1998).

The rationale that underlies the scholastic paradigm seems to be a formal and *technical-rational concept of practice,* implying a view of action as goal-directed and instrumental, based on a more or less explicit, theoretical knowledge base. The knowledge base is assumed to comprise factual, declarative knowledge ("knowing-that") and task-specific procedural knowledge ("knowing-how" represented as if-then rules) governing the choice and execution of actions (cf. Anderson, 1983). The task is assumed to be well-defined and known with high certainty in terms of objective measurements. Action is assumed to follow from a process of deliberate analysis of different action alternatives based on knowledge of the task and the consequences of the alternatives in terms of goal attainment, i.e. rational calculation based on the application of relevant knowledge. As argued by Hammond (1993), while this technical-rational mode is "certainty-geared" and likely to produce few errors, when the errors do occur they are greater and more likely to be catastrophic.

In contrast to this view of practice, it is possible to formulate a *pragmatic concept of practice* that appears to be more in line with current requirements in many sectors of the labour market (Ellström, 1999 a). According to this view of practice, the task is often assumed to be complex and ill-defined. The knowledge base for action comprises contextual, interpretative knowledge with a focus on explanatory concepts and principles, but also to a large extent practical, experience-based knowledge of an implicit character, including a repertoire of examples and models for action. Rather than viewing human action as determined by preconceived goals and plans, it is seen as continuously evolving through a process of mutual adaptation between the actor and the possibilities and limitations offered by a changing environment (partly as the result of the actor's own performance). In line with this orientation, problems are seen as being worked out and "solved" in action, or through social interaction, rather than through analytical problem solving (Lindblom & Cohen, 1979; Reason, 1980).

In order to conceptualize a teaching culture that has a potential to contribute to the development of occupational competence for a dynamic labour market it seems necessary to put a stronger emphasis on what we here call a pragmatic concept of practice, not to the exclusion of a technical-rational conception of practice, but rather as *complementary* to this still predominant view. Such a changing conception of practice has implications not only for what is considered as occupational competence, but also for how we conceive of successful teaching practices. In contrast to the dominant scholastic paradigm of teaching, a pragmatic view of practice would imply a non-scholastic paradigm (Wackerhausen, 1997) emphasizing, among other things:

* non-propositional knowledge, i.e. knowledge not expressed or not fully expressible in sentences and texts;
* a broader conception of competence, including e.g. personal development and social skills;
* the importance of non-personal knowledge, e.g. knowledge embodied in communities of practices, organizational routines and rituals;
* models of teaching and learning that recognize the importance of situated knowing and learning as participation in social practice.

As argued by Wackerhausen (1997), parts of what is here called the non-scholastic paradigm, together with the recent interest in apprenticeship models of learning, has become somewhat "the dogmatic solution" to the limitations observed in the scholastic paradigm. However, apprenticeship models and the current interest in situated learning are not without their problems. There is, for example, a risk that the current interest in situated learning and apprenticeship models favour a conservatism with respect to the acquisition of new knowledge and competence, something which would hardly be adequate for a dynamic and changeable labour market. As is also argued by Wackerhausen (1997), what seems to be needed is rather a kind of *complementarity* and an *integration* between theoretical reflection and situated learning, and, perhaps also, between scholastic and non-scholastic paradigms of teaching.

Summary and Conclusions

After the introductory section, Sections 3 and 4 of this paper sketched the development of the Swedish Labour Market Training (LMT) from the mid 1940s to the early 1990s. An analysis of this development was also made in terms of the marginal position of the Swedish LMT-system between what was seen as two, partly inconsistent, institutional environments, called the world of work and the world of education, respectively. It was concluded from this analysis that the reorganization in 1986 and perhaps also the reorganization in 1992, may be analysed as attempts to handle the asymmetry in influence between the two institutional environments, and also to tighten the loose couplings between the policy level and the area of policy realization (the operational levels) of the LMT-system. Thus, inconsistencies at the institutional level appear in this case to have been a *latent* driving force for a series of reorganizations of the LMT-system.

Using neo-institutional theory of organizations as a point of departure, the fifth section focused on the possible cultural shaping of the LMT-system. More specifically, it was asked to what extent the marginal position of LMT between the world of work and education, respectively, is mirrored in the teaching culture, and the content and practices of teaching. On the basis of a broad empirical study carried out a few years after the restructuring of the LMT-system in 1986, it was possible to identify two teaching cultures with their roots at an institutional level, i.e. in the world of work and education. The two cultures were called a factory culture and a school culture, respectively. The two teaching cultures were shown to differ in a number of respects, such as their teaching goals and content; teacher roles, and communication style.

Based on this, and on the observation of considerable homogeneity in the observed patterns of teacher beliefs and teaching practices between different schools and counties, it was concluded that cultural factors and the professional orientation of the teachers were more important determinants of the teaching practices within LMT than organizational factors related to the individual school, and perhaps also more important than decisions on new VET-policies and curricula at a regional or national level.

In addition, it was shown that whether teachers had completed a teacher training course and had received a teacher certification proved to be an important determinant of their "cultural orientation". This, of course, has implications for strategies of educational reform. First, it underlines the limits of policy driven attempts to change teaching practices by administrative decisions and decrees. Second, it also underlines the importance of factors such as: (a) the socialization to the teacher role and the important role of teacher training in this process; (b) the content, practices and organization of teacher training; and (c) "organizational demographics", i.e. the composition of the group of teachers within a VET-system, and its role for the strength of different teaching cultures, and, thereby, possibly also for the cultural shaping of teaching and learning processes.

Finally in Section 6, finally, an attempt was made to discuss the teaching cultures that were identified in relation to a dynamic labour market with changing competence requirements. In relation to this issue a distinction was made between a scholastic and a non-scholastic teaching paradigm, and it was concluded that the identified teaching cultures within the Swedish Labour Market Training seem to be closely related to a scholastic type of paradigm. A further conclusion was that this paradigm of teaching may be a serious obstacle to the development of competencies that are required by emerging concepts of production. Rather, what seems to be needed, in the context of current developments in the labour market, is some kind of integration, or middle way, between these two paradigms of teaching.

References

AMU Gruppen. *Annual Report 1997.* Stockholm: AMU Gruppen, AB.

Anderson, J. R. (1983). *The Architecture of Cognition.* Cambridge, MA: Harvard University Press.

Berner, B. (1989). *Kunskapens vägar. Teknik och lärande i skola och arbetsliv. (Ways of Knowing. Technology and learning in school and working life).* Lund: Arkiv förlag.

Bernstein, B. (1977). *Class, Codes, and Control, Vol 3: Towards a theory of educational transmissions* (2nd ed.). London: Routledge & Kegan Paul.

Berryman, S. & Bailey, T. (1992). *The Double Helix of Education and the Economy.* New York: Teachers College, Columbia University.

Bowles, S. & Gintis, H. (1976). *Schooling in Capitalist America.* New York: Basic Books.

Brunsson, N. (1989). *The Organization of Hypocrisy. Talk, decisions, and actions in organizations.* Chicester: John Wiley & Sons.

Carnoy, M. & Levin, H. (1985). *Schooling and Work in the Democratic State.* Stanford: Stanford University Press.

Collins, R. (1979). *The Credential Society. A historical sociology of education and stratification.* New York: Academic Press.

Collins, R. (1981). Micro-translation as a theory-building strategy. In K. D. Knorr-Cetina & A. V. Cicourel (Eds.), *Advances in social theory and methodology. Toward an Integration of Micro- and Macro Sociologies.* Boston: Routledge & Kegan Paul.

Dahlberg, Å. & Tuijnman, A. (1991). Development of Human Resources in Internal Labour Markets: Implications for Swedish Labour Market Policy. *Economic and Industrial Democracy, 12,* 151-171.

Dale, R. (1982). Education and the Capitalist State. In M. Apple (Ed.) *Cultural and Economic Reproduction in Education.* London: Routledge.

Dale, R. (1997). The State and the Governance of Education: An Analysis of the Restructuring of the State-Education Relationship. In A.H. Halsey, H. Lauder, P. Brown & A. Stuart Wells (Eds.) *Education. Culture, Economy, and Society.* Oxford: Oxford University Press.

DiMaggio, P. J. & Powell, W. W. (1983). The Iron Cage Revisited: Institutional Isomorphism and Collective Rationality in Organizational Fields. *American Sociological Review, 48,* 147-160.

Ellström, P.-E. (1992). Understanding Educational Organizations: An Institutional Perspective. *The Portuguese Journal of Education,* 5, 3, 9 - 22.

Ellström, P.-E. (1999 a). Understanding the Role of Knowledge in Practical Action. *Paper presented at the HSS-99 Conference, University of Dalarna, March 16-18, 1999.*

Ellström, P.-E. (1999 b). The Role of Labor Market Programs in Skill Formation: The Case of Sweden. In W. J. Nijhof & J. Brandsma (Eds.) *Bridging the Skills Gap Between Work and Education.* Dordrecht: Kluwer Academic Publishers.

Ellström, P.-E., Davidson, B., & Rönnqvist, D. (1990). *Kontext, kultur och verksamhet. En analys av AMU:s organisation och pedagogiska miljö. (Context, culture, and activity. An analysis of the organization and learning environment of LMT).* Linköping: Department of Education and Psychology, University of Linköping.

Ellström, P.-E. & Svedin, P.-O. (1989). Between Work and Education. In S. Larsson & S. J. Ball (Eds.), *The Struggle for Democratic Education. Equality and Participation in Sweden.* London: The Falmer Press.

Government Bill 1984/85:59.

Hammond, K. R. (1993). Naturalistic Decision Making from a Brunswikian Viewpoint: Its Past, Present, Future. In G. A. Klein, J. Orasanu, R. Calderwood & C. Zsambok (Eds.) *Decision Making in Action: Models and Methods.* Norwood, N.J.: Ablex Publ. Co.

Lindblom, C. E. & Cohen, D. K. (1979). *Usable Knowledge. Social Science and Social Problem Solving.* New Haven, Conn.: Yale University Press.

Lindensjö, B. & Lundgren, U. P. (1986). *Politisk styrning och utbildningsreformer. (Political Steering and Educational Reforms)*. Stockholm: Skolöverstyrelsen, B 86:3.

Lortie, D. C. (1975). *Schoolteacher. A Sociological Study.* Chicago: University of Chicago Press.

Lundgren, U. P. (1984). *Between Hope and Happening. Text and Context in Curriculum Development.* Geelong, Aust.: Deakin University Press.

March, J.G., & Olsen, J.P. (1989). *Rediscovering Institutions. The Organizational Basis of Politics.* New York: The Free Press.

Marklund, S. (1982). *Skolsverige 1950 - 1975. Del 3. Från Visbykompromissen till SIA.* Stockholm: Liber Utbildningsförlaget.

Meyer, J. W. & Rowan, B. (1977). Institutional organizations: Formal structure as myth and ceremony. *American Journal of Sociology, 83*, 340-363.

Meyer, J. W. & Scott, W. R. (Eds.) (1983).*Organizational Environments: Ritual and Rationality.* Beverly Hills, CA: Sage.

Murray, M. (1988). *Utbildningsexpansion, jämlikhet och avlänkning. Studier i utbildningspolitik och utbildningsplanering 1933 - 1985.* Göteborg Studies in Educational Sciences 66. Göteborg: Acta Universitatis Gothoburgensis.

Nijhof, W.J. (1998). Qualifying for the Future. In W. J. Nijhof & J. N. Streumer (Eds.) *Key Qualifications in Work and Education.* Dordrecht: Kluwer Academic Publishers.

Nijhof, W. J. & Brandsma, J. (Eds.) (1999). *Bridging the Skills Gap Between Work and Education.* Dordrecht: Kluwer Academic Publishers.

Offe, C. (1985) *Disorganized Capitalism. Contemporary Transformations of Work and Politics.* Cambridge: Polity Press.

Pfeffer, J. (1983). Organizational Demography. In L. L. Cummings & B. M. Staw (Eds.), *Research in Organizational Behavior. Vol. 5.* Greenwich, Conn.: JAI Press.

Pfeffer, J. (1995). *Competitive Advantage Through People.* Boston: Harvard Business School Press.

Reason, J. (1990). *Human Error.* Cambridge: Cambridge University Press.

Rothstein, B. (1986) *Den socialdemokratiska staten. (The Socialdemocratic State).* Lund: Arkiv avhandlingsserie.

Scott, W.R. (1987). The Adolescence of Institutional Theory. *Administrative Science Quarterly,* 32, 493-511.

Scott, W. R. (1991). Unpacking Institutional Arguments. In W. W. Powell & DiMaggio, P. J. (Eds.) *The New Institutionalism in Organizational Analysis.* Chicago: The University of Chicago Press.

Scott, W. R. (1995). *Institutions and Organizations.* Thousand Oaks: Sage.

Stern, D. (1992). Institutions and Incentives for Developing Work-Related Knowledge and Skill. In P. S. Adler (Ed.)*Technology and the Future of Work.* New York: Oxford University Press.

Swidler, A. (1986). Culture in Action: Symbols and Strategies. *American Sociological Review, 51,* 273 - 286.

Thomas, G. M., Meyer, J. W., Ramirez, F. O. & Boli, J. (Eds.) (1987). *Institutional Structure: Constituting State, Society and the Individual.* Newbury Park, CA: Sage.

Wackerhausen, S. (1997). The Scholastic Paradigm. *Journal of Nordic Educational Research,* 4, 195-204.

THE PRODUCTION GROUP AS A LEARNING ENVIRONMENT - ILLUSTRATED BY A CASE AND VARIOUS ASPECTS OF THE CONCEPT OF LEARNING

Steen Høyrup

Preface

In various forms a number of Danish private and public firms work upon implementing the Danish Confederation of Trade Unions´ vision of "The Developing Work". Empirical research concerning this matter has collected a number of experiences which form the basis of further theoretical perspectives within a research project Working Life, Learning Processes, and Democratization.

The major issue of the experience of implementing the developing work is that the places of work are or have a learning environment that partly is an attraction and benefit to the individual worker, and partly an important element of the economy, development, and survival of the firm. Just as the firm has an economic account it may also have a competence account: A current survey, evaluation and development of activities of education at the work place.

These facts demand for a clarification and re-definition of the concept of learning. This has been attempted below through reflections concerning different spheres of learning. Finally, it is considered how teams or production groups can function as learning environments, and attempts have been made to establish such groups under various names in many places of work, based upon an idea of changing the organization of the work. Thus a starting point has been laid out to a further study of learning environments and their reciprocal interplay, referring both to the development of competences within the firm, and learning in general educational institutions.

This article aims at analysing the problem: which possibilities of learning can be established within some of the developments we notice in the organization of the work in the firms? What is characteristic of the learning sphere in the new production groups/teams in the firms?

An Outline of the Concept of Learning

A description of various developmental tendencies concerning the thematizing of the concept of learning is now given. It must be emphasized that there is no black or white pole in each dimension, it is a spectrum between which the concept of learning is expanded. Finally, there is no progress from dimension to dimension, rather the various meanings are part of a complex concept of learning in which various theorists emphasize various aspects of the concept.

1. From cognitive development to whole-person-learning
One of the most deeply anchored concepts of learning is that learning is the acquisition of information and knowledge. Learning is "development of cognition". Changes of cognition or development is the most important element of learning and is the focus of examination and concept formation. Even though Piaget's ideas are broader - action is important, and effective aspects are part of the learning - the development of cognitive aspects of the personality is emphasized to a very high degree. The cognitive aspect of learning is an important part of the learning psychology.

When Staffan Larsson states, that learning can be defined as changes of the interpretation of aspects of the outer world, or changes of the way of acting which mirror an increased ability - cognition and action are emphasized, not only cognition is defined as knowledge, but also direct perception.

Lave is critical towards the cognitive understanding of learning:

> *Conventional explanations view learning as a process by which a learner internalizes knowledge, whether "discovered", "transmitted" from others, or "experienced" in interaction"...*
> *Furthermore, learning as internalization is too easily constructed as an unproblematic process of absorbing the given as a matter of transmission and assimilation.* (Lave, 1991)

Here Lave criticizes a primitive concept of cognition and a confused concept of internalization: learning takes place when the outer in some way becomes the inner. For instance, there is no communication between active inner and outer systems, which results in development and which is expressed in various types of system-thinking.

Bradford (1961) gives an example of whole-person-learning. He defines learning as follows:

It is a process of internal re-organization of a complex of thought patterns, perceptions, assumptions, attitudes, feelings and skills, and of successfully testing this re-organization in relation to problems of learning.

Bradford's concept of learning is like Piaget's, emphasizing a re-organization of structures in the individual. However, Bradford makes a number of aspects of the personality more explicit: cognition, attitudes, feelings, and actions.

Steen Larsen says, "A learning person becomes another person". (TV, February 1999). Jane Lave writes, "learning as increasing participation in communities of action concerns the whole person acting in the world. The individual defines and is defined by his social relations, and learning implies that the individual becomes another person in regard to his possibilities in a social community. Learning involves the construction of identities".

We can recognize a development in the concept of learning from stressing cognition, an aspect of personality, to the concept of learning as the whole person changes.

2. From whole-person learning to learning as social interaction

For a number of years - from 1961 to 1997 - Edgar H. Schein has developed a theory concerning "Personal and organizational learning" in which the most important aspect of the learning aspect is communication between the individual and the social environments. The theory is not repeated here, however, it can be mentioned that in many ways the learning process becomes social processes: the surroundings communicate acknowledgement, denial, or lack of denial of the concepts, ideas, and ways of understanding of the individual, all of which are stimulating learning. If the individual learns, thus changing his personality and actions, this results in social conflicts with the social environment, conflicts that may continue and support the learning process, or stop it, or make it recede, a sort of "unlearning".

When learning processes are seen as social processes, cues in the social environment are important to create a lack of balance of systems - for instance cognitive systems - in the individual, and learning is connected with the solution of an intrapersonal conflict. The indivdual's actions connect the individual with the social environment with possibilities of creating social conflicts. The solution of the two kinds of conflicts - created by and imbedded in social processes - is the focus of learning.

Consequently, learning becomes social interaction. This way of thinking can be seen with Elleström who refers to a common actions model as being the basis of drawing the attention to the preconditions of learning. There are two stages of the interplay individual-environment: Feed-forward where the individual tries to influence his/her environment according to his/her aims, intentions, and plans of action. The environment consists of not only people, objects/machinery, but also of cultural-symbolic environments such as organizational cultures and discourses. Central elements are the ideological-cultural ideas concerning what is desired or possible to do, or not, in various connections. The second stage of the interplay between the individual and the environment is the feedback stage: the perception/ observation of the individual of "answers" from the environment and the interpretation and reflections that concern these answers. Learning is a complex of individual/surroundings/interplay, and thus the step has been taken towards the concept of organizational learning.

3. From internalization of knowledge as the "substance" of constructivism
The position which Lave criticizes is based upon a specific conception of knowledge and the relationship between the individual and the environment and how the world is cognitively constituted. Knowledge is a substance existing independently of the subject, however, during various processes it can be implemented into the individual. This is a very unpsychological way of thinking as it is fundamental in psychological thinking that sense impressions, perception, and experiences are subjective creations, based upon activities of the brain and subjective structures of concepts, language, theoretical frames of reference, attitudes, motivation, and social allegiances, just to mention a few. Various tendencies within constructivism emphasize the old psychological wisdom that knowledge is constructed. Man plays an active part in the construction of reality and knowledge.

4. From adaptive learning to generative learning
These concepts illustrate the depth of learning and attach the individual process of learning closely to the environment or place of work.

> *Adaptive learning is applying the same old concepts or skills in new ways.*
> (Schein, 1997)

Generative learning is equivalent to what Argyris and Schön (1996) call "double-loop-learning" and Bateson´s "deutero learning", likewise, it corresponds with the concept of "learning to learn". In single-loop-learning the changes of the individual´s ways of behaviour and acting constitute the improvements, however, still within the established framework and conditions of the place of work. The individual is active and examining, and relates his/her results to the existing norms. When there is a "gap", it is diminished through corrective actions. Basic structures and values are consistent, both with the individual and in the environment. In double-loop-learning the individual is also examining if there are gaps and more basic framework and the culture of the workplace are questioned. As the culture is also internalized in the individual more basic spheres of the psychic system are affected.

Generative learning, writes Schein,

> *requires the learner to reframe, to develop new concepts and points of view, to cognitively re-define old categories and to change standards of judgement. Such changes increase the learner's capacity to deal with situations in new ways and lay the basis for developing radically new skills.*

Generative learning implies that the individual's basic attitudes, values, and basis of understanding are questioned. In a working situation the workers may have worked within an integrated "moral" and basic conception of work and education. Therefore, these questions, and the learning process they are part of may provoke anxiety, and other strong elements are necessary to maintain the worker in the process of learning if he or she does not refuse to learn.

Some theorists, among them Schein, evidently equal double-loop- learning and learning to learn, whereas others work with more levels of learning, among them Bateson and Elleström. The individual learns basic attitudes and methods to create order, meaning, and experiences in new and unsafe situations.

5. From individual learning to collective learning

Even though learning takes place in a social context - maybe in classes or groups in an educational institution - learning can be individual and individualized, because the basis of learning consists of changes of the individual. However, it is not only individuals that learn. Groups also learn, in connection with team-building. And organizations can learn. The learning organization is a complicated concept with many different theoretical bases which will not be further discussed here. However, it must be mentioned that it is problematic how organizations learn, but it is generally agreed that the individual's learning is a precondition that organizations can learn. Still, individuals can learn when organizations do not learn. For instance, a collective learning may consist of individuals - in various positions in the organization and with different interests - who each carry their own mental pictures of the organization. These pictures can be rendered visible and common in a learning process (Source). Just as group-self-study was fundamental to individual learning and development of the group in the laboratory method, these ideas are forwarded by Argyris and Schön (1978): one link of the organizational learning is that the workers explore their own working processes and situation, both on the individual and organizational levels. Organizational learning takes place when individual members continually modify their imagination and pictures of the organization, and when they act against the background of their mental pictures and discover conditions where expectations and profit do not correspond. The discoveries and experiences of the learner must be included in the memory of the organization.

Organizational learning takes place when mistakes, inexpedient actions, and processes take place and are corrected after a research that includes reflections concerning the individual's own acts, resulting in consequences for the collective actions of the organization. (Elkjær, 1994).

6. From institutionalized learning to informal learning

The traditional concept is that learning takes place in schools through education. Another view is that learning takes place all the time and in many different contexts.

Alan Roger distinguishes between four types of learning by applying intentionality - in the environment and with the teacher - as the criterion of separation:

In the individual's environment there may be agents, frameworks, and regulations that intend that the individual learns, versus: there being no such intentions.

In the same way the individual may have the intention to learn - in each of the two environments - or he/she has no such intention, again in each environment. This gives four possibilities:

Figures 1: Four types of learning.

	The learner intends learning to take place	The learner does not intend to learn
The source of learning intends that learning is to take place	Planned, purposeful and intended learning	Informal learning
The source of the learning does not intend to promote learning	Non-formal learning	Incidental learning. Casual learning

This extension of the concept of learning gives many perspectives: In the box with purposeful learning the individual sometimes learns something which is different from that which is intended (the hidden curriculum). The individual also learns in situations where nobody tries to teach him/her, and where the learner has no intention to be taught. A research of these learning processes might give us a knowledge we might use in the spheres where an agent or an environment intend that learning takes place. The workplace can be where learning occurs without it being intended, or it can be a sphere of learning where the optimal possibilities of learning are organized and workers can meet these intentions with corresponding or non-existing intentions.

7. From learning, thematized as permanent changes of the individual (as a result of the individual's interplay with the environment) to learning, understood as participation in and being an integrated part of a common practice (situated learning).

Lave states that,

> *there is no activity that is not situated.*

The problem is our understanding of what learning is and the possibilities of conveying knowledge from one connection to another. The traditional concept of knowledge is that knowledge mirrors the objective world and can be made independent through the language. The internalized knowledge is available to the individual when he/she is faced with a new situation. With the concept of distributed cognition Lave moves cognition (knowledge) from the individual to an aspect of the social community and attached to this:

> *The perspective-situated learning emphasizes an activity in and with the world; and on the view that agent, activity, and the world mutually constitute each other.*

Individual, action and social community thus constitute a unity, and the elements constitute each other mutually. In other words, knowledge or understanding are attached to the social communities we enter and the ways of organizing these communities. The social relations in the sphere where the social practice takes place become fundamental to learning. Klaus Nielsen isolates the concept of "situated" as follows,

> *In everyday life the situated refers to the fact that at first it may be difficult to give precise and reliable instructions how to act in future*

> situations, because these situations are very often rather complex, and only in the very situation is it possible to find the correct line of action.

And further,

> This means that learning, cognition, and knowledge must be understood according to the individual's participation in a complex network of relations, and it is the analysis of the relations that illucidates each element and not the elements that explain the relations. (DPT, p. 29)

The basic question of situated learning is whether our knowledge and learning processes are more sensitive to the context than is generally supposed in our educational thinking.

As far as possible some implications of education and learning are stated below:
* The aim must be that learning takes place in the situation where the knowledge is going to be used, i.e. at the place of work
* Practical training must be emphasized
* The principle of interaction must be emphasized (alternation between theory and practical work)
* Methods of working and learning environment at the training schools must be as much like the methods in practical life as possible, e. g. case-methods, role playing etc.
* It must be emphasized in the planning of courses to work with learning in different spheres of learning, each with their own potential, and systematically combine the use of the different spheres. Theoretically and in research this paradigm gives rise to moving focus and analysis from the individual to social relations, structures, and conditions, and the development of these, to be the basis of understanding learning at the workplace.

Below is a survey of the statement

The above thematic exposition of the concept of learning gives rise to several basic questions:

Which spheres of learning can be found?
Which types of learning processes can be found, and what are the basic factors and preconditions of these?
Which spheres of learning create the optimal possibilities of learning in which learning processes?

Figure 2: Different concepts of learning.

From	To
Cognitive development	Whole-person-development
Whole-person-development	Learning as social interaction
Internalization of knowledge	Constructivism
Adaptive learning (single-loop-learning	Generative learning (double-loop-learning) meta-learning, learning to learn
Individual learning	Collective learning, organizational learning
Institutionalized learning	Informal learning
Permanent changes of the individual	Learning viewed as situated activity. Participation in a community of practice

According to the experience from research concerning the implementation of the developing work, a short survey of possible spheres of learning is stated below, including considerations concerning the conditions of learning in one of the spheres: the production team as learning environment.

Spheres of Learning/Learning Environments

We can differentiate between four different spheres of learning:
(1) Spheres of learning in educational institutions
(2) The work as a sphere of learning
(3) Practical training as a sphere of learning
(4) Spheres of learning in "temporary systems"

Previously, the dominating understanding was to attach learning to education which took place in properly organized institutions. These were controlled by laws, executive orders, and government circulars, and they were rather isolated from places of work and Business life. (In Denmark, in 1998, the Ministry of Education worked out a programme "Education, Trade and Industry", and one of the visions is a close coorperation between education, business and industry.)

Learning at work implies the philosophy that the place of work and the company are primarily organized according to principles that ensure productivity, effectiveness, and quality of the products/work. However, at the same time, work in itself is a sphere which may contain considerable learning potentials. The work may contain conditions of learning which are almost impossible to carry into effect in the educational institutions. It is an everyday experience, also mentioned in research, that many people have experienced that they have learnt and learn most at work. In the companies the foremen, managers, etc. are in charge of the firm and the work done at various levels. In this situation, the personnel manager is the person who is responsible for further educating the workers and often has the possibility of contributing to organize the work according to pegagogical ideas.

Practical training is an integrated part of some of the formalized education, especially education that qualifies for a certain profession: vocational education, training to become a nurse, teacher, or educationalist etc. The sphere of learning which the educational institution offers is insufficient when the issue is to create the necessary qualifications which the profession demands. Some of these qualifications must be learnt by practical training. Or rather: a connection between theory and practical training which is created in the interplay between the educational institution and the place of training.

The place of training as a learning sphere is interesting in relation to the two spheres of learning first mentioned: the educational institutions work rather isolated from companies, and the working life (education, the creation of frames of learning) is organized according to a pedagogical logic (and, of course, other practical and economic conditions). Primarily, the place of work is organized according to the logic of the work. It can be said that the place of training consists of two overlapping systems: a work system and a pedagogical system. The actual places of training are organized differently, however, it is common to both that "proper" work is the primary function, but still, at the same time, that certain roles and obligations concerning the learning aspect of the students´ activities are built-in in the system.

"The temporary system" - which ordinarily is called residential courses - is a social system which is established to attend to a specific learning task. A distinctive feature of this sphere of learning is that it can be organized to function in a different way than the place of work. And - which is just as important - a number of social relations and attitudes are created in a certain social context, viz. the place of work. These relations and attitudes do not just disappear because they are moved to another context which differs from the context where they were created and developed.

The 4 spheres of learning each contain various potentials for learning and obstacles to learning. Thus, educational planning is to a very high degree a question of combining the different spheres of learning. Therefore, a closer insight in these spheres of learning is an important concern for the the people who are responsible for the education - in institutions and in the places of work.

In recent years, a connection with the development of the concept of learning is that these spheres of learning have become prominent in the philosophy of learning processes and educational thinking.

Which Learning is a Necessary Precondition that the Employees Function in Production Groups (Teams)?

In some of the Danish firms that work on implementing "The developing work" there are plans or concrete initiatives to change the organization of the work in different ways. Several companies want to implement changes that are known under different names: team-structure, co-managing groups, production groups.

The question is: What is the connection between the implementation of production groups and the learning processes that are related to this implementation, among other things as seen in the light of the above-mentioned concepts of learning?

I would now like to present some results and experience from the research project Working Life, Learning Processes and Democratization, in which I participated.

Questions can be asked concerning learning on two levels:
* What is the participant intended to learn to be able to enter into the new means of organizing of the work?
* What can the employees learn in the production group as a learning environment?

Below is a description from the management of a concrete firm with the demands on the employees and their role in the team:

Field of activity - production worker
 - read production schedules, order sheets, prescriptions
 - implement self-control "quality" labels
 - adjust machinery
 - understand and use the proper tools, object/quality
 - clean own place of work
 - know the products they work with
 - participate in problem-solving in their own group
 - contribute to planning the order of production
 - cooperate with colleagues in their own and in other sections
 - readjust own machinery

- daily maintenance and lubricating
- carry out simple repairs
- control of the quality of own work
- prevent mistakes
- plan the daily work
- be able to notice and correct defects in the machinery and processes
- be able to implement repairs of defects
- be able to read technical manuals
- be able to register and get experience

Analysis:
It is evident that in more dimensions there are changes in the work and function of the worker.
(1) There is a move away from an isolated and narrow functioning. A number of new functions are implemented in the work so that it is both a job extension and a job enrichment: planning, prevention of errors, maintenance, correction of defects, quality control.
(2) Some social functions in the shape of participating in problem-solving in own group, registration and collection of experience.
(3) Implementation of some outward focused functions that are connected with the interplay of the team with the entirety: cooperation with own and other sections. New role and interplay with the planners.
(4) The worker must learn on a broad spectrum in many fields:

The Cognitive Field:
- read and understand - sometimes very complicated technical manuals
- knowledge concerning the products that are used in the production
- planning, prevention of defects

Technical Skills:
Adjusting machinery, master the use of tools, re-adjust machinery and small repairs of machinery

Social Competences:
Problem-solving in the group, internal and external communication, cooperation.
To summarize there are both much greater demands in the work (compared to the isolated work) and a greater independence and challenges and thus presumably more satisfaction (challenges and learning potentials).

Attitudes, Values in the Work (Moral)
- Implement control of own work, quality control
- Initiative: stop the machinery when defect, prevent defects
- Daily maintenance
- Responsibility and understanding of the entirety
- Reciprocal help and support

Learn to Learn
- Be able to register and collect experience

Learning as Social Practice
The various types of competences must be carried out in a new social sphere. It was characteristic of the former team - the working team at the assembly line - that every man/woman had his/her own function or task. No rotation. Little communication, reciprocal help, cooperation, planning or problem-solving in the team. In the production group there is rotation, everyone is able to manage the machinery, and there is a great need for internal social adjustment and cooperation.

To summarize it is evident that the implementation of production teams is a complicated enterprise, viewed from a learning point of view (our concepts of learning).
* Learning must be in the shape of acquiring new knowledge (about new machinery). The employees express that this is their dominating need concerning learning
* The issue is "whole-person-learning", learning in the shape of a complex development of the whole person
* The issue is social learning: the production team is the intimate social sphere where the individual perceives new demands and challenges, and where his/her actions affect the other members of the group and stimulate their learning
* Each employee's subjective conception and valuation of his/her own work performance is decisive to the attitude towards changes of the organization of the work and the motivation to learn

Subjectively some of the workers in the actual case - who have slowly developed towards the new organization of the work - have the experience, among other things that
* Nothing much has happened in their daily work. The difference between new and the old organizaton of the work is not very great

* They have no experience of having any influence upon their own work or a greater freedom of organizing their work - in spite of the fact that the concept and the frames aim at this.
* The employees "guess" that their fellow workers in the old organization of the work - with a permanent function at the assembly line, without rotation, and with repeated and monotonous work - prefer this "old" work to the new organization of the work.

It is a vital perspective here that the emphasis of constructivism is that we construct our own reality and that this subjective reality is the basis of our actions.

The issue is both single-loop and double-loop-learning. The former is much emphasized in the shape of learning which results in a reduction of mistakes. However, at the same time there is an openness in the team-philosophy of the firm: some differences among the various production teams are acceptable, they may - within certain limits - find their own way of functioning. Each group works out a plan concerning its own functions and development, and the plans are not meant to be identical. So, there are possibilities of double-loop-learning.

The outlined learning situation is complicated by the fact that it is not the intention that an individual acts differently and with new competences in the same social situation (work situation). The individual and the context must change at the same time. The issue is both individual learning and organizational learning.

Lave is of the opinion that learning, practice, and the relations of the social system form an entirety and it is impossible to analytically differentiate each element of it. However, these elements mutually constitute and support each other and they may help us understand the opposition against teams and self-governing groups which appears with the workers in general and in many places of work: the object of the learning and developmental process is that many persons are brought together in a new social unity, viz. the group. In their past social organization the workers have developed norms, control, mutual relations concerning influence and closeness, etc. This social context is changing: will I be able to settle down in this new group structure? Maybe there is anxiety that a new group dynamics is developing resulting in other kinds of pressure against the individual. Besides, there is the possibility that this group dynamics becomes a stricter and more complicated employer than the previous one which was more simple, visible, and plain?

The firm has implemented an extensive educational programme in order to support the synchronous development of the individual and the organization of the work. The programme consists of both a formalized education managed by outside educational institutions, and various types of practical learning at work, for instance by teaching the person who is working at the machinery next to you. The idea of the concept is that learning is a continuous process at work, and consequently both an institutionalized and an informal learning take place.

Teams as Learning Environment

The Work and the Educational Institution as a Learning Sphere - Evaluated in General
The two spheres of learning are characterized by some general features (Fagermoen, 1993).

In the educational situation the contents are often more abstract, often consisting of linguistic expressions and symbols. In principle it is possible to work with something concrete, for instance the experience of the participants, shots of reality (tapes and video), or reality itself may be brought into the classroom (tissue, organs, etc.). In a concrete situation the concrete is often removed from its natural context. At work we are "part of real life" with concrete people, tools, and work processes.

In an educational situation, broad global perspectives can be applied concerning the work, historical and personal history, individual and societal perspectives can be emphasized. At work the perspective is often rather limited, viz. a local perspective, the job at hand.

Fagermoen understands the educational situation as being more static in relation to the more dynamical developmental work situation. Maybe this is not correct, each situation has its own dynamics. However, in an educational situation, subject-related courses, and a sequence of impressions, contents, topics, problems, concepts, and theories can be planned. When working with these subjects the group has its own dynamics and development. At work it is the logics of the work itself and the organization of the work that take over. The speed of the assembly line, piecework, rationalization, effectiveness etc. set the pace. The distinct learning situations cannot be planned in the same way, they must be grasped when the opportunity is there.

The educational situation is a sphere where the student is supposed to be active and responsible, however without the distinct compulsion to act which is characteristic of practical training. At work, the worker is supposed to act all the time, often against a background of ambiguous and insufficient information and antagonistic situations.

The work demands a nearness and attention, often in close contact with machinery and/or persons. Maybe it is difficult to get a possibility of focusing attention upon the subject which has to be learnt, and difficult to get a distance to occurrences, and - from various perspectives - notice situations and courses in which you are participating yourself.

Contrary to this the students are more "protected" in an educational situation, they are able to - mentally - withdraw a little and think and reflect, and get a distance to the subject and the experiences.

Finally, the work situation is often connected with a considerable responsibility and may result in serious consequences. In an educational situation there are greater possibilities of experimenting, and a bargain needs not be a bargain in the same way when there are mistakes or inexpedient actions.

The social relations are different in the two spheres. In a work situation people often function very closely together for many years, and one worker's behaviour may result in serious consequences for his co-worker: another person's work can be facilitated or a situation can be made impossible. The relationship is very important: a bad personal relation between two persons may result in an almost impossible work situation, thus being an important stress factor in the work.

In educational situations the students are often conscious of the fact that they are together only for these lessons. Of course, bad relations are a strain in the sphere of learning, however, they are not as threatening as bad relations at work.

The team as a learning sphere
Some characteristics about the teams that were to be implemented into the firm:
* More and diversified tasks and, consequently
* Greater demands, more challenges
* Each team is allowed to organize itself (flow sheets)
* Demand for ability to survey in general and responsibility for the work as a whole
* Greater independence

A very interesting aspect of the learning process in the teams is the dimension mentioned previously: adaptive learning versus generative learning. These two concepts are very close and correspond to Ellström's categories: adaptive learning versus developmental learning.

He gives two types of characteristics about these dual kinds of learning (Ellström, 1996)

Figure 3: Adaptive Learning and Developmental Learning.

Adaptive Learning to be able to:	Developmental Learning to be able to:
carry out tasks concerning a section or a component	carry out tasks concerning the general and the system
solve problems which the worker has met before	formulate problems, analyse how problems arise and can be solved
carry out for instance gauging or control	critically estimate the value of gauging and implementing appropriate initiatives
be responsible for assigned and specific tasks	be responsible for greater fields of work or processes

Against the background of the above stated basis the arrangement of the teams in our case may be learning environments for both types of learning, however, with considerable possibilities of a development orientated learning in the team. Thus the team has a possibility of being both a new organization of the work - in relation to the philosophy of the firm concerning the quality of the production etc. - and as a learning environment containing new learning potentials to the employees.

Summary

It is stated, referring to a concrete firm where the orientation of the work is changed to being production groups/teams, and referring to various aspects of the concept of learning - that - as a precondition to enter into a team the employee must learn a very wide spectrum of competences. On the other, hand attention is called to the fact that a team at a place of work contains considerable potential for being a learning environment where generative or developmental learning may take place.

References

Argyris, C. & Schön, D.A.(1996). *Organizational Learning II. Theory, Method, and Practice*. Addison-Wesley Publishing Company.

Bradford (ed.) (1961). *Forces in learning*. Selected Reading Series.

Elkjær, B. (1994): Arbejde som en kontinuerlig læreproces. Loke, nr. 3.

Ellström, Gustavsson and Larsson (ed.) (1966). *Livslångt lärande*. Studentlitteratur.

Fagermoen, M. S. (1993). *Sykepleie i teori og praksis - et fagdidaktisk perspektiv*. Universitetsforlaget.

Hermansen, Mads (ed.) (1998). *Fra læringens horisont - en antologi*. Klim.

Klavs Nielsen (1998). Viden og læring i et situeret perspektiv. *Dansk Pædagogisk Tidsskrift*, april.

Lave, J. and Wenger, E. (1991). *Situated learning. Legitimate peripheral participation*. Cambridge University Press.

Larsson, Staffan (1994). *Vardagslärande och vuxenstudier*. Paper presented at the conference "Forskning i Norden " Göteborg, 1-2 June 1995.

Schein & Bennis (1965). *Personal and organizational change through group methods*. New York, Wiley & Sons.

Schein, E. H. (1997). *Organizational Learning as Cognitive Re-definition: Coercive Persuasion Revisited*. Copyright 1997 The Society for Organizational Learning. (From Inter-Net).

AGEING WORKERS, HRM AND TRAINING IN SMEs

Erika Löfström & Maarit Pitkänen[*]

Abstract

The ageing of the work force and early exit/retirement are challenges facing the Finnish labour market. This study intends to map human resources practices in small and medium sized enterprises. The focus of the analysis is on human resources management and attitudes towards work force the ageing in SMEs. Special areas for the training of ageing workers are also investigated.

Most of the 100 enterprises in this study have participated in training and development projects. The most commonly used human resources development measures in SMEs were health promotion and training. The suggested training areas for ageing employees seem to be based on both realities and stereotypic assumptions. An important finding is that special training programmes and other measures especially designed for ageing workers are rare. Although the attitude towards ageing is positive overall, significant differences between age groups persist. Differences in attitude stem rather from differences in age and position in the organization. The greatest differences are to be found between younger managers and older workers. There might be a need for SMEs to tackle prejudice towards other age groups in order to promote a more positive atmosphere.

1. Introduction

This study focuses on one of the most important issues facing the Finnish labour market: the ageing labour force and the effect of human resource management policies as a means of combating early exit/retirement. The viewpoint of this study is that of small and medium-sized enterprises.

The role of SMEs in the labour market increased in the 1980s with a typical small or medium-sized company in Finland employing an average of only 4.2 employees. Indeed, one third of all enterprises are microcompanies, employing

---

[*] Sections 4., 5., 7.2., 7.3 by Löfström, E.
Sections 1., 2., 7.1. by Pitkänen, M.
Sections 3., 6., 8. by Löfström, E. & Pitkänen, M.

5 or less (Lindström & Schrey 1997). The Finnish labour market is experiencing, and will increasingly experience, the phenomenon of an ageing labour force. The baby boom in Finland, which occurred at the end of the 1940s and the beginning of the 1950s, is the reason for the age of the Finnish working population being high; in 1997 a quarter of the labour force was 50 or older. (Lindgren 1990; Miettinen et. al. 1998).

Most studies on ageing in the labour market concentrate on general issues such as the position of ageing workers in the labour market, unemployment, combating ageist policies and practices, and the marginalization of ageing workers. Another approach includes living conditions, health care services and social integration. The Finnish research tradition has focused mainly on microlevel analysis (individuals) and on the medical and physical abilities of ageing workers. An instance of this is the 'Respect for the Ageing in Finland' project (Ahola & Huuhtanen 1995; Piispa & Huuhtanen 1995). Recently, the volume of debate on ageing workers and the need for research on ageing, learning and education has increased. On the other hand, work on the organizational approach has been more limited. Research on learning, education and ageing workers could be summarized as follows: the focus has been mainly on retirees and learning and education in other than work contexts; age has been considered only as a background variable. Theoretical frameworks and concepts have been adopted uncritically and non-analytically and the low level of participation by ageing workers in education has been explained in terms of either age or poor motivation. Few studies have focused on work organization, job mobility, management practices and learning opportunities at work. In addition to this, studies have neglected the individual differences which exist among the ageing work force (Tikkanen 1998). However, as the work force ages over the coming decades, employers will need to transform the skills of the work force to meet new demands. This will entail new practices in human resource management, training and health care, and the design and organization of work (Pearson 1996).

Our present research task is that of analysing HRM as a means of combating the push and pull factors of early exit/retirement. The focus of the recent study is on the organizational level.

2. Early Exit Culture

The dominant characteristic of the labour market experience of ageing workers in the industrialized countries is the steady decline in the labour participation rate over the last 20 years. This decline can be analysed from three aspects (Kohli & Rein 1991): retirement, early exit and pathways.

Early exit means the preference to retire before reaching the official age for retirement. Early exit is popular in Finland: in the age group 50-64 almost 36 per cent chose early exit in 1996 and the percentage was 77 in the age group 60-64 (Miettinen et. al. 1998). Pathways are construed by institutional actors, such as the state, firms or employer's associations. Pathways such as part-time jobs and partial retirement have not been popular in Finland. Only 9 per cent of the 45-54 year-olds had part-time or short-term jobs. Part-time jobs do not seem to fit in with the Finnish full-time job culture. The social security system also functions as a disincentive for part-time solutions such as partial retirement. (Nätti 1996; Nätti & Julkunen 1994).

The main factors underlying early exit, i.e. recession, unemployment and redundancy, are demand-related. A secondary (but important) factor is the general attitude towards early exit - it had become acceptable in the work climate of the 1980s to encourage early exit from the labour market. This policy was favourable to employers who could then reduce the size of their work force or even obtain subsidies for doing so (Walker 1995; Kohli & Rein 1991; Tikkanen 1998). Other individual factors encouraging early exit include poor educational level, poor health and heavy work. However, this combination of attitude and early exit policy has served to reinforce a general devaluation of ageing. As a result, early exit tends to become self-sustaining, thus marginalizing more and more wage earners. (Puurula 1996; Guillemard & van Gunsteren 1991). Gradually, ageing workers become discriminated against in recruitment and training.

A recent survey on the quality of Finnish working life (Ylöstalo & Rahikainen 1998) provides interesting information on age discrimination. Eight per cent of wage earners have experienced age discrimination, while the oldest employees detected age discrimination the most frequently.

Early exit is one of the labour market's paradoxes. Ageing workers possess many good qualities such as a lower rate of absenteeism and long-term job commitment and they often show greater responsibility with regard to their duties (Johnson & Falkingham 1992; Piispa & Huuhtanen 1995). Ageing workers are also seen to have gained organizational experience, wisdom, maturity, age-related intellectual and personality-related abilities and life experience which can help others understand their own ageing (Chené & Sigouin 1995). Clearly, it must be in the interests of organizations to make an effort to keep this knowledge within the organization, and to find the means and methods by which to pass it on to younger employees.

Ageing workers are not alone in being responsible for developments. A generation ago, small and medium-sized companies in needed of unskilled workers who were loyal to the entrepreneur. Now, changes in working life are happening so quickly that neither the companies nor the ageing employees have been aware of the development. The modern workplace continually challenges ageing workers. They are expected to be physically and psychologically mobile and their identity tied to their talent, not their employer. In addition to this, retirement decisions are supposed to come about through the mutual agreement of individuals and the companies from which they retire (Kohli & Rein 1991; Chusmir 1990).

3. The Early Exit Culture as A Challenge For HRM

The early exit culture is an interplay of pull and push factors on macro, organizational and individual levels. From a microeconomic point of view, an individual's retirement decision is the result of a personal evaluation of the work-leisure trade-off. The greater the benefits of leisure are perceived to be, the weaker the inclination to work. Retirement in itself is felt to be a valuable time (Kohli & Rein 1991). On an individual level, pulling factors are the desire to gain more leisure time, the view that one has worked long enough, the existence of sufficient financial resources, the diminishing of physiological and psychological strength and endurance and the attitudes towards work. On the organizational level these can be challenged by the improvement of working conditions, rehabilitation, continuing education and training and a change in attitudes (Forss & Karisalmi 1997; Solem & Mykletun 1997; Rasku & Kinnunen 1995; Lilja 1990).

Push factors on the macro level are the general attitude against ageing workers in society at large, the belief that they should make way to younger people, and retirement policies affecting pension, or salary reductions. Other push factors are poor working conditions, poor atmosphere at work, lack of appreciation and respect for the work of the ageing worker and a lack of education and training opportunities. On an individual level, push factors are the poor level of basic education among ageing workers, the perceived difficulty of keeping up with the developments in the work itself, and the closely related feelings that work has become too demanding and that expectations of working life cannot be lived up to anymore. Ageing workers' skills might also have become outdated, and the learning of new technologies, for example, may not be considered worthwhile either by employers or by the employees themselves. Other factors are too heavy work load, a psychological and physiological burden, the loss of a sense of the meaningfulness of work, and individual values (Forss & Karisalmi 1997; Rasku & Kinnunen 1995; Lilja 1990). The fact that the impact of push factors is stronger than that of pull (Gould, Takala & Lundqvist 1992) poses a serious question concerning the realities of human resource management. Challenges for the management of ageing human resources and examples of measures for combating these are shown in Table 1.

Attempts have been made to map out age-specific programmes in European organizations and enterprises. Apparently only a minority of companies are implementing measures to combat age barriers. In enterprises employing less than 100 employees the most frequently utilized measures were related to different aspects of job recruitment, such as training programmes to promote recruitment policies and positive discrimination. Also development of training and educational programmes particularly for ageing workers were utilized to some extent in the European companies. In organizations employing more than 500 employees the range of measures implemented was much wider. The lack of actions in SMEs seems to reflect the actual situation. Nevertheless, it has been important to investigate good practices of age-aware HRM. Based on the number of initiatives of good practice gathered in the EU countries, companies in the UK, the Netherlands, Germany, Greece, and France have been among the most active ones. In the UK the most frequently utilized measures are concerned with job recruitment and flexible working practices, the latter also frequently utilized in France. Other measures utilized in French, Greek, German, and Dutch companies are those related to training, development and promotion (Walker & Taylor 1997). Age-awareness training for managers seems rare, although a few good examples, mainly Dutch, have been recorded (Taylor 1998).

The size of the companies partly explains why training or any other measures for employees are often neglected. The companies have neither resource managers nor units which take care of the personnel. Small enterprises are more like teams with joint targets. However, small enterprises do possess several advantages: decision making is democratic and the job offers freedom and responsibility (Lindström and Schrey 1997). As mentioned before, the only available HRM tool for ageing workers has too often been retirement. The options of retraining, redesign or organization of work, flexible work arrangements, counselling and health promotion are either not known or are not utilized by employers.

In this study emphasis is on attitudes towards ageing workers and HRM measures utilized in the SMEs as push and pull factors on the individual and organizational levels. Beyond the scope of this research are the macro level value systems, organizational level atmosphere and work load, and individual attitudes towards work and retirement.

Table 1 Challenges for the management of ageing human resources and examples of measures for combating these (adapted from Pearson 1996; Walker 1997).

CHALLENGES FOR HRM Push Factors	MEASURES
MACRO LEVEL • pension systems and policies • labour market demand • values, attitudes and beliefs ORGANIZATIONAL LEVEL • working conditions • atmosphere • workload • lack of opportunities for training INDIVIDUAL LEVEL • psychological/physiological burden • level of basic education • loss of meaningfulness of work, values	• improving facilities, ergonomic planning • interaction, openness • job sharing, part-time jobs • providing training, incorporating learning in daily activities • rehabilitation • providing training leading to diploma, e.g. apprenticeship training • job redesign, job rotation
Pull Factors	
MACRO & ORGANIZATIONAL LEVEL • values, attitudes and beliefs INDIVIDUAL LEVEL • attitudes towards work and ageing • one has worked long enough • leisure time and family • diminishing strength • existing financial resources	• enhancing positive attitudes • part-time jobs, gradual retirement • create opportunities for mentoring novices, increase meaningfulness of work • part-time jobs, gradual retirement • increase meaningfulness of work

4. Attitudes and HRM

The exclusion of the ageing workers from HRM policies is often justified as being in accord with the general attitude towards ageing workers.

Ageing workers have a more positive view of the ageing than younger employees. There is a clear relationship between age and attitudes: the younger the person, the less positive are the attributes attached to ageing. A Finnish study (Ahola & Huuhtanen 1995) confirms the previous findings of international researchers - although the attitudes found are neither extremely positive nor extremely negative, and differences are marginal, except for the assessment of social competence. Differences were also observed between attitude and position in the organization. In general, blue-collar workers considered the ageing worker to have less capacity and lower performance ability than younger employees. Opinions common to all groups were that the ageing workers know their work better because of their considerable experience, that they work accurately and calmly, and they have certain routines which they have difficulty changing. Younger employees were thought to bring new elements into work: changing it, being more flexible and faster, quicker learners. The younger workers considered themselves to be less spontaneous, liable to make more mistakes, having less power - even to the extent of being belittled in the workplace (ibid.). Apparently, there are negative attitudes both ways.

Age-related changes have also been evaluated as mainly positive, but once again with slightly less positive evaluations presented by younger respondents (Åhsberg, Gamberale & Hallsten 1993). The ageing workers ascribe more positive than negative changes to ageing, and the impact of these changes on working ability was basically considered positive. Concerning abilities related to intellectual flexibility, such as creativity, stress tolerance, adjustment, and tolerance of differences, younger and older respondents seemed to have opposite conceptions of the direction of change; the younger seeing a negative, and the older a positive change with increasing age. Results indicate that the older workers regard themselves as increasingly capable of managing complex situations. Why the younger ones do not acknowledge these same changes is an interesting question (ibid.).

A person with a negative attitude towards his own ageing certainly detects negative changes in the ageing of others, whereas a person with a positive attitude realizes the strengths of ageing workers. The ageing are important to any organization as they are experienced and committed to the organization. They also provide managers and developers of human resource management with valuable information about the atmosphere and well-being of the employees by expressing their feelings openly. Furthermore, a manager's values and attitudes are reflected in the practices and atmosphere of a workplace (Puurula 1996). A manager might be younger or find himself/herself in a position where the employee has more knowledge about the work itself and is highly regarded because of his experience. In these situations, the manager might feel the authority of ageing workers as a threat to his/her position as leader. By taking on the role of a coach, leading people instead of assigning tasks, a manager might find powerful support among the ageing workers: they are often unofficial leaders of groups and informants possessing valuable resources (Juuti 1994).

A study of managers' attitudes towards older workers indicates that while there seems to have been an improvement, stereotypic assumptions are still endorsed (Legge, Cant, O'Loughlin & Sinclair 1997). Older workers were perceived as both less willing and less able to learn and resistant to new technologies. Moreover, the assumption that younger employees take more sick leaves was confirmed. However, while records show that this is actually the case, the scales are balanced because younger workers have many short absences while older workers tend to take a few long leaves. Older workers were also described as reliable and possessing a high work ethic, paying attention to detail, and providing quality customer service (ibid.).

The influence of external attitudes and values is clearly demonstrated by the fact that ageing workers themselves ascribe stereotypic characteristics to the ageing process. Naturally enough, these tend to become self-fulfilling prophesies. New technology, a very low or very high average age in the company, lack of flexibility in the organization, conflicts between generations together with prejudice and ageism appear to be reasons for employers' reluctance to hire ageing workers. Age, too, appears to be a hindrance in the recruitment process. Ageing workers have also been ascribed unflattering attributes, such as being inflexible, opposing change, having an attitude of superiority, a low level of commitment, being negative, tired, and too expensive (Johansson 1997). Even though costs do tend to rise through higher wages, social security and pension payments, the result does not have to be negative from an organization's point of view if the human resources of the ageing are fully utilized (OECD 1996).

Ageing workers participate actively in adult education. Wage earners aged 45-54 received work related training the most. In the older age groups other than work related education and training has been more dominant. (Blomqvist,

Koskinen, Niemi & Simpanen 1997). A Finnish study on staff's opinions of on-the-job training in the retail and hotel business show that the level of formal education was higher among the younger age groups, but participation in courses arranged by the employer was the highest in the oldest age group, i.e. 55 and over. The need that was felt for extra vocational training decreased after the age of 45, but the older employees were more satisfied with the on-the-job training provided (Puurula 1995).

Here the ageing workers are a highly motivated group: the complete reverse of negative stereotypic assumptions. In order to maintain the ageing workers in gainful activity and to increase their attachment to the labour market and working life, emphasis should be placed on the framework of lifelong learning. This approach is needed to promote productivity, to adjust employees' competencies, and to enhance their capacity to adapt to the changing demands of work and the labour market (OECD 1996).

5. Management of Ageing Human Resources in SMEs - Principles and Realities

Human resources practices and the value placed on ageing workers in an organization have varied during different phases in the development of HRM. Having focused on job performance and loyalty in the 1970s, job performance and individual development in the 1980s, it has in the 1990s leaned towards human and organizational learning and development. Sources of knowledge have shifted from managers and experts to teams of workers and consultants. Even so, the perceived value of ageing workers in the organization has been low and ambivalent. It is anticipated that in the first decade of the 21st century the focus will be on lifelong learning, education and personal growth and development. Core teams, cooperation and personal portfolios will be the sources of knowledge in the organization. Through this development in HRM, it is anticipated that the value of ageing workers will increase and that age will become less of an issue (Tikkanen, Valkeavaara & Lunde 1996).

SMEs often lack human resource development and training schemes. Nevertheless, they can be ideal sites for human resource development because of the more direct communication, flexibility in work, flatter hierarchy, the relatively greater impact of a single employee's actions on the whole organization and a greater insecurity which makes an organization be more responsive to labour market changes and customer demands. More informal development programmes may have a greater impact than the rigid programmes in large organizations (Bacon, Ackers, Storey & Coates 1996).

Ageing workers have specialized knowledge. To be able to pass this on to younger employees, it is important that they obtain opportunities to refine and update their vocational and trainer's skills. Unfortunately, there are employers who find interest in such practices only if the financial or commercial advantage is immediately evident (Pearson 1996). Employers refer to the ageing workers' lack of skills - although that in itself is often the result of a lower level of formal training (Forteza & Prieto 1994). HRD practices often exclude the peripheral labour force. This includes part-time and temporary workers and minority groups such as women, ethnic minorities and ageing workers. Selective training policies easily exclude those who would benefit most from training (Forrester, Payne & Ward 1995). Vocational education or training is seldom considered a viable way of managing the ageing employees' final years before retirement (Puurula 1996). Excluding employees from training on the basis of age - not to mention current discussions which concern them - and taking a superior position displays insensitivity and an attitude which ignores the skills and knowledge of the ageing. A lack of knowledge and skills cannot be cited as justification as this is seldom solely the fault of the individual enough reasons may be found in the management of the human resources of the organization (Tikkanen 1998.)

Within the diversity of human resource management issues, including corporate and human resource planning, policy, recruitment and selection, rewarding, and organization design and development, we will especially emphasize training as it is one of the main approaches to increase the organization's adaptability and raise the competence of its employees.

Human resources strategies employed in organizations can be grouped into four main categories based on continuity and availability of training. These are also the main criteria for lifelong learning. The categories are (Juhela 1994):
- a preventive strategy, in which training is neither continuous nor available for the entire personnel,
- a segmentation strategy, in which training is continuous but not available for the entire personnel,
- a strategy for managing change, in which training is not continuous but is available for the entire personnel, and
- a prospective strategy, in which training is both continuous and available for the entire personnel.

The preventive strategy is common in organizations where employees are considered merely a necessity for the production and do not possess any skills that are important to the organization from a strategic point of view.

Characteristic of these organizations is a reluctance to invest in their employees - and if such actions are called for, it is on an ad hoc basis with an emphasis on temporary training, not continuous development. The adoption of a preventive strategy has often been justified by arguments which undermine an individual's interest in developing himself/herself and his/her work. This non-continuous training neither offers real challenges for the employees nor enhances lifelong learning (ibid.)

The segmentation strategy is clearly connected to developing the qualifications of key employees in the organization. This policy easily strengthens the division between different groups in the organization as it does not cover the entire personnel (Juhela 1994). Managers are naturally influenced by their individual goals, which might include maintaining standing or avoiding conflict. In exercising personnel policy, the training of certain individuals is then used as a tool for achieving these goals (Keep 1992). This is typical of the segmentation strategy, where the problem is that the strategy is not intended to cover the change of work organization (Juhela 1994).

The strategy for managing change and the prospective strategy differ from each other in terms of how one defines the aim of human resources management. Is the aim to develop the management of new technology or is change seen as a continuous process requiring constant development through training and education? The strategy for managing change is based on the assumption that change is manageable through the development of human resources at all levels of the organization. Training is not continuous, and the time periods might be short and limited only to cover major changes (ibid.).

A prospective strategy is implemented in an organization's strategies at large and is based on the view that HRD is a continuous process essential for the optimal utilization of employees' knowledge and a systematic accumulation of that knowledge. In a prospective strategy organization all employees, including the ageing, are treated equally in human resources management. Typically, training and development are tied both to the other areas of organizational strategy and to the more individual goals of the employees, thus enhancing productivity and personal well-being at work. This does not necessarily mean rising personnel costs, but an efficient utilization of existing funds. The main obstacle for successful HRM is the lack of organization and planning systems (ibid.).

Productivity, job satisfaction, well-being, health and safety are determined by factors falling into two categories: those fitting the job to the person, and those fitting the person to the job. Ergonomics, job redesign and career development fall into the first category. Processes in the second category are institutional selection and training (Hesketh & Bochner 1994). Some common prerequisites for the management of human resources, especially regarding the ageing, are the analysis of tasks, and the redesigning of them, or the matching of employees to suitable jobs, improvement of assessment of actual competencies, investigation of performance appraisal, career development practices and ergonomics and training adjusted to meet the special needs of the ageing (Warr 1994). Arrangements for the ageing usually also suit younger workers, but not necessarily vice versa (Pearson 1996).

The flexibility of the work force depends on its ability to continuously acquire new knowledge. Older workers with a poor level of basic education initially need to learn how to learn. Building new information on existing knowledge, according to the principles of the constructivist view, supports the older employees' learning. Learning is always contextual, also taking place outside formal training (Rauste-von Wright 1994). The employer may introduce mentoring, job rotation, study circles, and incorporate learning tasks in the activities of teams and groups to connect learning with everyday working life (Martinsuo, Otala & Keltikangas 1997). Even though on-the-job training is regarded as difficult to identify, evaluate, and calculate costs for effectively, it is a highly contextual form of training and is well suited to workers with lengthy experience (Pearson 1996).

Large organizations and SMEs differ in that the latter seldom have specific personnel assigned to the development of HRM. The smallest enterprises struggling on the edge of existence do not have development and implementation of training schemes as their top priority (Pearson 1996). Short-term financial pressures dictate to what extent investments in human resource management and development are actually planned and carried through. Accounting systems count the costs of such investments, not the consequences of failure to invest in the development of human resources (Keep 1992). Even so, continuous learning is vital and should be implemented in the everyday practices and policies of these companies. With the ageing of the work force in mind, organizations will have to solve the dilemma of implementing the vision of employees being their main resource as they aim for increasing competitiveness (Tikkanen et. al. 1996).

6. Research Task

This study intends to map out human resource practices in small and medium-sized enterprises. The focus of the analysis is on human resources management and attitudes towards the ageing in SMEs. Special areas for the training of ageing workers are also investigated as HRM is traditionally training-centred.
Questions of interest:
1. To what extent do human resource practices exist in SMEs?
2. In what areas do leaders/managers and employees consider that ageing workers need further training ?
3. Is there a relationship between age, gender, position, and educational background and the attitude towards ageing workers?

Although SMEs usually lack specific human resource development and training schemes, for the purpose of this study companies were primarily selected among firms participating in training and development projects in Finland. A total of 100 enterprises of which 75 per cent had participated in the ESF funded projects 'Skilled Uusimaa' (a region in southern Finland, including the Capital) and GRAM - a development project for the printing industry were selected. In the selection of the enterprises the researchers aimed at obtaining a sample representative of both region and field of industry - though the focus is primarily on fields with an exceptionally difficult situation with regard to an ageing work force, e.g. the printing industry. Other fields represented in the sample are metal, electronics, plastic, textile and food industries, and in the service sector real estate, transportation, travel, hotel, and retail business, book-keeping, and health care (Graph 1).

On average the companies employed 66 employees. As these organizations have already participated in training and development projects, they might bias the sample and thus not represent the actual situation in Finnish SMEs generally. For this reason 25 randomly chosen enterprises were included in the sample as an ex post facto control group.

6.1 Sample

The sample consists of 228 individuals of whom 100 were leaders or human resource managers and 118 employees. In the companies either the leader or the human resource manager was chosen for the interview based on who had the responsibility for personnel matters. Criteria for selection of the subordinates were age (an ageing employee if available) and the number of years in the company (preferably at least one year). In companies that have remotely located branches, the location of the employees' work place was also a criterion for selection. On the basis of the information available, the subordinates were chosen either randomly or in some enterprises by their manager beforehand, or at the time of the interviewer's visit in the company. The researchers have aimed at a random selection in order to minimize bias.

GRAPH 1. Companies by industry (percentage).

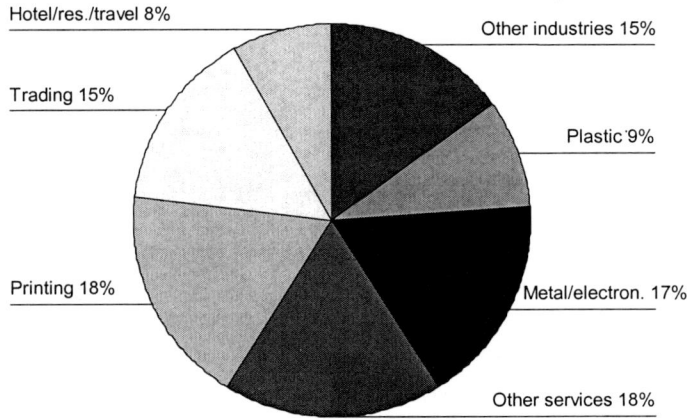

6.2 Interviews

The interviews were conducted between October 1998 and March 1999. Data, both quantitative and qualitative, was gathered through interviews using structured questionnaires with instruments and open-ended questions incorporated.

The following main themes were included in the interviews: background information (personal/organizational), personnel policy, organization, leadership, human resource management, recruitment, and retirement. The interviews with the leaders and human resource managers lasted approximately one hour. The focus was on organization and human resource development, whereas the focus in the interviews with the subordinates was on individual experiences of ageing in working life. Interviews with the subordinates lasted approximately half an hour. All interviews were taped, and the researchers took notes during the interviews. The results have been analysed by means of a package for statistical analysis (SPSS).

7. Results

Of the interviewees, 46 % were women, 54 % men. 32 % of the managers, and 57 % of the workers were women. The average age of all interviewees was 47 (ranging from 19 to 63) being slightly higher for the workers (48 vs. 46), as older workers were deliberately sought after for the interviews so as to gain insight into questions concerning willingness to stay on in working life and the wish to retire (these results remain beyond the scope of this article). Of the managers, 53 % were aged 45 or over. The corresponding percentage for workers was 78 %. As expected, the level of education was higher among the managers.

7.1 HRM measures

We divided the HRM measures into three basic categories: health-promoting measures, training, and flexible design and organization of work. The first category involved medical services and information sharing (personalized and written), exercise and fitness programmes along with occupational safety and health services. The second category included a diverse set of measures starting from various types of training, guidance, mentoring, workshops, and individual feedback. The design and organization of work involved work time, leave of absence, job rotation, changes in work process and other measures.

These categories seem to be equally utilized, although some single measures are more widely employed than others. The most utilized measure was the medical inspection (92%). The reason is logical: the medical inspection is compulsory in many fields. The inspections were considered the best functioning measure by 12 per cent of the respondents. The second most frequently utilized measure was training, including further and vocational training (85% of respondents). These were considered to be the best by 9 per cent of the respondents. Basic vocational education, considered the best measure by 9 per cent, was used in 58 per cent of the enterprises. Automation and new technology have forced companies to invest in training. As one director explained it, two workers out of 40 are continuously taking part in some sort of on-the-job training. For instance, team work and management training also proved to be popular. Surprisingly, work safety measures appeared only in 82 per cent of the companies despite the regulations and laws relating to work safety. This means that at the company level the measures based on laws and regulations have often failed.

The use of measures differed between small and medium-sized companies. The smaller companies had employed only one or two measures while the medium-sized companies possessed experience of a wider variety of measures. The results also confirm the statement that Finland has no tradition of part-time jobs. Partial employment before or after retirement is rare. Despite the fact that the companies were for the most part organizations in which extensive training and development projects have been carried out, few had implemented any special arrangements for the ageing workers. This was simply because there was no awareness of the issue. This was a particularly important finding as it shows that much work still is to be done on raising the level of awareness before systematic strategies and improvements can be expected. This is also supported by the fact that systematic strategies for personnel development are rare.

Human resources management is training-orientated, often based on a traditional trainer-centred pedagogy (Hesketh & Bochner 1994). The emphasis on training is also evident in the present study. The use of group work, mentoring and guidance is still quite limited. For instance, mentoring was a concept that was most often misunderstood or unknown to the interviewees.

The findings are in line with a study of shop-stewards by Laukkanen (1998). Only one fifth of all workplaces had evaluated the development needs of ageing workers. Health promotion targeted at the ageing worker was the most utilized measure, followed by work safety and training. The companies in our sample were more active in human resource development than those in the study of Laukkanen; this is mainly due to the fact that these companies were involved in development projects. The companies have received consultation and funding for training and other types of public support for their human resource development.

7.2 Training for ageing workers

The interview included an open-ended question concerning the ageing workers' training needs (Table 2). When asked in which areas the managers and employees considered ageing workers to need further training, almost half of the respondents replied "computers" or "new technology". Older people who have not grown up surrounded by new technology doubt their ability to learn to use computers. Computer anxiety appears to be quite common among ageing workers.

Vocational training was recommended for ageing workers by one fourth of the interviewees. Also the management of change and process-thinking, guidance

Challenges and development 57

in physiological and psychological well-being and working capacity, changing attitudes, and languages and international issues were occasionally mentioned. Surprisingly, the training of trainers and leadership training were not cited as important topics for ageing workers.

The results are similar to those in a recent study on vocational competence and training needs in Finnish SMEs (Alppivuori & Vuorio 1997), where leadership, team work, co-operation, multi-skills, customer relations, and computer technology were suggested as training areas. From an HRM point of view, emphasizing the development of skills specifically possessed by the ageing seems reasonable. Utilizing the special potential of ageing workers - for example developing trainer's skills - certainly benefits an organization.

Table 2. *"In which areas do you consider ageing workers to need further training ?" Groups identified in the open-ended question. Question answered by managers and employees.*

1. Computers, new technology	48 % of interviewees
2. Vocational training	26 %
3. Guidance in physiological and psychological well-being and working capacity, changing attitudes,	
4. Managing change, process-thinking	11 %
5. Languages, international issues	9 %
6. Teamwork, social skills	7 %
7. Other training (entrepreneurship, training of trainers, occupational safety, quality, pre-retirement counselling and leadership)	7 % 9 %

7.3 Attitudes towards ageing workers

All interviewees were asked to rate their assumptions about ageing workers on a scale from 1 (strongly disagree) to 5 (strongly agree) in a 20-variable index. The statements loaded on four factors describing
- Innovation, e.g. "Ageing workers are highly motivated to learn", "... take others into consideration", (Alpha = .73),
- Cognitive capacity, e.g. "... know how to state arguments", "... are flexible", (Alpha = .80),
- Work commitment, e.g. "... want what is best for the company", "... are committed to the company", (Alpha = .65), and
- Slowness, e.g. "... are slow", "... learn slowly", (Alpha = .74).

On average, the respondents considered a person as 'ageing' after reaching the age of 53 with the range varying from 10 to 65 years. The younger the interviewee, the lower was the perceived time of "ageing". The number of answers to this question was 186 as not all interviewees wished to make a statement.

Overall the attitudes towards the ageing were quite positive (mean 3.67). There were no significant differences in attitudes between male and female interviewees or educational backgrounds. The workers had a slightly more positive view of the ageing workers than the managers. This result is contradictory to previous research (Ahola & Huuhtanen 1995), where blue-collar workers had a less positive attitude towards the ageing. This might be explained by the higher mean age of the workers over that of the managers between age groups of managers and workers. Significant differences of opinion were found on innovation (Tables 3.1 and 3.2).

Workers aged 45 and over had a more positive view of ageing employees than other groups. They also had a significantly more positive view of the innovative capacity of ageing employees than both managers and workers under 45. Regarding slowness, cognitive capacity and work commitment there were no differences between the age groups.

Differences in attitude stem rather from both differences in age and position in the organization. The greatest differences are to be found between younger managers and older workers. Those who are 45 and older seem to have a more positive view of themselves concerning their innovative capacity. Innovation, in a broad sense, includes not only creativity, but also aspects of tacit knowledge, such as strategic thinking.

The differences in attitudes can create problems in communication between the two age groups and employees in different positions who have such different conceptions of the abilities of one of the groups. During training, the use of heterogeneous groups might help overcome barriers, but it is crucial that the trainer is aware of existing attitudes.

8. Conclusions and Further Research

In this study we have attempted to analyse attitudes towards ageing workers and HRM measures, especially training, utilized in SMEs as push and pull factors on the individual and organizational levels.

Tables 3.1 and 3.2. Differences in attitudes between age groups in different positions.

ANOVA

		Sum of Squares	df	Mean Square	F	Sig.
INNOVATION	Between Groups	43.575	3	14.525	18.222	.000
	Within Groups	159.425	200	.797		
	Total	203.000	203			
COGN.CAPACITY	Between Groups	2.808	3	.936	.935	.425
	Within Groups	200.192	200	1.001		
	Total	203.000	203			
COMMITMENT	Between Groups	4.397	3	1.466	1.476	.222
	Within Groups	198.603	200	.993		
	Total	203.000	203			
SLOWLESS	Between Groups	1.139	3	.380	.376	.770
	Within Groups	201.861	200	1.009		
	Total	203.000	203			

Position & Age		INNOVA	COGNIT	COMMIT	SLOW
Manag < 45	Mean	3.0889	3.8385	3.8389	2.5815
	N	45	45	45	46
	Std. Deviation	.5162	.5364	.5505	.6792
Empl < 45	Mean	3.2214	3.6429	3.6571	2.6786
	N	28	28	28	28
	Std. Deviation	.5287	.5245	.6033	.6731
Manag > 45	Mean	3.2760	3.8387	3.9120	2.6200
	N	50	50	50	50
	Std. Deviation	.4710	.3971	.4868	.5895
Empl < 45	Mean	3.6381	3.9852	4.0067	2.6641
	N	97	98	97	99
	Std. Deviation	.5472	.5985	.4840	.8911
Total	Mean	3.3905	3.8788	3.9064	2.6390
	N	220	221	220	223
	Std. Deviation	.5669	.5452	.5243	.7597

The early retirement culture has become more or less institutionalized in Finland and changes in this culture cannot be expected. The interviewed employees and managers wanted to retire three to five years earlier than the official retirement age. The early retirement culture presents challenges for human resources development in that it gives employers an opportunity to avoid the question of the positive management of ageing human resources. These include training, flexible working practices, ergonomics and health promotion.

The overall positive attitude towards ageing is an encouraging result and should increase the attachment of the ageing to the work force. Even so, a difference between age groups and position in the organization persists and it was remarkable with regard to evaluation of innovative capacity. There might be a need in SMEs to tackle prejudice towards other age groups in order to promote a more positive atmosphere.

One of the central findings of this study was that an awareness of the issue of ageing, in general, did not exist. A prerequisite for the implementation of the management of ageing human resources is an awareness of the age issue. The high figures on participation in adult education in Finland (Blomqvist et. al. 1997) does not yet mean that an awareness exists. It did not exist in most of the organizations which took part in the present study. This is illustrated by the fact that most managers did not know the age distribution in their organization. Most had some idea as to the age structure, but precise calculations had not been made - except in a handful of cases in the printing industry, where on average the work force is ageing even more rapidly than in many other trades. The lack of any kind of calculations was usually explained by the novelty of the issue; the managers had never thought of the ageing workers as being separate from other workers. There are two sides to this: the fact that the managers had not really thought of age issues is a positive sign indicating equality between different age groups, at least in some respects. But, by ignoring some realities about ageing we run the risk of overlooking special needs and wasting the potential of the ageing workers in the organization.

Training, as one of the most frequently utilized HRM tools, has covered certain groups - in some cases the entire personnel - but the training has not been continuous. A mix between the segmentation strategy and the strategy for managing change (cf. Juhela 1994) appears to be common in the SMEs in the present study. Nevertheless, the training and development projects seem to have sparked an interest in continuing such projects in the future. However, there are many companies that did not have any kind of strategy, written or oral. This makes the participation in development projects all the more important for SMEs lacking HRM personnel and a stated HRM policy.

The most commonly used human resources development measures in SMEs were health promotion and training. The study did not reveal if the employees had had the opportunities to influence the participation and the content of the development programmes. The suggested training areas for ageing employees seem to be based on both realities and stereotypic assumptions. An important finding is that special training programmes and other measures especially designed for the ageing workers are rare. This is partly due to the unawareness of the ageing in general. However, we could ask if it is necessary to design programmes only for them? The ageing employees have more positive attitudes with respect to their capabilities and social skills than their younger counterparts. What effect would a programme only for the ageing have in a small or medium-sized company? Would it create or strengthen existing gaps between generations?

The aim has been to describe the state of human resources management in SMEs with regard to ageing employees. HRM practices, or the lack of them, reflect the attitudes of leaders and management towards the ageing workers in the organization. Most of the enterprises in this study have participated in training and development. These are organizations, open to innovation and renewal, which might be adopted as models in the implementation of different HRM measures, and the overall positive view of ageing. It would not be fair, however, to claim on the basis of this limited sample that the situation in Finnish SMEs at large is so positive. Another limit to any such generalization is the age structure in the sample; the older age groups being over-represented.

Beyond the scope of this research were macro level value systems, organizational level atmosphere and work load, and individual attitudes towards work and retirement. It is the intention of the researchers to investigate the dynamics of attitudes and push and pull factors on an individual level. Other interesting topics requiring further investigation are how attitudes influence the interaction between different age groups, how the groups perceive the interaction and what role age awareness or the lack of it plays in these situations. In practice this knowledge could increase understanding, and help build constructive interaction between groups - thus decreasing conflict. If the aforementioned visions of lifelong learning, education, personal growth and development, and the increasing value of ageing workers (Tikkanen et. al. 1996) are to become reality in the 21st century, fundamental issues in HRM need to be reconsidered.

References

Age and Learning in Working Life. (1996). Nygård, C.-H. & Kilbom, Å. (Eds.). Arbete och Hälsa vetenskaplig skriftserie 16. Stockholm: National Institute for Working Life.

Ahola, K. & Huuhtanen, P. (1995). Ikäasenteet ja oikeudenmukaisuus työssä. Helsinki: Finnish Institute of Occupational Health.

Alppivuori, K. & Vuorio, R. (1997). Ammattitaito ja koulutustarve pienyrityksissä. In M. Bergström, M. S. Huuskonen, K. Koskinen, K. Lindström, S. Kaleva, G. Ahonen, J. Järvisalo, S. Forss, A. Järvikoski & R. Vuorio. *Työ ja ihminen. Työkyky yksilön, pienyrityksen ja yhteiskunnan menestystekijänä.* Research Reports 10. Helsinki: Finnish Institute of Occupational Health.

Bacon, N., Ackers, P., Storey, J. & Coates, D. (1996). It's a Small World: Managing human resources in small businesses. *The International Journal of Human Resource Management,* 7(1).

Blomqvist, I., Koskinen, R., Niemi, H. & Simpanen, M. (1997). *Adult Education Survey 1995. Adult Education in Finland.* Helsinki: Statistics Finland.

Chené, A. & Sigouin, R. (1995). Never Old Older Learners. *International Journal of Lifelong Education,* vol. 14, no. 6, 434-443.

Chusmir L.H. (1990) A Shift in Values in Squeezing Older People. Personnel Journal. January 1990. 48-52.

Elinikäinen oppiminen. (1994). A. Kajanto & J. Tuomisto (Eds.). 4th Ed (1997). Helsinki: KVS Foundation and Adult Education Research Society in Finland.

Forrester, K., Payne, J. & Ward, K. (1995). Lifelong Education and the Workplace: a critical analysis. *International Journal of Lifelong Education,* vol. 14, no. 4, 292-305.

Forteza, J. A. & Prieto, J. M. (1994). Aging and Work Behavior. In *Handbook of Industrial & Organizational Psychology.* (1994). Vol. 4, 2nd Ed. H. C.

Triandis, M. D. Dunnette & L. M. Hough (Eds.). Palo Alto: Consulting Psychologists Press, Inc.

Forss, S. & Karisalmi, S. (1997). 50 vuotta täyttäneiden työssä pysyminen ja sen taustatekijöitä. In M. Bergström, M. S. Huuskonen, K. Koskinen, K. Lindström, S. Kaleva, G. Ahonen, J. Järvisalo, S. Forss, A. Järvikoski & R. Vuorio. *Työ ja ihminen. Työkyky yksilön, pienyrityksen ja yhteiskunnan menestystekijänä.* Research Reports 10. Helsinki: Finnish Institute of Occupational Health.

Gould, R., Takala, M. & Lundqvist, B. (1992). *Varhaiseläkkeelle hakeutuminen ja sen vaihtoehdot.* Helsinki: The Central Pension Security Institute 1992:1.

Guillemard, A.-M. & van Gunsteren, H. (1991). Pathways and their prospectives: A comparative interpretation of the meaning of early exit. In M. Kohli, M. Rein, A.-M. Guillemard & H. v. Gunsteren (Eds.) *Time for Retirement. Comparative Studies of Early Exit from the Labor Force.* Cambridge: Cambridge University Press.

Handbook of Industrial & Organizational Psychology. (1994). Vol. 4, 2nd Ed. H. C. Triandis, M. D. Dunnette & L. M. Hough (Eds.). Palo Alto: Consulting Psychologists Press, Inc.

Hesketh, B. & Bochner, S. (1994). Technological Change in a Multicultural Context: Implications for Training and Career Planning. In H. C. Triandis, M. D. Dunnette & L. M. Hough (Eds.). *Handbook of Industrial & Organizational Psychology.* Vol. 4, 2nd Ed. Palo Alto: Consulting Psychologists Press, Inc.

Human Resouce Strategies. (1992). G. Salaman (Ed.). London: Sage Publications.

Ikääntyminen ja työ. (1994). J. Kuusinen, E. Heikkinen, P. Huuhtanen, J. Ilmarinen, J. Kirjonen, I. Ruoppila, T. Vaherva, O. Mustapää & S. Rautoja (Eds.) Helsinki: WSOY & Finnish Institute of Occupational Health.

Johansson, I. (1997). *Ålder och arbete. Föreställningar om ålderns betydelse för medelålders tjänstemän.* Stockholms universitet, pedagogiska institutionen.

Johnson, P. & Falkingham, J. (1992). Ageing and Economic Welfare. Sage Publications. London.

Juhela, A. (1994). Teollisuuden koulutusstrategiat elinikäisen oppimisen perspektiivistä. In A. Kajanto & J. Tuomisto (Eds.). *Elinikäinen oppiminen.* 4th Ed (1997). Helsinki: KVS Foundation and Adult Education Research Society in Finland.

Julkunen, R. & Nätti, J. (1994). Joustavaan työaikaan vai työajan uusjakoon? Tampere: Vastapaino.

Juuti. P. (1994). Johtaminen, työmotivaatio ja töiden organisointi sekä kehittäminen. In J. Kuusinen, E. Heikkinen, P. Huuhtanen, J. Ilmarinen, J. Kirjonen, I. Ruoppila, T. Vaherva, O. Mustapää & S. Rautoja. (Eds.). *Ikääntyminen ja työ.* Helsinki: WSOY & Finnish Institute of Occupational Health.

Keep, E. (1992). Corporate training strategies: the vital component? In G. Salaman (Ed.). *Human Resouce Strategies.* London: Sage Publications.

Kohli, M. & Rein, M. (1991). The Changing Balance of Work and Retirement. In M. Kohli, M. Rein, A.-M. Guillemard & H. v. Gunsteren (Eds.). *Time for Retirement. Comparative Studies of Early Exit from the Labor Force.* Cambridge: Cambridge University Press.

Laukkanen, E. (1998). *Tulevaisuus työpaikoilla. SAK:n ennakointihanke.* ESF Publications 38/98. Helsinki: Edita.

Legge, V., Cant, R., O'Loughlin, K. & Sinclair, G. (1997). Australian Managers' Attitudes towards Older Workers. In Å. Kilbom, P. Westerholm, L. Hallsten & B. Furåker (Eds.). *Work after 45?* Arbete och hälsa, vetenskaplig skriftserie 29, Vol 2. Stockholm: National Institute for Working Life.

Lilja, R. (1990*). Older Workers at the Crossroads - Early retirement in Finland.* Helsinki: Labour Institute for Economic Research.

Lindgren, J. (1990). *Towards an Ageing Society. Some Demographic and Socioconomic Aspects of Population Aging in Finland.* Väestöntutkimuslaitoksen julkaisusarja D 25/1990. Helsinki.

Lindström, M. & Schrey K. (1997). Pientyöpaikat työyhteisöinä. Organisaation terveys, tuottavuus ja yhteiskunnalliset muutospaineet. In M. Bergström, M. S. Huuskonen, K. Koskinen, K. Lindström, S. Kaleva, G. Ahonen, J. Järvisalo, S. Forss, A. Järvikoski & R. Vuorio. *Työ ja ihminen. Työkyky yksilön, pienyrityksen ja yhteiskunnan menestystekijänä.* Research Reports 10. Helsinki: Finnish Institute of Occupational Health.

Martinsuo, M., Otala, L.& Keltikangas, K. (1997.) *Jatkuvan oppimisen valmiudet ja niiden kehittäminen. Esimerkkejä metalliteollisuudesta.* Industrial Management and Work and Organizational Psychology, Working Papers No 6. Espoo: Helsinki University of Technology.

Miettinen, N., Söderling, I., Ehrnrooth, A., Heikkilä, E., Hjerppe, R., Martelin, T., Nieminen, M. & Shemeikka R. (1998). *Suomen väestö 2031 - Miten, mistä ja kuinka paljon?* Väestöpoliittinen raportti Suomen väestön kehityksestä vuoteen 2030. Väestöliitto Väestöntutkimuslaitos E 5/1998.

Nätti, J. (1996). Ikääntyvät, epätyypillinen työllisyys ja työn puute. Gerontologia 4/1996. 262-264.

OECD. (1996). *Ageing in OECD Countries. A Critical Policy Challenge.* Social Policy Studies No. 20. Paris.

Pearson, M. (1996). *Experience, Skill and Competitiveness: The implications of an ageing population for the workplace.* EF/96/02/EN. Dublin: European Foundation for the Improvement of Living and Working Conditions.

Piispa, M. & Huuhtanen, P. (1995). *Eläkeajatukset murroksessa. Muutokset työ- ja eläkeajatuksissa 1990-1994.* Ikääntyvä arvoonsa -työterveyden, työkyvyn ja hyvinvoinnin edistämisohjelman julkaisuja nro 19. Helsinki.

Puurula, A. (1996). Elderly Employees as Students in Retail Business. In C.-H. Nygård & Å. Kilbom (Eds.). *Age and Learning in Working Life.* Arbete och hälsa, vetenskaplig skriftserie 16. Stockholm: National Institute for Working Life.

Puurula, A. (1995). The Generation Gap: a case study on staff's opinions of on-the-job training in the retail and hotel business. In A. Kauppi, S. Kontiainen, K. E. Nurmi, J. Tuomisto & T. Vaherva. *Adult Learning in a Cultural Context.* Adult Education Research Society in Finland & University of Helsinki, Lahti Research and Training Centre.

Rasku, A. & Kinnunen, U. (1995). Ikääntyvien opettajien eläkehakuisuuden yleisyys ja syyt. *Gerontologia,* 9(2): 125-133.

Rauste-von Wright, M. (1994). Opetussuunnitelma ja oppimiskäsitys. In A. Kajanto & J. Tuomisto (Eds.). *Elinikäinen oppiminen.* 4th Ed. Helsinki: KVS Foundation and Adult Education Research Society in Finland.

Solem, P. E. & Mykletun R. (1997) Work Environment and Early Exit from Work. In Å. Kilbom, P. Westerholm, L. Hallsten & B. Furåker (Eds.) *Work after 45?* Arbete och hälsa, vetenskaplig skriftserie 29, Vol. 2. Stockholm: National Institute for Working Life.

Taylor, P. (Ed. and co-Author) (1998). *Projects Assisting Older Workers in European Countries. A review of the findings of Eurowork Age.* Luxembourg: European Communities, Employment and Social Affairs.

Tikkanen, T. (1998). *Learning and Education of Older Workers. Lifelong Learning at the Margin.* University of Jyväskylä, Jyväskylä Studies in Education, Psychology and Social Research 137.

Tikkanen, T., Valkevaara, T. & Lunde. Å. (1996). The ageing work force and life-long learning: an organizational perspective. *Education and Ageing.* 11(2), 100-114.

Time for Retirement. Comparative studies of early exit from the labor force. (1991). M. Kohli, M. Rein, A.-M. Guillemard, H. v. Gunsteren. (Eds.) Cambridge: Cambridge University Press.

Työ ja ihminen. Työkyky yksilön, pienyrityksen ja yhteiskunnan menestystekijänä. (1997). M. Bergström, M. S. Huuskonen, K. Koskinen, K. Lindström, S. Kaleva, G. Ahonen, J. Järvisalo, S. Forss, A. Järvikoski & R. Vuorio. Research Reports 10. Helsinki: Finnish Institute of Occupational Health.

Walker, A. (1997). *Combating Age Barriers in Employment. European Research Project.* Dublin: European Foundation of the Improvement of Living and Working Conditions.

Walker, A. (1995). *Investing in Ageing Workers - a framework for analysing good practise in Europe.* Backround paper for the European Foundation Project Combating Age Barriers in Job Recruitment and Training 1994-

1995. Dublin: European Foundation for the Improvement of Living and Working Conditions. WP/95/33/EN.

Walker, A. & Taylor, P. (1997). *Combating Age Barriers in Employment. A European portfolio of good practice.* Dublin: European Foundation for the Improvement of Living and Working Conditions. WP/97/53/EN.

Warr, P. (1994). Age and Employment. In H. C. Triandis, M. D. Dunnette & L. M. Hough (Eds.). *Handbook of Industrial & Organizational Psychology.* (1994). Vol. 4, 2nd Ed. Palo Alto: Consulting Psychologists Press, Inc.

Work after 45? (1997). Å. Kilbom, P. Westerholm, L. Hallsten & B. Furåker (Eds.) *Arbete och hälsa, vetenskaplig skriftserie* 29, Vol 2. Stockholm: National Institute for Working Life.

Ylöstalo, P. & Rahikainen, O. (1998). *Työolobarometri Lokakuu 1997.* Työpoliittinen tutkimus 186. Työministeriö. Helsinki 1998.

Åhsberg, E., Gamberale, F. & Hallsten, L. (1993). *Föreställningar om åldersförändringar och arbetsprestation.* En enkätundersökning bland yngre och äldre tjänstemän. Arbete och hälsa, vetenskaplig skriftserie 8. Stockholm: National Institute for Working Life.

ENTREPRENEURSHIP AND EDUCATION SEARCH FOR EACH OTHER IN THE POSTMODERN TRANSITION

Paula Kyrö

Entrepreneurship and education have not usually been related to the same scientific knowledge base, rather the contrary. Entrepreneurship, as a new field in science, has established itself in economics. Education for its part has established its place as its own separate field in science. It is suggested, however, in this article that these two phenomena and their scientific knowledge bases have, in the present postmodern transition a close relationship to each other. It can even be suggested that entrepreneurship provides education with those characteristics that are needed as construction material for a new emerging postmodern learning paradigm. When entrepreneurship and education are approached from the historical, cultural, multidisciplinary perspective the relationship between education and entrepreneurship and further between the postmodern learning paradigm and entrepreneurship can be delineated.

Entrepreneurship and education in cultural transitions

This study describes the meaning and purpose of entrepreneurship as an ever-changing reflection of culture, as a phenomenon searching for new forms in the course of history. From an epistemological point of view, this study represents postmodernism. The data consist, on the one hand, of historical events and on the other, of the comprehension of entrepreneurship and learning inherent in scientific models of economics, sociology and education. The holistic perspective used in this study allowed a reinterpretation of the understanding of entrepreneurship that for its own part reveals the relationship between education and entrepreneurship.

I start this analysis by employing first the concepts of culture and cultural phases as tools to approach entrepreneurship and education. Then I will position the ideas of entrepreneurship and learning into these phases to be able to reveal how they are searching for and interacting with each other in cultural transitions.

Culture itself, as a term, is a product of culture. The content and meaning of different explanations of culture are reflections of the time and place of birth (for the concept of culture see e.g. Aaltio-Marjosola 1991, Keesing 1981 or Murphy 1989).

Even though different scholars have a different focus in their definitions, culture can generally be regarded as referring to collectively created, accumulated history, a sort of heritage, which is transferred intentionally or unintentionally from past to present and from present to future. As a life-long learning process and as a collectively created reality, culture is at the same time collective and individual by nature. In this process the models found to be most successful will be transmitted. This process has conscious as well as unconscious aspects. Thus past models of behaviour are guiding our behaviour today, and our behaviour will in turn affect our understanding of the world.

Society does not transfer all the models, but only those which have resulted in success. When circumstances change, culture has to renew itself. This is difficult, because culture has a certain stability. It is constituted of collectively created norms and behaviour, and it carries in itself an interpretation of the world. This interpretation is mostly unconscious, involving rules on how to think about the world and how to behave (see e.g. Aaltio-Marjosola 1991). As a collective phenomenon culture has also a latent meaning which can only be seen through interpretation. This refers to the cohesion needed for the existence of society and for changing its models of behaviour when needed. How this socially-created heritage comes into being can be seen in the development of scientific paradigms. They are manifestations of society's idea of the world, human beings and the essential elements for its own success.

During the development of industrialization we can identify two culturally constituted transitions and two eras preceding them. In times of transition, past and present emerge as contradictory streams of ideas. Different ideas collide with each other. When past models do not guarantee success in the new circumstances, society attempts to reconcile the different ideas (for Levi-Strauss's dualism of mind see e.g. Sturrock 1981). It consciously or unconsciously makes choices between the different values. Those choices are the foundation for the ethos of the incoming era. They guide the behaviour of society.

The first modern transition took place at the beginning of industrialization during the 18th and 19th centuries, when the traditional era came to a close. Out of this transition developed the modern era, which, for its part, started to end in the 1970s, when the postmodern transition occurred. From a historical perspective the connection between entrepreneurship and learning can be seen as emerging in these two transitions - modern and postmodern. (E.g. Beck et. al. 1995, Dillard 1967, Harvey 1990, Turner 1990) Both entrepreneurship and learning can be positioned and analysed through and within these culturally constituted phases, which represent different ideas of human beings, society, learning and their interaction.

The first point of transition - detachment from the crafts and feudalism

The roots of an entrepreneurship

The roots of an entrepreneur for and in the industrial revolution can be retraced to the semantic development of the term (Haahti 1989). The first meaning can be found from the French verb 'entreprendre' in the twelfth century. It meant to do something referring to action without any economic connotation. In England the terms adventurer and undertaker were used to denote an entrepreneur, followed by such terms as projector and contractor from the 14th century onwards. These terms referred to such functions and qualities as an exciting, unknown experience, at one's own risk and a certain task or assignment from the Crown. All these were characteristics unknown to the social order of feudalism and the medieval crafts system. The seeds of free man can be identified in them.

Only from the 18th century onwards did a more outlined approach start to describe the phenomenon of 'entrepreneurship'. The concept emerged along with industrialization and developed as a product of it. First conceived by Cantillon and further developed by French physiocrats and their followers, entrepreneurship took a more specific, scientific meaning (Barreto 1989, Casson 1982, Entrepreneurship development in public enterprises 1991, Kirzner 1991, Kovalainen 1993, Wilken 1979).

Scientific models describing entrepreneurship

At the end of the Middle Ages in France, two systems, feudalism and the crafts system were coming to an end. People were tired of the court's profligacy and heavy taxation. Peasants were burdened with continous new regulations, which restricted their life.

The monopoly, the predictable social order and secure life of the crafts system was threatened by industrialisation. (Dillard 1967, Ethier 1988, Grubel 1981). The crafts system operated within a secure, controlled and organized environment and granted a modest but secure standard of living to its members. Industrialization, for its part, required risk-taking, capital and abilities to trade in unknown international markets. In this process, instead of hereditary, citizens started to demand freedom of trade and industry; in general, freedom to decide how to earn their livings.

Science started to model and describe this new environment. Its interests turned to these new, unknown circumstances, success in which required new models. In this diversity, with its new ideas of the human being, lay the seeds of entrepreneurship and the idea of education as the right of all members of society. The roots of entrepreneurship can be found in the economic writings of the French physiocrats. They opposed mercantilism and the power of money. For them money was only the symbol of wealth, whereas wealth itself lay in the land. Industry only changed its nature, and commerce transported it from place to place. (Lindeqvist 1905) Entrepreneurship referred to a farmer and farming in free circumstances. Along with the efforts of the physiocrats, the monopoly of the crafts system began to come to an end, and the term entrepreneurship started to be applied to emerging industry. It started to refer to extraordinary human beings that by their own efforts and thinking, created something new, which in turn created economic progress. (E.g. Barreto 1989, Casson 1982, Wilken 1979). This was the opposite of the traditional idea of a human being as a product of his inborn place in society.

From these roots developed different approaches to entrepreneurship theory building in economics, sociology and psychology (Kovalainen 1993, Vesala 1992). Amazingly few differences can be found in the theories of early contributors. They describe entrepreneurship as a special kind of management and ownership. The entrepreneur is a holistic, extraordinary human being who, by combining resources in a novel way, by applying new knowledge, taking risks and making decisions involved in that, creates something new. Some of the theories focus more on ownership, some on management.

What is different in the various explanations is connected to the time at which each of them was born. In each phase entrepreneurship describes a new phenomenon of the era or the transition. This journey we will follow, after describing the ideas of learning and education in the modern transition.

Table 1. Entrepreneurship and education in the transition from traditional to modern

THE ERA	THE IDEA OF THE HUMAN BEING AND LEARNING	THE IDEA OF ENTREPRENEURSHIP
TRADITIONAL - consumption and production in the same entity - social order created by feudalism and the craft system	*"God's unique creation, whose place in society was based on his class at birth"* learning by doing or learning as the privilege of a small elite	ENTREPRENEURSHIP STARTED ITS JOURNEY IN SEMANTICS - adventurer, risk- taker - project-based assignments from the Crown
THE TRANSITION FROM TRADITIONAL TO MODERN FROM THE EARLY 1700s TO THE LATE 1800s Towards industrialization - the decline of feudalism and the crafts system - liberalism and democracy as ideals - demand and supply start to diverge	*"God's unique creation vs. human being is created in the course of his upbringing"* Theories of learning start to take shape - the diversity of ideas - moral bases in theories - tension between the unique and equal man and man as a product of society and his own initiative, as a product of objective science	THE ENTREPRENEUR AS AN INDIVIDUAL AND ENTREPRENEUR- SHIP AS THE CREATION OF ECO- NOMIC SUCCESS * entrepreneurship breaks old models of behaviour and old systems, crafts and feudalism * creates new forms of work and ownership * innovator, co-ordinator * takes responsibility and risks * applies new knowledge

The ideas of learning

Education, as the right of all citizens, also has its roots in France during the Enlightenment. At that time learning was still the privilege of a small elite. In the 17th and 18th centuries there was no formal education for ordinary people. Education meant for them life-long learning by doing in the context into which they were born. The essential idea of the Enlightenment was to create an educational system for all, not only for those of noble birth. However, only in the 19th century were an educational system and theoretical bases for learning created.

This stream of ideas in the modern transition changed the idea of the human being and brought with it the bases for learning theories. Actually at that time two different ideas of the human being were fighting for dominance. The first one started in France. It valued the human being as a unique creature and as an essential part of Nature. In learning theories these thoughts are represented, for example, in the writings of Rousseau (1712-1778) and Pestalozzi (1746-1827) (Bowen 1981, Connell 1980). The other idea followed the British empiricists, who believed that the human being is created in the course of his upbringing. His behaviour could be studied objectively by perception. The seeds for this view can be found e.g. in the ideas of the British empiricists John Locke (1632-1704) and David Hume (1711-1776). Next we will see how these ideas of the British empiricists became dominant in the modern era, first in Britain and later in the Western world. Along with this development, entrepreneurship was no longer valued. Its meaning in society became marginal and it escaped to the realm of a small firm.

The modern era of organizing and growth

The dominance of growth suppresses entrepreneurship

At the time when the physiocrats were fighting for their beliefs and ideas in France, Adam Smith (1723-1790) made a visit there. He disagreed with the ideas of the physiocrats and started to write his best seller "The Wealth of Nations". Above all, Smith based his ideas on free trade. For him it was not land but work that had the greatest value, and it was of the utmost importance for the wealth of nations to expand the demand for it. Smith thought that by expanding trade, it was possible to create work and also to satisfy citizens' self-interests.

The followers of Adam Smith, the classical and later neo-classical schools in economics, were not interested in entrepreneurship. At the beginning their interest lay in macroeconomics and later in the behaviour of organization in the environment of large-scale enterprises. The efforts, made in many contexts, to combine these explanations with entrepreneurship are misleading (Lahti 1991). These theories are telling the story of industrialization, but not from entrepreneurship's point of view (Bell 1981, Kirzner 1991, Kyrö 1997). Barreto (1989) describes this story as the disappearance of the entrepreneur from microeconomic theories.

Their descriptions concentrate on large-scale enterprises, growing markets as well as rational decision-making and a rational mechanism between supply and demand (Bell 1981, Kirzner 1991, Kyrö 1997). The core of entrepreneurship theories, on the other hand, rests in the human, extraordinary and holistic, free individual who creates prosperity and welfare. It is therefore essential to be able to identify the distinction between these two.

When supply and demand were detached from each other, growing demand created the illusion of an "invisible hand" that was guiding the market. On this basis the classical school of economics was born, followed later by the neo-classical school with basically similar ideas. Theories of macroeconomics and, later, of microeconomics relied on the idea of rational actors in open markets with full information and rational decision-making. (Barreto 1989, Bell 1981). It is amazing how strongly the ideas of Adam Smith have followed us into the modern era, even though it has been observed in many contexts that the world is not predictable, that actors in society do not form a rational and homogeneous group and that, neither competition nor information is perfect. It was, however, possible to develop this illusion because demand was growing giving work and prosperity to the Western world. Its ideas of economic success remained pre-dominant throughout the modern era. By separating the story of Adam Smith from entrepreneurship theories we can reveal the very nature of entrepreneurship and follow its journey through history.

In modern time entrepreneurship theories lost their connection with the economic progress that was adopted by the story of growth. Instead, a new connection was born. Entrepreneurship began to describe a small enterprise, where management and ownership are manifested in the same entity. Thus the connection between the human being and the micro-level was born. Especially in the USA this approach achieved dominance in the entrepreneurship theory building of the modern era. Max Weber brought this idea from the USA to Europe at the beginning of the 20th century. The nature of entrepreneurship, however, remained the same as ever. It involved innovative, holistic risk-taking and the coordinating of ways of behaviour. It broke old systems and institutions and brought new forms of work and ownership.

Order – the idol of the modern age

While industrialization was expanding, another kind of ethos started to spread in Western industrialized countries from the late 19th century onwards. This was the dominance of organization. Denhard has located its origin in the 1870s. He describes it as an era dominated by organizational ethics, which in itself offers a way of living in our society. Gradually all our activities became organized outside ourselves. We have implicitly followed the very first interpretation of culture in our lives. The theme of cultural evolution started in the 18th century and dominated 19th-century anthropology (Murphy 1989). Basically culture was connected with 'order'. Provocatively expressed, it almost became synonymous with order. Through culture order was created from chaos or in uncivilized communities. All societies have tended to pass through the same stages in the same order toward a civilized, organized society. This unilinear path had as its idol the white race and Western, European civilization. (Murphy 1989).

We have organized our lives and nature believing that organizing is a way of securing our existence and success. Psychologists have divided our lives up into stages. Different organizations have then been founded for each stage. The efficient citizen follows these steps using the services that various organizations offer for each of them. Nature has been organized as well. We swim in winter, ski in summer, and so on. In welfare states more and more activities concerning our everyday life have been taken over by the government. This organizing can also be identified in the idea of the human being and learning.

Empiricism and order in learning theories

The ideas of organizing and growth also changed the idea of the human being. From the two different ideas of the modern transition, the modern era chose that of the British not only in economics, but also in learning and education. As the idea of the human being as the product of his upbringing and evolution took dominance, the human being was categorized and classified. Following the ideas of Charles Darwin (1809-1882) the human being came to be regarded as an animal among other animals, and later as a part of a machine or system (e.g. Bowen 1981, Fiske & Taylor 1984). This was followed by the notion that the world can be controlled and changed through order and technology. Not only was economics organised, but also human beings and society (e.g. Etzioni 1968, Halsey et. al. 1997, Morgan 1986, Zuboff 1988). As Etzion (1968) expressed it "society produced individuals suitable for organisation".

Table 2. Entrepreneurship and learning in the modern era.

MODERN ERA	THE IDEA OF THE HUMAN BEING AND LEARNING	THE IDEA OF ENTREPRENEURSHIP
IN THE EARLY 1900s Industrialization - continuous, implied growth, - expanding markets - growing prosperity and public sector - full employment - supply oriented, historical rationality - efficiency - standardization - bureaucracy, hierarchy, control - unified culture - the domination of the Western world	*"from animal to a machine or a part of a system"* BEHAVIOURISM STARTS TO DEVELOP - no difference between man and animal - learner as object of indoctrination and control - learning as a sum of reactions THE COGNITIVE PARADIGM BORN - man as an information producer and processor - learning treated as changes in information structure - the analogies of a computer or software	ENTREPRENEURSHIP SMALL BUSINESS MANAGEMENT AND OWNERSHIP * fighting for survival in a small firm

These thoughts can also be identified in learning theories at first in the behaviourist's learning paradigm and later in the thoughts of early cognitive paradigm. Behaviourism recognized no difference between man and animal. The learner was regarded as an object, which can be controlled. Learning could be seen as the sum of reactions. The early cognitive ideas for their part regarded the learner as an information producer. Learning was seen as changes in the information structure. Analogies were sought either from computers as machines or from their programmes. Thus the British story of rationality and order became dominant not only in economy but also in the ideas of learning. This was followed by diversity and expert knowledge. All of these violated the idea of the holistic, free and self-supporting human being.

The Postmodern transition

Entrepreneurship re-emerges in the postmodern transition

Now that we have found that the world around us is changing and that the illusion of continuous, implied growth, ever-growing prosperity, full employment and the domination of the Western world, with its large companies and institutions, has not in fact produced welfare, a new discussion is about to begin. There is much similarity between this conversation and that in France during the transition from traditional to modern. Our stable predictable environment has been replaced by turbulent, unpredictable circumstances in which the old models do not guarantee success. As a heritage from the modern era we have a large, rational, diversified story, global technology and global markets. On the other hand, however, the demands for local initiatives, a holistic human being and small narratives have raised their heads. These two ideas are manifested in many polarized phenomena that characterize this transition, such as rich and poor, employed and unemployed, young and old, segregation and networking, successes and failures. On the one hand, we are proceeding toward more and more centralised and ever larger organizations (EU, Nafta, Nasa), while on the other hand we have started to realize the meaning of small enterprises.

The basic problem behind these conflicts is that society has met up with new circumstances where the old models of behaviour do not guarantee success and welfare, although they still implicitly guide our behaviour. The notion that demand has its limits is too hard to realize and accept. Society is confused with the notion that even though its gross national product is growing, this does not guarantee work for its citizens. As a result, society cannot afford to maintain the services people have become used to expect from it. We face the very same problem as Adam Smith faced in 18th century Britain. The only problem is that we also have to notice that the solution for that is not the same as during the modern era, since circumstances have changed. Once again, as in the modern transition, we have turned our expectations toward entrepreneurship. First, we have noticed that it was the only sector that could create work. For example, in Finland according to the latest enterprise statistics for 1996, large firms have cut back on their employees by 1.6 % (7 400 employees), while middle-sized firms have increased their employees by 2.3 % (4 200 employees) and small firms by 7.6% (34 000 employees) (Statistics Finland 1998). With this notion entrepreneurship has been connected with other contexts in working life. Different service sectors in society, such as education and nursing, are searching for new structures, and entrepreneurship is a phenomenon harnessed to that (e.g. Halsey et. al 1997). Individuals, for their part, have become acquainted with it when stable careers have been replaced by project assignments.

In science, entrepreneurship has invaded organization theories, as well as other fields of economics, learning theories and so on, maintaining its original features. (Argyris et. al. 1985, Minzberg & Quinn 1991, Morgan 1968, Näsi 1991). In the transition from modern to postmodern, it has again found a new object, which is a product of the modern era, namely the organization. Now a new form of entrepreneurship has been created. The new term "intrapreneur" has been invented by Gifford Pinchot (1986). "Numerous, small intrapreneurial groups interact in voluntary patterns too complex and synergistic to be planned from above" (Pinchot 1986, 11). Intrapreneur refers to activities inside the organisation. This interpretation involves, though, two phenomena: collective behaviour and individual behaviour. The implicit assumption behind this is that entrepreneurship is always an individual category. However the organization is, as a phenomenon, collective by nature. Now that entrepreneurship has been harnessed to break an organized way of behaviour, it has received a new meaning and a new category. An organisation is not the same as a group of people. As an organization it has a history and culture of its own. The basic element in the term organisation is its collective nature. Organization is needed when the individual cannot accomplish his goals or fulfil his needs by himself.

Now three forms of entrepreneurship have been created. Entrepreneurship refers to entrepreneurs outside the organization, while intrapreneur means entrepreneurial activities conducted by the collective unit, organization. It refers to an organizational culture. This interpretation involves, however, two kinds of phenomenon: collective behaviour and individual behaviour. As an organization it has a history and culture of its own. It is thus something different from the actors of today, even though it is the actors of today who can change its way of behaviour in the present and in the future.

Thus time has actually produced three forms of entrepreneurship:

1. Entrepreneurship, referring to the individual entrepreneur and his or her firm

2. Intrapreneurship, referring to an organization's collective behaviour

3. Individual entrepreneurship, referring to an individual's self-oriented behaviour.

Entrepreneurship has thus been found to be important and meaningful in society at two points of transition, first at the transition from traditional to modern, and now at the transition from modern to postmodern. However whatever form entrepreneurship has taken in the course of history, it has always involved the human being as a free, holistic, risk-taking and self-supporting individual. This individual has the ability to perceive environment in order to find its possibilities, to combine resources in an innovative way and to negotiate with the environment in order to get them. He has the ability of solving the problems in unknown circumstances and to achieve success there.

At both points of transition, entrepreneurship has been harnessed to break old stable and hierarchical habits and institutions, and to introduce new ways of work and management. Its role has been in both cases to work as an instrument in society's efforts towards changing its culture.

The shift in the paradigms of the theories can also be identified in three forms of entrepreneurship. The first shift occurred when the economic process was lost and attention was addressed towards the small enterprise, the second when the organization was selected as the target. Is the third shift about to occur, i.e. can entrepreneurship again find and connect with the economic process? Only the future can tell us this. There are however some signals of this happening. When we turn our attention to changes in learning paradigms, we can discover signs of this. Education is society's media for manifesting its ideas. Thus the learning theories adopted reflect society's ideas about its success. The last step in this article interconnects postmodern learning and entrepreneurship. It will start first by delineating the knowledge bases of the different forms of entrepreneurship. Then a few principles adopted from entrepreneurship will be sketched, which can be seen as unifying features in a new emerging postmodern learning paradigm.

Learning paradigms diversify

Table 3 has gathered a summary of the development of entrepreneurship and learning. As can be noticed from the development of learning paradigms in the modern era, they are reflections of the ideas and tools for achieving society's goals. In the modern era they served the goals of organizing and the needs of large units in the private as well as in the public sector (see e.g. Halsey et. al. 1997). Now, as a reflection of the postmodern transition learning theories have also started to search for new models.

Table 3. The phases reforming the dialogue between entrepreneurship and learning

THE ERA	THE IDEA OF THE HUMAN BEING AND LEARNING	THE IDEA OF ENTREPRENEURSHIP
TRADITIONAL - consumption and production in the same entity - social order created by feudalism and the craft system	"God's unique creation, whose place in society was based on his class at birth" learning by doing or learning as the privilege of a small elite	ENTREPRENEURSHIP STARTED ITS JOURNEY IN SEMANTICS - adventurer, risk-taker - project-based assignments from the Crown
THE TRANSITION FROM TRADITIONAL TO MODERN FROM THE EARLY 1700s TO THE LATE 1800s Toward industrialization - the decline of feudalism and the crafts system - liberalism and democracy as ideals - demand and supply start to diverge	"God's unique creation vs. human being is created in the course of his upbringing" Theories of learning start to take shape - the diversity of ideas - moral bases in theories - tension between the unique and equal man and MAN AS THE PRODUCT OF SOCIETY AND HIS OWN INITIATIVE, AS A PRODUCT OF OBJECTIVE SCIENCE	ENTREPRENEUR AS AN INDIVIDUAL AND ENTREPRENEURSHIP AS THE CREATION OF ECONOMIC SUCCESS * entrepreneurship breaks old models of behaviour and old systems, crafts and feudalism * creates new forms of work and ownership * innovator, coordinator * takes responsibility and risks his own life * applies new kongelige
MODERN IN THE EARLY 1900s Industrialization - continuous, implied growth, - expanding markets - growing prosperity and public sector - full employment - supply oriented, ahistorical rationality - efficiency - standardization - bureaucracy, hierarchy, control - unified culture - the domination of the Western world	"from animal to a machine or a part of a system" BEHAVIOURISM STARTS TO DEVELOP - no difference between man and animal - learner as object of indoctrination and control - learning is a sum of reactions COGNITIVE PARADIGM WAS BORN - man as an information producer and processor - learning treated as changes in information structure the analogies to a computer or software	ENTREPRENEURSHIP SMALL BUSINESS MANAGEMENT AND OWNERSHIP * fighting for survival in a small firm

POSTMODERN TRANSITION	"the uniqueness as a universal feature in each human being"	THREE FORMS OF ENTREPRENEURSHIP
1970 -	"human being as a feeling entity and social actor"	1. The small enterprise, meaning the individual entrepreneur and his firm
Post-industrial phase	"woman as a human being among other human beings"	2. Intrapreneurship, meaning an organization's collective behaviour
Information society	COGNITIVE PARADIGM	3. Individual, self-oriented entrepreneurship, meaning an individual's self-oriented behaviour.
- more complicated environment and systems	- uniting paradigm start to take shape	ENTREPRENEURSHIP
- saturation of consumer demand	- it enlarges, takes different forms and has various applications	An instrument for changing culture.
- demand-oriented, fragmented markets	- it starts to be questioned	
- polarization, diversity, discontinuity, unemployment and insecurity	HUMANISTIC PARADIGM	
-public sector fulfils more complicated roles in society	Challenges the cognitive paradigm and its idea of the human being	
	CONSTRUCTIVISM, LATER SOCIAL CONSTRUCTIVISM	
	- individual him/herself constructs knowledge based on his/her past experiences	
	- social dimension in this process other people are involved as well	
	EXPECTATION FOR A NEW EMERGING POSTMODERN PARADIGM	
	- holistic approach to world and the human being	
	- human being is an actor with other human beings	
	-learning as a complex and diverse process	
	Human being as an extraordinary, risk-taking, creative, free and responsible actor.	

The cognitive paradigm has gathered itself together and found more complex forms. The holistic approach can be identified in the formulations of humanistic ideas. This tradition, however, has not formed a separate paradigm. It has rather questioned the mechanistic ideas of the human being in other paradigms and its contribution can be identified within their development. For example, the latest paradigm, constructivism, at the same time both follows and questions cognitivism. Its main point is that information is not transferred, but that the individual him/herself constructs information. He/she chooses and interprets information, assimilates and accommodates it, constructing new knowledge based on previous experiences. This learning process is always situational tied up with the culture the learner lives in and with (Von Wright & Von Wright 1998).

Thus we start to return to those ideas of the human being expressed during the Enlightenment. The connection between these two transitions in learning and education has also been identified by many scientists (see e.g. Halsey et. al. 1997). The combination of learning and postmodernism has attracted and inspired many writers. Some of them have started to develop the idea of a postmodern paradigm. There are, however, many similarities, but also differences between the focus of the prevailing paradigm of constructivism and the demands of postmodern society. What is suggested here is that we can learn some essential ideas and elements needed for that new paradigm from the phenomenon of entrepreneurship. There are resemblances between many present ideas of learning and features of entrepreneurship. They are still, however, fragmented pieces of knowledge, which the features of entrepreneurship can bind together. Resemblances from a cultural perspective give us an opportunity for suggesting that the combination of entrepreneurship and education is valuable for society in the present transition. Next with the help of the different forms of entrepreneurship, a sketch will be drawn of how the scientific knowledge bases for learning and entrepreneurship have a natural connection. Then, a description will be given of how a few essential principles adopted from entrepreneurship can be combined into the postmodern paradigm.

Scientific knowledge bases for entrepreneurship

If we look at the scientific knowledge bases that can delineate the different forms of entrepreneurship in this transition, we can notice that, besides economics, this transition has also brought in the science of education. The three forms and their relationship to each other are illustrated in Figure 1.

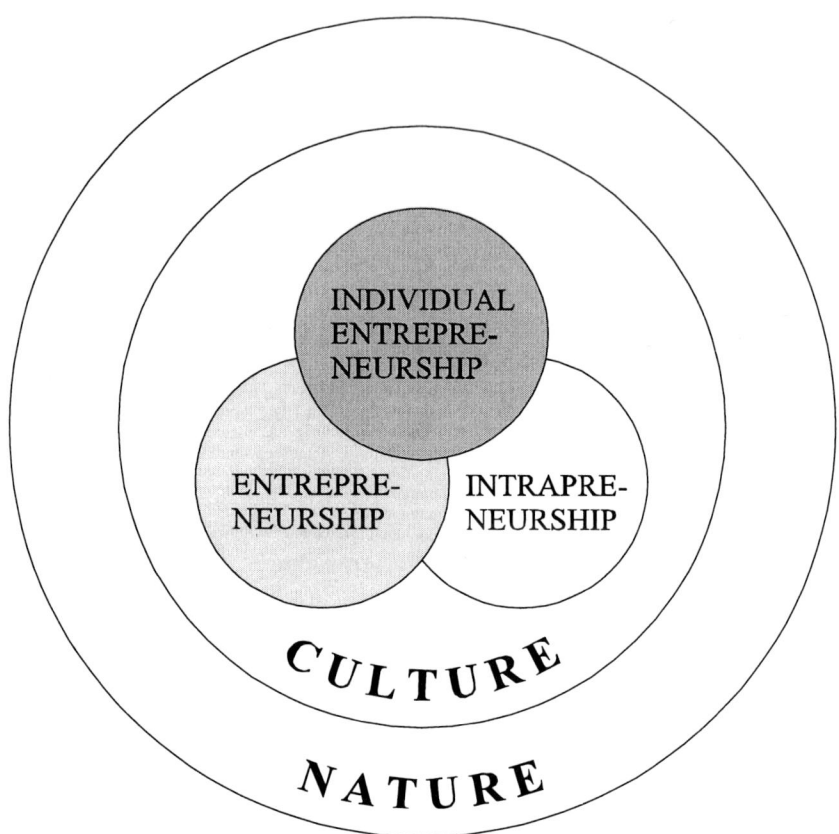

FIGURE 1: *Different forms of entrepreneurship (Kyrö 1997)*

The invention of the modern era, small business management and ownership has its natural knowledge base in economics. Intrapreneurship, the organization's collective behaviour has two different scientific knowledge bases. In economics it has been described by the latest organisation theories and strategic thinking (Argyris et. al. 1985, Johannisson 1984, Juuti & Soikkanen 1994, Kanter 1989, Minzberg & Quinn 1991, Morgan 1968, Näsi 1991, Peters & Waterman 1982, Schein 1985). Learning theories comprise, however, another field that has focused its interest on this collective phenomenon. Many scientists in education have delineated learning organization, cultural perspective and team building (Halsey et. al. Ed. 1997, Ruohotie & Grimmett ed. 1994, Sarala 1996, Kauppi et. al. 1994). Thus intrapreneurship has its knowledge base in both education and economics. Finally the oldest form and the very essence of entrepreneurship, the individual form of it, actually has its natural base in education. Economics does not provide many tools for individual behaviour, while education has always studied learning and individual learners. As far as individual entrepreneurship is concerned education has much to offer to the discussion about the different forms of entrepreneurship. Actually it is suggested here that the features and qualities of entrepreneurship comprise just those elements which have attracted attention in many new models and ideas of learning and have been delineated by many scientists. This can raise expectations for a new paradigm in which, in this postmodern transition entrepreneurship and learning find each other.

The Postmodern paradigm and entrepreneurship

We can search for the idea of a postmodern paradigm from those qualities that characterize entrepreneurship. The core of entrepreneurship theories as illustrated in this article, rest upon the human, extraordinary and holistic, free individual who is responsible for his own life and who, with his own actions creates prosperity and welfare by combining resources in a novel way, by applying new knowledge, taking risks and making decisions involved in that. He questions old hierarchies, rules and norms and creates new ways of behaviour.

If we look at the assumptions concerning the idea of human existence involved in these qualities, we can identify three basic elements: first **a** *holistic attitude towards the world, second a holistic view of the human being and thirdly the human being as an extraordinary, risk-taking, creative, free and responsible actor.* These three elements can be regarded as principles guiding the postmodern paradigm.

Holistic attitude towards the world

If we ponder what the holistic attitude means in learning, we can compare it to other paradigms, their ideas of the relation between the knower and what is supposed to be known (Mozer & Vander Nat 1987, 186-190), between the learner and what is supposed to be learnt.

The dominant paradigms of the modern era, behaviourism and cognitivism, both meet some difficulties with these. Behaviourism based on empiricism claims that sense impressions and observations are the criteria for knowledge (e.g. Niiniluoto 1984, 140, Sarvimäki 1988, 16-19). The justification of knowledge in empiricism is provided by observations and deduced from them (e.g.

Boed 1991, 5). The cognitive paradigm following the ideas of rationalism, thinks that it is possible to accomplish true knowledge through intellectual intuition or reasoning. There exists 'a priori' truth, which does not need empirical support (Niiniluoto 1984, Sarvimäki 1988). Neither of these meets the holistic principle's requirements. One assumes that learning takes place outside the person, the other inside a person. The knower in rationalism is a rational isolated thinker and in empiricism an outside observed object, whose world is restricted to the part of the world he can observe. Both of these viewpoints, however, are needed in the holistic approach to learning. Even together they do not provide a sufficient basis for the holistic approach.

In a changing reality we are facing the fact that what one is supposed to know and learn is changing, too[1]. In the diverse reality of the postmodern transition, these changing factors are numerous. How can we get a holistic view of this changing diversity? We have to choose the factors we are interested in. This means that we are also actors in this knowing and learning process and that our interests guide it. To describe these difficult matters we can ask for help from two directions; on the one hand from the pragmatists, whose basic element in knowing and learning is action and change guided by human meaning and human interests; on the other hand, help can be sought from those who have pondered the connection between meaning and language, that is, from the Swiss structuralist Ferdinand de Saussure and the French postmodernist Jean-Francois Lyotard.

Ferninand de Saussure, a linguist, who extended the idea of language into the field of meaning, semiotics, suggested that language was a social communication structure. It has two components: the signifier and the signified (Giddens, 1984, Sturrcok, 1981). Both are needed if we want to give a meaning to a phenomenon. They are the two sides in the process of producing a meaning. Thus the signifier and signified are in an interaction process with each other.

When we apply these ideas of language to human beings we turn to the pragmatists. For them, knowledge is born and evaluated through and for action.

---

[1] The modern time these ideas were accompanied by the stability. What was supposed to be true and known was stable and the development toward it was stable, both knower and known were regarded as stable. According to Niiniluoto (1984) "Truth and untruth are stable, characteristics independent of time... Pragmatists, however, consider truth as an acquired quality. According to Dewey truth is something that is happening to an idea while verifying it. According to James, (1913) truth means ultimately the same as the process of verification."

What guide the action and evaluation are meanings and subjective interests. They are represented in the ideas of Charles S. Pierce (1839-1914), William James (1842-1910), John Dewey (1859-1952) and C.I. Lewis (1883-1964), early contributors to pragmatism (Dewey 1951, James 1913, Rorty 1982, Thayer 1968). The problem with these ideas in a holistic approach concerns other knowers. There are not many ideas about that. Dewey (1951) saw man as a living being in interaction with the world. There is a confrontation with things in the interaction process. That is how meaning, emotions and interests are born. In this process, knowledge is created and tested by its consequences. In the holistic approach we must assume that interaction with the world concerns other human beings as well. Meanings are like culture, at the same time collective and individual. From this perspective knowing is also a social phenomenon. This means interaction with other people. Social constructivists have noticed this.

How can we create a holistic attitude towards the world, when the actors' subjective interests are involved and guiding that process? We can get some ideas from Lyotard. He suggests that in the postmodern transition the nature and position of knowledge, especially of scientific knowledge, is changing. As a solution he offers narrative knowledge (Lyotard 1985). Narratives have lost their meaning and value in modern times. Diversified scientific knowledge has taken their place. Whereas scientific knowledge tells us how things are, narratives tell us how to speak, how to listen and how to act. These comprise a holistic attitude towards the world. In narratives, past is present here and now, and also readies us for the future. A nation, which has narratives, does not need to remember its past. The criteria for narrative lie in its competence to be presented. It is valid if it will be transmitted, that is, if it has some meaning for others.

By perceiving how the world is approached today and in the near past, we can identify the elements of narrative. When we met with an unpredictable environment, we started to simulate it. Instead of one explanation we needed a separate explanation for each situation and for each variable. The quantitative measurements also accreted qualitative descriptions with cases. Instead of theories, we got a tremendous number of models and cases (Altman et. al., 1985, 1979, Minzber & Quinn, 1991). These are small holistic pictures of the world. From a sociological perspective Bauman's term habitant and other similar terms have been launched, referring to the social unit, where people gather together (Jallinoja 1995). They build holistic entities according to their interests. These are signals of the need to see around us realities, which we can understand and handle. These examples pursue the idea that the human beings have a need to construct a holistic and integrated picture to be able to act. He does this consciously or unconsciously, intentionally or unintentionally.

Entrepreneurship has always involved the idea that when people, look around, and combining different elements, they create holistic realities, which have their consequences in action. Even when the environment is full of paradoxes and inconsistent events, the entrepreneur chooses that are suitable for his/her ideas. These elements are not selected from a single environment; on the contrary, his/her ideas can spring from anywhere. When this is applied to learning, we can quickly notice how narrow the idea of learning has been in the modern era. We thought that learning takes place at school, at an age before the start of one's working life. Home, work, hobbies and learning were all separate environments (e.g. Hilgard & Bower, 1966, Julkunen ed. 1997). At school we got, and still do get, information from separate fields of knowledge. Now, however, we have started to question these restrictions (e.g. Engeström 1987, Julkunen 1997, Linturi 1999, Lonka & Joram & Bryson 1996, Miettinen 1993, Ruohotie & Grimmett 1994, Räsänen 1997, Sarala & Sarala 1996, Suojanen 1996). The ideas of an open learning environment and life-long learning have been launched (e.g. Life long learning in Europe). We have got the terms integration and mainstreaming in our curriculum. We have got learning models like problem solving (e.g. Life Long Learning 2/1997, Ruohotie & Grimmett 1994. Multiscientific approaches have started to be accorded some value in scientific discourse (e.g. Kyrö 1997, Kyrö & Suojanen 1998). There is still however a lot of difficulty in realizing what an open learning environment is. In some connections it has been called learning independent of time and space. This approach has often been connected to the virtual learning environment (e.g. Linturi 1999). Distant learning is another term connected with this. If it is connected only to these, we have a narrow realization of the holistic approach. From entrepreneurship we can learn that when the environment changes, we change our reality as well. From these ideas we can turn to our second principle concerning the human being.

The holistic view of a human being

The holistic view of a human being has lately attracted much attention from various scientists. We have finally started to consider emotions as the essential part of a human being. As recently as 1980s, feelings were very rare in scientific writings other than psychology. For example, the Finnish researcher Jaana Venkula (1994) found, from 235 000 scientific articles and publications, only 50 mentions of feelings, and no mention at all of joy. The Finnish professor, Eero Ropo (1996), who studies the postmodern paradigm, uses the term medias or channels to oneself. According to him, these are metacognitions, emotions, ethics and aesthetics. Learning for him is a constructive process between self, key experiences, themes, the learning environment, knowledge and competence. We have started to enlarge our ideas of the human being from that of an object, rational thinker and decision-maker towards a complex, holistic creator (e.g. Lonka & Bryson 1996, Räsänen,1997). To these ideas can also be added skills. Besides knowledge and feelings, skills have been found to be part of the human being as well (Kyrö & Suojanen 1998, Seitamaa-Hakkarainen & Uotila 1997, Suojanen, 1996). This is nothing particularly new, since skills were very highly valued e.g. by Pestalozzi. Plato had already identified knowing how as one kind of knowledge. This is a combination of knowledge and action – know-how. In the present transition it has started to interest science, especially in the field of expertise research (Engeström 1987, Miettinen 1993, Seitamaa-Hakkarainen & Uotila 1997). Sciences like craft and home economics have got their own scientific knowledge bases too.

What makes these things important in this transition is that in the modern era we tried, in the name of democracy and equality, to find similarities in human beings to be able to treat them as an equal, homogeneous group, which could be equally organized. In a changing environment we have started to realize that there is a similarity between us, but this common denominator is the difference, the extraordinarity. These features taken together mean that each individual is a different entity and that his/her holistic attitude towards the world is different. Applied to learning this means that there is not just one way of learning, but rather a diversity of ways and different combinations. The lack of a holistic attitude and extraordinarity has influenced the scientific discourse concerning entrepreneurship and education. It is questioned whether, entrepreneurship is an art or science, whether it can be taught or not (Rise 1996). Instead we should turn the question around, and ask what entrepreneurship can give to education, what we can learn about it.

The human being as an extraordinary, risk-taking, creative, free and responsible actor

If we think of the creativeness involved in entrepreneurship we soon can notice that creative methods of learning have started to interest scientists (Engeström 1987, Julkunen 1997, Miettinen 1993, Ropo, 1996, Räsänen 1997, Sarala & Sarala 1996, Suojanen 1996). In the transition this has a special meaning. We are used to thinking, comparing and legitimating our knowledge with the past, with what has been known before (Lyotard, 1985). In stable conditions this means that in the course of time, we can obtain more and better knowledge, which strengthens the behaviour we expect to achieve success. However, when circumstances change, this behaviour turns against us. For example, Lyotard suggests that should we be more interested in inventing new games and rules, instead of verifying our knowledge against the past. Lyotard's suggestion has actually got support, since research into the future, futurology has received some attention in the present transition (Linturi 1999). The essential feature in entrepreneurship has always been innovativeness. The most exciting dilemma is, how can we invent new things if we are supposed to justify our existence through the past. The tool for that in entrepreneurship has been action. Instead of arguing, entrepreneurs have put knowledge into practice. If they have not succeeded they have been responsible for the consequences. This is called risk. Risk-taking has probably received least attention in learning theories so far. How to learn to fail. Failure and innovation are related to each other. If we want to create something new, risk is always present. In the modern era and even today, I believe, we are used to evaluate learning through success, which means something other than failure. If we can learn this from entrepreneurship, we have tools to educate for survival and learning in transitions.

Finally we have the most difficult features of all to learn from entrepreneurship. What is, and what is meant by, a free actor. The simple idea that a person has the right to choose how to act and how to learn, how to earn her/his living and how to think, as a holistic phenomenon is awfully difficult. We rather tell and order, give instructions and make systems, than rely on a person's ability to act. We have started to study this feature, for example, as self-supportive learning, with the term empowerment, etc (e.g. Ahteenmäki-Pelkonen 1994). At the same time, society gives us ever more rules and laws on how to act. The dilemma between these two is the key for society's ability to adopt entrepreneurship-like behaviour. If it is solved we have already adopted entrepreneurship in our every-day life and the change in culture has taken place.

Conclusions

This short description has highlighted some of the essential features of entrepreneurship, which could be used as society's tools when it has to change its culture. We can identify several resemblances between the present ideas about learning and entrepreneurship. The title of this article "Entrepreneurship and education search for each other in the postmodern transition" has been approached from a cultural, historical perspective, and has then been developed as relating to learning in the present transition from different perspectives. Various elements have been combined from different ideas of learning in an entrepreneurial way. Like narrative it comprises past and present, and makes suggestions for the future. These suggestions concern some unifying principles for a postmodern paradigm. It was suggested that in this postmodern transition, learning theories have started to value those qualities involved in entrepreneurship. As always with narratives, the validity of them depends on action and involves the taking of risks. Will somebody see some sense in it and will they take up some of the ideas, enriching them with his/her own ideas and telling it further? Thus, what entrepreneurship can give to education will be seen in the future. Like the existential knowledge of Bahtin, there is potential knowledge that does not yet exist, but which we have the possibility of achieving. It is only dependent on our actions.

References

Aaltio-Marjosola, I. (1991). *Cultural Change in a Business Enterprise. Studying a Major Organizational Change and Its Impact on Culture.* Helsinki. The Helsinki School of Economics and Business Administration. Acta Academiae Oeconomicae Helsingiensis. Series A: 80

Ahteenmäki-Pelkonen L. (1994). From self-directedness to interdependence? An analysis of Mezirow's Conceptualization of self-directed learning. In: *Social Change and adult education research. Adult education research in Nordic Countries 1992/93.* Trondheim.

Altman, S., Valenzi, E., Hodgetts, R. M. (1985). *Organizational Behaviour: Theory and Practice.* Academic Press, Inc. Orlando.

Argyris, C. - Schön D. (1978). *Organizational Learning: The Theory of Action Perspective.* Massachusettes: Reading, Addison & Wesley.

Barreto, H. (1989). *The Entrepreneur in Microeconomic Theory. Disappearence and Explanation.* London-New York. Routledge

Beck, Giddens, Lash (1995). *Nykyajan jäljillä.* Vastapaino. Tampere.

Bell, D. (1981). Models and reality in economic discourse. In the publication: *The crisis in economic theory.* ed. by Bell, D., Kristol, I. p. 46-80. Basic Books. USA.

Bowen, J. (1981). *A History of Western Education.* Volume two. Civilization of Europe sixth to sixteenth century. Methuen & Co Ltd. London.

Bowen, J. (1981). *A History of Western Education.* Volume three. The modern West, Europe and the New World. Methuen & Co Ltd. London.

Boyd, R. (1991). Confirmation, semantics, and interpretation of scientific theories. In: *The Philosophy of science*, ed. Boyd, R. - Gasper, P. - Trout J. D. 2nd edition pp. 3-35. Massachusetts Institute of Technology, MIT Press. Cambridge, Massachusetts.

Cameron, R. (1995). *Maailman taloushistoria paleoliittiselta kaudelta nykypäivään..* Suom. Tapio Helen. WSOY Suomen Historiallinen Seura. Juva.

Casson, M. (1982). *The Entrepreneur. An Economic Theory*. Great Britain

Connell, W.F. (1980). *A History of education in the twentieth century world*. Teachers College press Columbia University. New York.

Dahmen, E., Hannah, L., Kirzner, I.M. (1994). *The Dynamics of Entrepreneurship*. Crafoord Lectures 5. Institute of Economic Research. Lund University Press. Malmö.

Dewey, J. (1951). *Experience and Education. 13th edition*. New York: The MacMillan Company.

Dillard, D. (1967). *Economic Development of the North Atlantic Community: Historical Introduction to Modern Economics*. Englewood Cliffs, New Jersey: Prentice-Hall. Inc.

Engeström, Y. (1987). *Learning by Expanding: An activity-theoretical approach to development reasearch*. Orientakonsultit Oy. Helsinki.

Ethier, W. J. (1988). *Modern International Economics*. 2 nd. ed. New York.

Etzioni, A. (1968). *Nykyajan organisaatiot*. Foorum Kirjasto. Kustannusosakeyhtiö Tammi. Helsinki.

Fiske, S.T., & Taylor, S.E. (1984). *Social Cognition*. Random House. New York.

Giddens, A. (1984). *Yhteiskuntateorian keskeisiä ongelmia. Toiminnan, rakenteen ja ristiriidan käsitteet yhteiskunta-analyysissä*. KustannusOy Otava. Keuruu.

Grubel, H.G. (1981). *International Economics*. USA.

Haahti, A.J. (1989). *Entrepreneurs' strategic orientation. Modelling Strategic Behaviour In small Industrial Owner-managed firms*. The Helsinki School of Economics and Business Administration, Helsinki. Acta Academiae Oeconomicae Helsingiensis. Series A: 64.

Halsey, A. H., Lauder H., Brown, P. & Wells A.S. (Ed.) (1997). *Education. Culture, Economy, and Society*. Oxford University Press. Oxford.

Harvey, D. (1990). *The Condition of Postmodernity.* Basil Blackwell. Great Britain.

Hilgard, E.R., Bower, G.H. (1966). *Theories of learning* 3rd edition The Century Psychology Series New York.

Hofstede, G. (1991). *Cultures and Organizations. Software of the Mind. Intercultural Co-operation and its Importance for Survival.* McGraw-Hill Book Company. London.

Jallinoja, R. (1995). Sosiologiaa postmodernisuudesta: Zygmunt Bauman. In Rahkonen, Keijo. (Ed.). *Sosiologisen teorian uusimmat virtaukset.* 30-54. Gaudeamus Helsinki.

Johannisson, B. (1984). *A Cultural Perspective on Small Business - Local Business Climate.* Småskrifter nr 23. Högskolan i Växjö. Centrum för Småföretagsutveckling.Sweden.

James, W. (1913). *Pragmatismi.* Otava. Helsinki.

Julkunen, M-L., ed. (1997). *Opetus, oppiminen, vuorovaikutus.* WSOY.

Juuti, P. & Soikkanen, A. (1994). Change to new organizational cultures. Paradigmatic Change. FEMDI. In: *Action Research in Finland.* Active Society with Action Research 25-27 August 1993. Helsinki. Labour Policy Studies 82. Ministry of Labour.

Kanter, R. M. (1989). *When giants learn to dance. Mastering the challenges of strategy, management and careers in the 1990s.*Simon and Schuster. New York.

Kauppi A., Kontiainen S., Nurmi K.E., Tuomisto & Vaherva T. (Ed.) (1994). *Adult Learning in a Cultural Context* Adult Education Research Society in Finland. University of Helsinki, Lahti Research and Training Centre.

Keesing, R. M. (1981). *Cultural Antropology. A Contemporary Approach.* 2nd. ed. Harcourt Brace Collage Publishers. Philadelphia.

Kenwood A. G., Lougheed A. L. (1971). *The Growth of the International Economy 1820-1960.* London.

Kirzner, I. M. (1991). Market processes versus market equilibrium. In Thompson, G., Frances, J., Levacic R. & Mitchell, J. *Markets, Hierarchies & Networks. The Co-ordination of Social Life.* (Ed.) by 24-34. Sage Publications. Great Britain.

Kovalainen, A. (1993). *At The Margins of The Economy. Women's self-employment in Finland 1960-1990.* Publications of The Turku School of Economics and Business Administration. Series A 9:1993.

Kyrö, P. (1996). *The Points of Transition in Reforming the Understanding and Meaning of Entrepreneurship.* Academy of Entrepreneurship Journal. Volume 2, Number 1, pp. 71-94. USA.

Kyrö, P. (1997). *Yrittäjyyden muodot ja tehtävä ajan murroksissa.* Jyväskylä studies in computer science and economics and statistics 38. University of Jyväskylä.

Kyrö, P., Suojanen, U. (1988). *The relationship between sustainable development and intrapreneurship in the postmodern transition.* Accepted as a refereed article in the Academy of Entrepreneurship Journal. European edition.

Lahti, A. (1991). Entrepreneurial Strategy Making. pp. 146-162. In Näsi, J. (Ed.). *Arenas of Strategic Thinking.* Foundation for Economic Education. 1991 Helsinki.

Life long learning in Europe (1997-1998). New scientific referee publication.

Lindeqvist, K. O. (1905). *Yleinen historia. Uusi Aika.* WSOY. Porvoo.

Linturi, H. (1999). *Educational polyphony and dialoque in information society-Futu-Themis project.* Internetix http://www.internetix.fi/tutkimus/internetix-tutkimus/futu/ppframe.htm. 30.6.1999.

Lonka, K. & Joram, E. & Bryson, M. (1996). *Conceptions of learning and knowledge – does training make a difference?* Contemporary Educationa Psychology, 21, 240-260.

Lyotard J. F. (1984). *The postmodern condition: a report on knowledge.* University of Manchester Press. Manchester.

Miettinen, R. (1993). *Oppitunnista oppimistoimintaan. Tutkimus opetuksen ja opettajankoulutuksen kehittämisestä.* Tampere. Gaudeamus.

Minzberg H. & Quinn, J. (1991). *The Strategy Process: concepts, contexts, cases.* Prentice-Hall, International Inc. USA.

Morgan, G. (1986). *Images of Organization.* Sage Publications Beverly Hills.

Mozer P. K & Vander Nat A. (1987). *Human Knowledge, Classical and contemporary approaches.* Oxford University Press. USA.

Murphy, R. F. (1989). *Cultural & Social Antropology an Overture.* 3rd. ed. Prentice Hall. Englewood Cliffs.

Niiniluoto, I. (1984). *Johdatus tieteen filosofiaan. Käsitteen ja teorianmuodostus.* Helsinki: Otava.

Näsi, J. (1991). Strategic Thinking as Doctrine: Development of Focus Areas and New Insights. In *Arenas of Strategic Thinking,* ed. by Näsi, J., pp. 26-66. Helsinki: Foundation for Economic Education.

Peters, T.J. & Waterman R.H Jr. (1982). *In search for excellence.* New York: Harper & Row.

Pinchot III, G. (1986). *Intraprenörerna. Entreprenörer som stannar i företaget.* Svenska Dagbladet. Södertälje.

Rise (1996). *Research on Innovative Strategies and Entrepreneurship.* Conference proceedings. *June 11-13 Jyväskylä.*

Ropo, E. (1996). *Toimiva oppimisympäristö.* Opetushallistuksen Opinnetpäivät. Syyskuu 1996. Järvenpää.

Rorty, R. (1986). *Consequences of Pragmatism* (Esseys: 1972-1980) 3. edition University of Minnesota Press, Minneapolis, USA.

Ruohotie, P. & Grimmett, P. P. (ed.) (1994). *New themes for education in a changing world.* University of Tampere and Simon Fraser University. Tampere.

Räsänen, M. (1997). *Building Bridges. Experiental art understanding. A work of art as a means of understanding and constructing self.* University of Art and Design. Helsinki.

Sarala, U. & Sarala, A. (1996). *Oppiva organisaatio.* Oppimisen, Laadun ja Tuottavuuden yhdistäminen. Helsingin Yliopiston Lahden tutkimus- ja kuolutuskeskus.Tampere.

Sarvimäki, A. (1988). *Knowledge in Interactive Practice Disciplines: An analysis of knowledge in education and health care.* Department of Education University of Helsinki. research Bulletin 68, Helsinki.

Schein, E. H. (1985). *Organisational Culture and Leadership. A Dynamic View.* Second Printing. San Francisco, California: Jossey-Bass Publishers.

Seitamaa-Hakkarainen, P. & Uotila, M. (Ed.) (1997). *Produkt, fenomen, upplevelse.* Proceedings of a Nordic symposium. Helsinki, November 7-9.1996. Nordic Forum for Research and Development in Craft and Design. Research in Sloyd Education and Crafts Science B no. 3 1997 Helsinki.

Statistics Finland (1998). *Enterprises in Finland 1996.* 1998:25. Helsinki.

Sturrock, J. (Ed.) (1981). *Structuralism and Since - From Levi-Strauss to Derrida.* Oxford University Press USA.

Suojanen, U. (1996). *Entrepreneurial aspects in Craft Education.* Paper presented at the Second International Symposium of Handicraft Teaching. Towards a creative teaching and learning. Vinalas Valley. Pinar del Rio, Cuba. November 18-23.

Sveiby, K.E. (1988). *Managing knowhow. Increase profits by harnessing the creativity.* Bloomsbury. London.

Thayer, H.S. (1968). *Meaning and Action. A Critical History of Pragmatism.* The Bobbs-Merrill Company. The City College of the City University of New York. USA.

Turner, B.S. (Ed.) (1990). *Theories of Modernity and Postmodernity. Theory, Culture and Society,* Sage Publications. London.

Weber, M. (1969). *The Theory of Social and Economic Organization.* First paperback 1947. Sixth printing. Introduction, T. Parsons. New York: A Free Press Paperback Collier-MacMillan Ltd.

Venkula, J. (1994). *Tiedon suhde toimintaan.* Yliopistopaino. Helsinki.

Vesala, K. M. (1992). *Pienyrittäjän kontrollipremissit. Sosiaalipsykologinen tarkastelu.* Acta Psychologica Fennica. Soveltavan psykologian monografioita 5. Suomen Psykologinen Seura. Rauma.

Wilken, Paul H. (1979). *Entrepreneurship. A Comparative and Historical Study.* Ablex Publishing Corporation. USA.

Von Wright, Maija-Liisa & Von Wright Johan (1998). *Oppiminen ja koulutus.* WSOY. Helsinki.

Zuboff, S. (1988). *In The Age of The Smart Machine. The Future of Work and Power.* New York.

SOCIAL STRUCTURE AND LIFELONG LEARNING

Critical analysis of learning opportunities in working life

Jukka Tuomisto

Point of departure

The current international discussion of lifelong learning has a clear individualistic emphasis. "Lifelong learning" in itself refers to the individual, since learning is generally understood as an indvidual process. This has resulted in emphasizing the significance of the individual as one who sets his or her own goals, as well as supervises and assesses his or her own learning. This is particularly true of adult education where the "self-directiveness" of adult learners has been used as a kind of "mantra" since the 1970s. Adults' activities and self-directiveness have been believed in firmly, and for a good reason. However, since a large proportion of adults still show no interest in studying and continuous self-development, researchers should investigate the reason for this. Are the differences in participation and the will to learn primarily a consequence of individual psychological personality differences or do they result from social structures, mainly sociological factors? It is obvious that both have an effect here, but which impact is more primary? Although no final answer to this question will be provided in this article, I shall still try to present some views of what the role of the social structures is in developing lifelong learning.

Choosing this viewpoint, I am not defending structural factors against individual psychological ones. It is worth pointing out, however, that the effect of socio-historical change on the development of learning opportunities in working life was of focal interest to me and my research group in the early 1990s (Tuomisto et al. 1996). The Academy of Finland funded a research project on lifelong learning and our study was part of it. This article is mainly based on the theoretical analyses and concrete results from our study.

In this context I will discuss the relationship of social structures and lifelong learning on three levels: first, the general changes in the labour market (the macro level); secondly, the strategies related to staff development in organizations (the meso level); and finally, the opportunities of staff development, career advancement and participation, as well as staff participation in education provided by the employer (the micro level). The target group consists mainly of employees in the private sector, but the views presented here are also relevant with regard to other groups of workers and white collar employees.

Development of the labour market system and learning opportunities

General development of the labour market system

The labour market system is an entity comprising employers, employees and the state. Since 1968, Finland has been living in a period of so-called social corporatism, which has meant centralized collective bargaining between the labour market partners (primarily the central organizations). The main goal has been to establish a long-term economic and incomes policy based on consensus between the government and the unions. This has enabled the development of a comprehensive labour and social policy. The system has created an urgent need for new knowledge and information for both employers and employees. This has of course mainly concerned people who have been elected to represent their fellow workers in the negotiations, and participation by ordinary rank and file workers has remained limited (Kauppinen 1992, 43-61).

For some time now Finland has been actively discussing the abolition of the centralized collective bargaining system. It has been suggested that it should be replaced by giving more negotiating power to the level of unions and workplaces. The present corporative system does not seem to correspond to the current demands for more flexibility and efficiency in production. However, the collective bargaining negotiations have so far continued within the framework of the centralized system, because this has been considered the best way of securing the stable development of the Finnish economy.

Central Europe, on the other hand, is characterized by corporatistic union solutions, while in Southern Europe workplace-related agreements are typical. In Finland, as well as in the other Nordic Countries, centralized agreements have been common and have secured a stable economy and the creation of the welfare state. The integration of Europe undoubtedly brings with it pressures to unify the agreement system. From the viewpoint of the Nordic Countries, such decentralized or union-related agreements are not without problems, because they may break down Nordic equality and justice (Kauppinen 1992, 295-296).

Both within the trade union movement and among employers in Finland there are at the moment very conflicting ideas about the need to reform the labour market system. If agreement power is shifted to workplaces, it will lead to a new situation in which both employers and trade unions will have to redefine their strategies in order to ensure their interests. This will have a direct impact on the educational activity of both partners.

At the moment it seems as if the Finnish labour market system should opt for local negotiations in the workplace, it will mean that all employees, at least in principle, will participate in the designing of the agreement system. So far relatively few decision-makers who already are in leading positions in society have been involved in the negotiations. The new system will require from all partners a more in-depth knowledge of the current situation in working life, as well as the will to cooperate. Are they prepared to this?

Structures are changing - or are they?

For the last century, Finnish working life has been characterized by the conflicting interests of employees and employers and this has had an effect on all developmental efforts as well as on the learning and education opportunities of the workforce. This conflict first emerged as a Taylorist, and later as a Fordian basic structure. The system presupposed that the actual production and the planning of work (the brawn and the brain; physical and mental work) should be kept apart. The employers, in particular, wanted this and it was the starting point for all supervisory work. The majority of workers have had to function in jobs in which they have had no possibility of developing or using their creative skills. According to a slogan frequently used by the supervisors, the worker does not need to think but simply follow the instructions given. Since this kind of work does not motivate anyone to develop himself or herself, or his or her creative skills, the result was alienation from work and a search for life content outside the working life. Today employers demand commitment, initiative and innovation from their employees, in other words, exactly those skills which the workers were not previously allowed to learn or use. Are we now saying goodbye to Taylorism? It is obviously too early to say, because the employers' changed attitude does not follow from their greater concern for the physical and mental well-being of their employees but rather from the new demands for productivity and efficiency resulting from increased competition. Human capital and its ongoing renewal are in a key role in this development.

Physical exploitation of the workforce has been replaced by mental exploitation. This is evident in the increased psychological ill-being and burnouts in the workforce, both on production and executive levels. According to a study made in 1997, about every fifth Finn in active workforce suffered from some degree of burnout, some of them seriously (Kalimo and Toppinen 1997). It seems that planning and other creative work will remain with the core workforce, while mechanical and repetitive work will be done by machines - creating redundancies among the people who previously performed these tasks. Only a small proportion of employees will possibly manage to move on to the core workforce and maintain their permanent jobs. A large part of the workforce will have to be satisfied with various atypical jobs, that is, short-term or temporary jobs. Frequently these jobs consist of fairly simple and mechanical tasks. In other words, Taylorism still seems to prevail, even though it is not so obvious a strategy as before in large-scale production. Instead, it forces individual "entrepreneurs" to concentrate on a very narrow field of know-how and to adapt to the requirements of working hours and efficiency of large enterprises. As a consequence of this development, there is a clear polarization of workforce into the successful and the marginalized. This is a central problem in today's working life. So far no solution has been found, nor has it been actively investigated.

Kevätsalo (1999, 120-135) talks about "wasting" of workforce resources in two ways. Firstly, the skills and potential of the unemployed are ignored, and secondly, the skills and potential of people who work are under-used. At the beginning of the 1990s, the rate of unemployment in Finland was about 20 %, while today it is about 12 %. The second form of "wasting" Kevätsalo studied in 1997 was by asking people who were working, whether they felt they had skills and potential for more demanding jobs than those they were doing at the time. About one third of the employed who responded were of the opinion that they had such skills. The perceptions of all groups of the employed were fairly similar, varying between 28 and 38 % (ibid, 124).

Conflicts of professional identity

One of the current problems in working life is related to the development of vocational or professional identity. This is an essential question in terms of learning on the job, because vocational development can only happen if the individual is supported by a group of people with whom he or she may identify, whose norms he or she can accept and with whom he or she can discuss vocational issues. Several trends in working life, such as the increase in atypical jobs and subcontracting, the emphasized productivity, the more instrumental role of trade unions, etc., have led to a situation in which the formation of a professional identity is becoming more and more difficult in workplaces.

Traditionally, employees have primarily identified with the labour and trade union movements, since it has helped them to improve their own status both at work and in society. Today trade union membership in Finland is no longer so ideological. It is only the most active members who still base their membership on an ideology and the view that workers share common interests. For ordinary members, the trade union has become a service organization, and they are only involved because everyone else is and because it is a way of ensuring a certain level of income even in a crisis situation, such as unemployment (Kevätsalo 1995, 37-40). At present the trade union culture seems to be breaking down, because the movement is no longer able to maintain the necessary trade union identity among its members on the local level (Ilmonen and Kevätsalo 1995, 197).

Trade union and organization cultures have developed in close interaction with each other (see e.g. Davies and Weiner 1985). It has been thought that the weakening of one culture gives the opponent a chance to strengthen its own. It could be said, though, that both partners will have to change their way of thinking and functioning. Employers today like to emphasize the significance of organization culture and staff commitment in terms of productivity and efficiency. For the core workforce, identification with the enterprise is natural, although their own professional group may also serve as a central object of identification. For others (peripheral workforce, employees in atypical jobs), the enterprise/workplace can hardly do that. It seems that the formation of employees' identity (working class and/or trade union culture) will no longer be as uniform as in the past but it will be divided into several smaller subcultures according to each task or work group. This has already happened, at least in part. With regard to lifelong learning, this is a worrying trend, because a strong (professional) identity provides a good foundation for continuous self-development.

Changes in working life and learning - an issue of trust?

Even in the simplest change situations, the central element defining functional solutions involves a game: the participants want more power and influence. Ultimately it is a struggle for societal and social existence. Changes are experienced as dangerous, if they limit the actors' game possibilities and the "zones of uncertainty" controlled by them (Koivisto 1995, 69).

On the level of society, a major barrier to changes and development of working life continues to be the conflict of interests of the central groups (employers/ employees). In negotiations, this is seen in that priority is given to divisive issues (such as questions related to salaries and wages, working hours, etc.) and in translating the vertical relationships of the workplace into a zero-sum game in which the win of one always means a loss for another. This design can be defended when the partners' interests are mutually exclusive, or are opposite to each other. Continuing to play the zero-sum game renews the culture of mutual juxtaposition in the workplace with the result that it is impossible to make a change that would be acceptable to both partners. This was a common situation in the past. In the present labour market situation, the employers' and employees' interests converge, at least in part. This concerns, for example, production issues related to the planning and organization of work. Such convergent advantages should be charted and brought up more concretely in the discussions of the development of working life, because this way it would be possible to break down, at least in part, the juxtaposition created by the zero-sum game.

The rules of working life (laws, agreements, etc.) define the economic, and also the legal, social and cultural relationships between employers and employees. They can be understood as expressions of the partners' mutual trust (or lack of it). Both employers and representatives of trade unions have lately begun to emphasize the significance of mutual understanding and *trust* for the efficiency of the enterprise (see e.g. Kevätsalo 1994). The greater trust there is between the different partners, the more committed they will be to the goals of action and the better opportunities there will be for flexibility in organizing the work. This creates a good foundation for developing the workplace into a learning community and a learning organization. If an atmosphere of distrust prevails in the workplace, it is necessary to lead and manage it in a controlling manner (Ibid, 111-113). This is not likely to improve the employees' work or learning motivation.

An example of a new kind of entrepreneurship and cooperation based on trust is provided by education offered jointly to enterprises and trade unions. The Murikka adult education centre of the Finnish Metal Workers' Union has successfully arranged courses like this for some time already (see Koivisto 1995). An atmosphere of trust, however, cannot be established if the job is only short-term or indefinite. That is why achieving an atmosphere of trust is probably possible only for the "core workforce", whereas with peripheral workforce it is much more difficult, if not impossible. It is obvious that in-service programmes in companies will in the future, too, primarily focus on educating the "key employees".

Reorganization of work is necessary - but how to do it?

Some central developmental features of work

The current trend of trying to lower the professional hierarchies in working life and expanding the work tasks ("lean production", for example) is positive from the viewpoint of learning on the job, since it increases teamwork and cooperation in the workplace and improves the employees' developmental opportunities. By changing the division of work and by improving the employees' opportunities to participate in developing and planning the work in the workplace it is possible to create a good environment for functional flexibility, and continuing self-development and study possibilities for employees.

Work psychologists and sociologists have for some time already been of the opinion that the traditional Taylorist or Fordian model of work does not provide sufficient stimuli for our mental growth and development (see Hacker 1982, 380-381; see also Thorsrud and Emery 1971; Konrbluh and Green 1989, 256-273). An OECD report, published in 1993, emphasizes the importance of reorganization of work and points out that if we want to motivate employees to develop their skills continuously:
- the work must be independent; employees must have more responsibility which helps them to understand that they need more knowledge and information continuously;
- the work must be diverse so that it will expand employees' skills and knowledge;
- the work must be meaningful/valuable so that employees can justify its value to others and that they have a need to improve their own performance;
- employees must get feedback regarding their work from fellow workers, the management and clients, that is, from all those who are involved; this helps them to see what they need to do to improve their productivity (Utbult 1988, 14; cit. Industry Training 1993, 37).

So in principle all agree that work tasks should be designed in such a way that they will provide development and participation possibilities for all employees. In practice, however, this is difficult, if not impossible, to achieve. Some work tasks will probably always be less stimulating, offering few challenges for development. Furthermore, some tasks continue to be performed in the old style because it is advantageous from the employer's point of view.

In addition to the nature of work, continuity/permanence is another essential quality factor in working life. Today it is threatened in many ways. The rate of unemployment has been high all through the 1990s (12-20 %) and even those who have been working cannot have been sure of their jobs continuing. The number of atypical jobs (part-time jobs or jobs for a specified period of time) has increased rapidly. According to a study made by Statistics Finland, every fourth employed person worked in an atypical job at the end of 1996 (Lähes...1997). Even though the situation in Finland is not quite so bad as in some other European countries, it is apparent that the number of atypical jobs will increase considerably when the present unemployment eases and a new workforce is hired once more (Kasvio 1995, 98-100).

People working in atypical jobs mainly belong to the peripheral workforce whose training and education do not interest the employer. On the one hand, small entrepreneurs and people working in atypical jobs must continuously try to "sell" themselves, so they they have no time or means for studying or self-development. On the other hand, the competition for jobs forces these people to improve their skills and knowledge in one way or another. There is a danger that as a consequence of the continuing competition and struggle for existence their world image will become narrow and their quality of life will deteriorate.

The present advanced divison of work has led to extreme specialization in many professional fields. From the point of view of learning, this is positive because generally people working in specialized jobs of this kind are very motivated to develop their skills and knowledge in their own field. From the perspective of individual development, however, this kind of specialization may be dangerous. Firstly, the person may become too dependent on his or her employer, which means that his or her opportunities in the general labour market are diminished. Secondly, in terms of personality development excessive specialization may be harmful, if the person's social views become too narrow and his or her interaction with other people decreases.

The other extreme in the development of occupations is formed by multi-professionality which has been defended lately in connection with flexible production. At best, these jobs offer great challenges, but at worst, they may lead to short-term training and superficial professional skills. Multi-professionality can improve a person's mobility and employment possibilities on the labour market, but in the long run it can become a problem, if it is only concerned with adopting rapidly and superficially "professional" skills of different occupations. On the other hand, learning a new job which is closely related to one's previous occupation and "expanding" one's job this may be regarded as a positive challenge.

Problems related to flexible production - who will have to be flexible and what can be learnt?

The issue of flexible production has been discussed a lot in relation to current changes in working life. Moving over to flexible production has been considered to radically change the traditional ways of using workforce. A number of different concepts of flexibility have emerged in the discussion; not all changes brought about by them have been positive from the viewpoint of learning. Atkinson and others (see Atkinson 1987) have developed a model of "flexible enterprise" in which they distinguish two basic types of flexibility: functional and quantitative flexibility.

Functional flexibility includes such measures as expanding work tasks, increasing multiprofessional skills among staff, and establishing self-directive teams, for example. These measures are only available to the core workforce of enterprises, however. These employees are expected to have wide-ranging professional skills, creative problem-solving and teamwork skills, and an ability to learn new things continuously (e.g. Ollus et al. 1990, 141-142; Kasvio 1995, 98-100). With regard to peripheral workforce, it is primarily strategies of *quantitative flexibility* that can be used. Fluctuation in production is levelled by regulating working hours and the number of staff as well as by shifting some of the work to be done by outside subcontractors. As to learning something new, the position of peripheral employees is weak, because their work is on the whole not very developmental, their incomes are smaller and the continuity of their work is uncertain.

Another feature of the change in working life has been the demand for increased flexibility in the labour market and the abolition of "unnecessary" regulation. To achieve this, the quantitative strategy has been used more than before (especially in the public sector). Since this strategy does not help workers and white-collar employees to develop and learn professionally, it cannot be recommended. From the viewpoint of learning new things, functional flexibility is clearly a better alternative for developing working life. What is of primary importance here is, how the quality of working life can be improved and how the changes as social processes can be controlled.

In the present discussion it has been claimed that as a consequence of the change in working life, the traditional conflict between work and capital will vanish altogether. However, this is not so. Foley (1994, 121-124) has noted that it is not a question of the "restructuring" of working life, but of "capitalist reorganization". According to Foley, in the present postmodern stage of society, the "thesis of flexible specialization" describing the change in working life acts as an ideological myth which is used only to conceal the present dynamics of the economic reorganization of the globe (ibid, 125).

It has been discovered in Finland that conflicts in workplaces have actually increased in the 1990s. Different conflicts between individuals and groups of staff in 1990 were considerably more serious than those in 1984 (Kolu 1992, 58-59). Valtee (1994), too, has found in his study entitled "Controlling conflicts in the work community" that the atmosphere in workplaces has deteriorated in the 1990s. It is especially noteworthy here that the conflicts (competitive atmosphere, conflicts between employees, between the management and subordinates, as well as between different groups of staff) have increased more than average in those workplaces where the working conditions have been changed to comply with the requirements of the model of flexible production.

According to Kortteinen (1992, 23-27), flexible production seems to lead to a situation in which the contrasts actually become emphasized. In other words, it appears that the goals of flexible production and the results in practice are in conflict. Greater contrasts do not result from ideological orientation; instead, they are related to the actual changed work performance which exacerbates relationships in the workplace. The more experience the respondents had with the changes related to the new model of flexible production, the more frequently they experienced conflicting interests in relation to their employer.

Education strategies of enterprises and lifelong learning

Juhela (1996, 439-448) has studied education provided by enterprises especially from the viewpoint of lifelong learning. He distinguishes four different education strategies used by enterprises:

1) The preventive strategy is characterized by the limited amount of education or at least by avoidance of educational costs. This strategy hardly offers employees any learning challenges or opportunities, or prospects of continuing education. The knowledge and skills of the staff (employees) are not considered strategically important for the company.

Challenges and development

2) The point of departure in the segmenting strategy is to organize work tasks into distinct vocational or professional groups and qualification requirements. Selecting the people who will be educated is a central issue. The know-how is concentrated on key people who will be offered opportunities for development at work and prospects of continuing education. The know-how and training of the rest of the staff is not considered important. It is typical of this strategy that the polarized structures of work tasks and participation in education become reinforced and mutually legitimized.
3) The strategy supporting management of change aims at controlling the reforms in production when a new production technology, for example, is introduced. Staff education and development is in principle directed to the whole personnel, but it is planned in the form of a project and is carried out only once. Long-range visions and staff development programmes are missing.
4) The prospective strategy is similarly directed to the whole personnel but it differs from the previous strategy in that the goal here is the comprehensive and systematic development of the workforce. Furthermore, this strategy aims at flexible professional skills, which demands that staff development is seen as a long-range and ongoing process. The first three strategies approach education and staff development from a more or less limited perspective, and staff development is clearly not a primary starting point for the development of the organization. In this respect, the prospective strategy is different. It should be used in all enterprises that want to develop into learning organizations.

Because of the limited data of Juhela's study, we cannot make conclusions about the extent to which the different education strategies are used. However, if we examine the results of a nation-wide survey of employees' opportunities for development and participation in their own work, it is obvious that there are not many enterprises in Finland that use the prospective strategy (see Table 1). The strategies most commonly used by enterprises today are the segmenting strategy and the strategy supporting management of change. The enterprises that have adopted the prospective strategy are generally large companies that are leaders in their own field (Nokia, for example).

Learning organizations - do they exist?

Organization researchers have frequently emphasized the organization's ability and willingness to change, the close relationship of the individual and the organization (cooperation and teamwork), consideration of the structures and operating models of organizations, and the close interrelationship of the organization and the environment (See e.g. Argyris & Schön 1978; Senge 1990; Sarala & Sarala 1996; Engeström 1993; Watkins & Marsick 1993; Docherty 1996).

As the new development models (such as learning organizations) are widely discussed in public, it is easy to imagine that they already are everyday reality in all enterprises. According to Alasoini and Heikkilä (1998, 40-41), however, the trendy talk about "teams", "networking", "empowerment", "continuing improvement" or "learning organization" has represented the rhetoric of the trend-conscious management rather than reality on the shopfloor. When the EPOC project of the European foundation for the development of working and living conditions collected data from ten EU countries, it was discovered that only about 10 % of the work places had introduced highly advanced team and group work models (Sisson 1997).

Some critical researchers have even asked, whether the learning organization really is a realistic development model or whether it is simply a beautiful label. They do admit, however, that even though such model organizations are hard to find in reality, studying organizations from the point of view of learning is important, because it helps organizations to develop their operation and their employees' self-directiveness and initiative (Docherty 1996, 31, 45; Sarala & Sarala 1996, 63-64).

Why is it that the ideal of the learning organization is practically impossible to implement? The Saralas (ibid) give many reasons, such as:
1) Full commitment to work, required by the learning organization, is extremely difficult to achieve.
2) It is Utopian to believe that all people want to learn and develop in their work continuously.
3) Since the restructuring of an organization is always related to power and a loss of authority for some individuals, it is hard to implement.
4) The management rarely wants to make a major contribution towards the development and learning of the whole staff, because it necessarily requires financial invenstments. It is also time-consuming and its beneficial effects will only be seen gradually. Furthermore, staff development and learning can never be converted to pure money terms.
5) The ideas of a learning organization are difficult to distinguish from other work on productivity and quality improvement.

It seems that enterprises often use the paradigm of the learning organization only as a tool to legitimize their own ideas. In a learning organization everyone has to learn to adapt to unpleasant changes, too. A critical attitude to change is often labelled as resistance to change and people expressing critical ideas are considered disruptive. From the perspective of employees, the learning organization is often experienced as "sweating" or pressuring, since the economic profit resulting from the more efficient work will generally only benefit the management and shareholders of the company.

Development, participation and study opportunities of employees

Development, career advancement and participation opportunities as experienced by staff

How do employees today experience their own work? Does it offer challenges and opportunities for development and career advancement, like a learning organization should? These issues, among other things, were studied in an adult education survey (AKU 90)(see Simpanen 1993, 66-75).

Table 1. Employees' perceptions of development, career advancement and participation opportunities offered by their workplace (%). (Tuomisto 1996, 43)

	Opportunities Development[1]	Career advancement[2]	Participation in decision-making[3]
Very many	9	3	3
Fairly many	52	15	18
Some	36	38	44
None	3	44	35
	100	100	100
N=	2333	2327	2327

Some 60 % of employees report that they have very many or quite a lot of opportunities for development at work. Only 3 % say they have no development opportunities at all.[2] The different groups of staff perceive their development

---

[2] In the question concerning development of opportunities, the respondents were asked: How much does your present work offer you opportunities for learning new things, using previously learnt knowledge and skills, choosing your own work methods and developing them, managing independently your pace of work, developing your abilities and professional skills, receiving recognition for work well done, experiencing yourself as a valuable member of your work community, and working in cooperation with others?

opportunities rather differently. About half (51 %) of workers consider they have either many or very many opportunities for development. Among the different groups of white-collar employees this percentage varies between 62% and 82 % (Tuomisto 1996, 47).

With regard to career advancement[3] the situation is clearly worse. Only 18% of the respondents experience that they have good or very good opportunities for career advancement. Nearly half of the respondents report having no opportunities for career advancement. We have to bear in mind two things when we look at these figures. First, with some of the respondents the result is obviously influenced by the "ceiling effect". If one already is at the top of one's career, it is difficult to advance any further. Secondly, statistics show that it is not possible for all people to have career advancement opportunities, at least if we think of rising in the hierarchy of the workplace. Only a small proportion of employees can work in management positions. Experiences of career advancement were surprisingly similar in the different groups of personnel (see ibid.).

Participation in the decision-making concerning one's own work, or the enterprise/workplace[4], can make the employee feel that he or she is a fully authorized member of his or her work community. Some 35 % of the respondents report having no such opportunities; in other words, they have to work in a work community which in no way appreciates their opinions and does not even ask for them. Nearly half of the respondents experience that they have some opportunities for participating in the decision-making of the workplace. About one fifth of the respondents have very many or many opportunities for this.

In Finland, different forms of participation in working life (industrial democracy, cooperation in enterprises) have been developed since World War II, but even today these reforms do not reach all employees. To a large extent,

---

[3] In the question concerning career advancement opportunities, the respondents were asked: To what extent in your latest job have you had opportunities for changing to another job in the same workplace, transferring to a more demanding job after gaining work experience, or being promoted in your career?

[4] In the question concerning opportunities for participation, the respondents were asked: To what extent in your latest job have you had opportunities for influencing the kind of education provided in the workplace, influencing the division of work and general functioning of your own workplace, or participating in the decision-making concerning the whole enterprise?

participation has been implemented by elected representatives, not as direct participation. Some enterprises have advanced much further than the formal regulations require, while some others do not even meet the formal requirements. This is a central problem in improving opportunities for employees' active participation and lifelong learning. The problem is made worse by the fact that the trade union organization, too, has been clearly divided into active members and rank-and-file members (see Tuomisto 1996; Ilmonen and Kevätsalo 1995). The "ordinary" members account for the majority of trade union members, but they participate in union activity only to a very limited degree or not at all. Irrespective of the organization, centralized power and control always seem to lead to passive rank-and-file members.

Participation in in-service education

A positive attitude towards staff development and education can be regarded as a fundamental point of departure for a learning organization and lifelong learning. In the last twenty years, in-service education has increased more rapidly than any other sector of adult education. More than half of employees (some 830,000 people) today participate in in-service education on an annual basis. However, participation is divided rather unevenly among the different groups of personnel.

Table 2. *Participation in in-service education in 1980, 1990 and 1995 by socioeconomic group (employees aged 18-64 years) (Blomqvist & Simpanen 1996).*

	1980	1990	1995	Change 1980/95
-Executives	41	72	69	+28
-Clerical workers	32	57	58	+26
-Workers	10	26	33	+23
All	25	47	52	+30

People working in clerical jobs are offered more in-service education than the other groups of personnel. The differences have levelled out somewhat in the 1990s, but they continue to be great between workers and clerical employees. Women in Finland participate in in-service education more (55 %) than men (49 %), contrary to other European countries (see OECD 1996, 151).

Private employers (43 %) educate their staff considerably less than public employers (the state 60 % and municipalities 63 %). This is common in other countries, too (Blomqvist 1997, 89; cf. OECD 1996, 151). In 1995, the length of in-service education in Finland was eight days per participant on average.

Summary and conclusions

It is obvious from the above that there are still several structural factors in working life which make the promotion of lifelong learning difficult and complex in practice. The conflicting interests of employers and employees - partly myth and partly reality - continue to be a major barrier to developing workplaces into real learning environments. The figure below illustrates the past development and presents a view on the future direction.

The future vision depicted by the above figure must be looked at critically, since development is only rarely linear. Most of the time it happens more or less dialectically. As can be seen from the above, the present development contains many conflicts and problems. How they will be resolved in time will influence the future development.

In the following I will briefly list the most essential developmental features of working life and their impact on workplaces, bearing in mind the development of workplaces into real learning environments:

- The shift from centralized labour market system to a more decentralized union or workplace centred system in principle increases the employees' opportunities for participation in the decision-making concerning their own salaries and working conditions. On the other hand, this may result in even more bitter disputes between the employer and workers in the workplace. If the employees no longer have common interests, it will, for example, be more difficult for an individual worker to defend his or her own interests in the workplace with regard to the pay or working conditions. A balanced change-over to a new system presupposes comprehensive education directed to all employees.
- Shifting the Taylorist type of work outside the large enterprises to subcontractors and part-time employees working in atypical jobs is a new problem. So far no attempts have been made to solve this problem. We should seriously consider how to take care of the learning opportunities of these groups of workers and employees, both at work and in society at large.

Figure 1. Cultural structures describing cooperation relationships and their impact on better opportunities for growth and lifelong learning (Tuomisto 1996, 72; cf. Kevätsalo 1990, 58).

	In the past	At present	In the future
Dominant feature of organizational culture	authoritative	negotiating	participatory (developing staff)
Dominant feature of trade union culture	counterculture	representative participation (pragmatic)	direct participation (commitment)
Cultural basic structure of workplace	relationships of distrust	--	relationships of trust
	BETTER OPPORTUNITIES FOR COOPERATION -- >>>		
	distinguishing between thinking and performing	--	integration
Looking after interests	divisive issues	--	production issues
Participation in development of production	none	limited, by representatives only	all in cooperation
Mode of production	Tayloristic	--	"new mode of production"
Work organization	hierarchical	--	"flexible"
System of agreement	onesided dictation	central organization and union level	local agreement
Opportunities for lifelong learning	very limited	limited, for part of employees only	for all together, self-directiveness

- Establishing professional identity is more and more frequently a dilemma in the pressures of enterprise and trade union cultures. "Commitment" to the goals of the enterprise is more or less obligatory in the present labour market situation (high unemployment). On what conditions should this happen? Will employees in fact have to adapt to demands and orders coming from the top down? From the point of view of self-directiveness and learning, this would mean regression.
- Can an atmosphere of trust be established in workplaces and can we finally get rid of the zero-sum game? This is essential for the development of learning opportunities.
- Is it possible to solve the problem of "good" work, that is work that would contain suitable developmental challenges for all? To make this happen, we should create the preconditions for functional flexibility for all employees.
- How to solve the problems caused by holistic and comprehensive human development by advanced specialization, on the one hand, and multi-professionality, on the other?
- The increasing conflicts in workplaces in the 1990s are not necessarily something negative. We can regard this phenomenon as an integral part of democratic decision-making and dialogue. A true change requires this kind of open and critical discussion. However, we need to learn the rules of a new kind of discussion culture.
- The employers should see to it that the different groups of personnel are provided with more equal opportunities for development and education. Furthermore, education should be economically profitable and rewarding to the employer, too. This could be achieved by founding an "educational fund" which could be used to equalize educational costs and implement such educational programmes that private enterprises cannot afford to carry out.

There are more questions than answers. At any rate, all the above structural problems are those which we will have to solve somehow, if we really want to change workplaces into learning environments and learning organizations. Employers in Finland have required willingness to self-development and lifelong learning from all employees. However, presenting this requirement without implementing the necessary structural changes in the supervision of work, etc., means that this principle is being onesidedly exploited to advance the employers' own interests. The concept has then been used in an ideological sense to legitimize the demands for efficiencey. The real "in-depth" structural change in working life is only possible when the partners have a greater trust in each other and when "common interests" are truly shared, and not just attempts to bluff the opponent.

References

Alasoini, T. & Heikkilä, A. (1998). *Kansallinen työelämän kehittämisohjelma - projektien itsearviointien väliaikatietoja.* Työpoliittinen Aikakauskirja 2.

Argyris, C. & Schön, D. A. (1978). *Organizational Learning: A Theory of Action Perspective.* Addison-Wesley Publishing Company, Reading.

Atkinson, J. (1987). Flexibility or fragmentation? The United Kingdom labour market in the eighties. In *Labour and Society* 1987, 12, 1, 87-105.

Blomqvist, I. et al. (1997). *Aikuiskoulutustutkimus 1995. Aikuisopiskelu Suomessa.* Tilastokeskus. Koulutus 1997/4. Helsinki: Yliopistopaino.

Davis, R. J. & Weiner, N. (1985). A Cultural Perspective on the Study of Industrial Relations. In Frost et al. (eds.) *Organizational Culture.* Sage Publications. Beverly Hills.

Docherty, P. (1996). *Läroriket -vägar och vägval i en lärande organization.* Solna: Arbetslivsinstitutet.

Engeström, Y. (1993). Organisaation oppiminen - sopeutumista vai uuden luomista? In Kontiainen & Nurmi (Ed.), *Muutos ja interventio työelämässä.* Helsingin yliopiston kasvatustieteen laitos. Tutkimuksia 139. Helsainki: Yliopistopaino.

Foley, G. (1994). Adult Education and Capitalist Reorganization. In *Studies in the Education of Adults.* Vol. 26, No. 2. October.

Hacker, W. (1982). *Yleinen työpsykologia.* Espoo: Weilin+Göös.

Ilmonen, K. & Kevätsalo, K. (1995). *Ay-liikkeen vaikeat valinnat.* Palkansaajien tutkimuslaitos, tutkimuksia 59. Helsinki.

Industry training in Australia, Sweden and the United States (1993). Paris: OECD.

Juhela, A., Tuomisto J., Heikkilä K., Juhela A., Poikela E. & Vuorikoski M. (1996). Henkilöstön kouluttamisesta työn kehittämiseen. In Tuomisto, *Yhteiskunnan rakenteet ja elinikäinen oppiminen.* Tampereen yliopisto. Kasvatustieteiden laito. Julkaisusarja A 59.

Kauppinen, Timo (1992). *Suomen työmarkkinamallin muutos.* Työpoliittinen Yhdistys R.Y:n julkaisu 1. Helsinki: Hakapaino.

Kalimo, R. & Toppinen, S. (1997). *Työuupumus Suomen työikäisellä väestöllä.* Työterveyslaitos.

Kasvio A. (199)5. *Uusi työn yhteiskunta.Suomalaisen työelämän muutokset ja kehittämismahdollisuudet.* Gaudeamaus. Jyväskylä: Gummerus Kirjapaino Oy.

Kevätsalo, K. (1990). *Kunnallishallinnon työelämän laadun ja palvelutuotannon tuloksellisuuden kehittämisen tutkimusohjelma.* Tampereen yliopisto. Työelämän tutkimuskeskus. Työraportteja N:o 16. Tampere.

Kevätsalo, K. (1994). *Yhteisymmärrystä, luottamusta ja tehokkuutta jäjittämässä.* Metallittyöväen Liitto ry. Turenki: Jaarli Oy.

Kevätsalo, K. (1995). *Edut aatteena ja vakuutus solidaarisuutena.* Metallityöväen liitto ry. Turenki: Jaarli Oy.

Kevätsalo, K. (1999). *Jäykät joustot ja tuhlatut resurssit.* Tampere: Vastapaino.

Koivisto, T. (1995). *PL-verstaan uudet toimintatavat. Analyysi osallistavan uudelleensuunnittelun prosessista.* Tampereen yliopisto. Yhteiskuntatieteiden tutkimuslaitos. Työelämän tutkimuskeskus. Työraportteja 51. Tampere.

Kolu, T. (1992). *Työelämän laatu 1977-1990. Hyvinvoinnin koettuja muutoksia työssä.* Työolokomitean mietinnön liiteselvitys. Komiteanmietintö 1991:38. Tilastokeskus, tutkimuksia 188. Helsinki.

Kortteinen, M. (1992). *Kunnian kenttä. Suomalainen palkkatyö kulttuurisena muotona.* Hämeenlinna: Hanki ja Jää.

Kornbluh & Green (1989). Learning, empowerment and partipative work processes: the educative work environment. In Leymann & Kornbluh (eds.), *Socialization and learning at work.* Aldershot: Avebury.

Lähes joka neljännen työsuhde epätyypillinen. Aamulehti 18.2.1997.

OECD (1996). *Lifelong learning for all.* Meeting of the Education Committee at Ministerial Level 16-17 January 1996. Paris: OECD.

Ollus, M., Lovio, R., Mieskonen. J., Vuorinen, P., Karko. J., Ylä-Anttila, P. (1990). *Joustava tuotanto ja verkostotalous - tekniikan, talouden ja yhteiskunnan vuorovaikutus 1990-luvulla.* SITRA nro 109. Helsinki.

Rinne R., Silvennoinen H. & Valanta J. (1995). *Työelämän aikuiskoulutus. Valta, vastuu ja intressit henkilöstökoulutuksessa.* Turun yliopisto. Koulutussosiologian tutkimuskeskus, raportti 29. Turku.

Sarala, U. & Sarala, A. (1996). *Oppiva organisaatio -oppimisen laadun ja tuottavuuden yhdistäminen.* Helsingin yliopiston Lahden tutkimus- ja koulutuskeksus. Tampere: Tammer-paino.

Senge, P. M. (1990). *The Fifth Discipline: The art and practice of the learning organization.* New Youk: Doubleday.

Simpanen, M. (1993). *Aikuiskoulutus ja työelämä.* Aikuiskoulutustutkimus 90. Tilastokeskus, tutkimuksia 201. Helsinki.

Sisson, K. (1997) (ed.). *New forms of work organization.: can Europe realise its potential?* European Foundation for the Improvement of Living and Working Conditions. Dublin.

Thorsrud, E. & Emery, F. (1971). *Osallistuminen ja vaikuttaminen työelämässä.* Helsinki: Weilin+Göös.

Tuomisto, J., Heikkilä K., Juhela A., Poikela E. & Vuorikoski M. (1996). Ammattiyhdistysliikkeen koulutuksen lähtökohdat. Teoksessa Tuomisto et al. *Yhteiskunnan rakenteet ja elinikäinen oppiminen. Tampereen yliopisto.* Kasvatustieteiden laitos. Julkaisusarja A/59. Tampere.

Tuomisto J., Heikkilä K., Juhela A., Poikela E. & Vuorikoski M. (1996). Yhteiskunnan rakenteet ja elinikäinen oppiminen. Tampereen yliopisto. Kasvatustieteiden laitos. Julkaisusarja A/59. Tampere.

Valtee, Pasi (1994). *Työyhteisön konfliktit ja niiden hallinta - teoreettisia ideoita ja empiirisiä havaintoja.* Tampereen yliopisto. Julkishallinnon lisensiaatintyö.Tampere.

Watkins, Karen E. & Marsick, Victoria J. (1993). *Sculpting the Learning Organization.* San Francisco: Jossey-Bass Publishers.

EDUCATION OF ADULTS VERSUS ADULT EDUCATION

Ove Korsgaard

Abstract

In this article I argue in favour of the expediency of distinguishing between educating adults and adult education. In Denmark the concepts of adult education and lifelong learning did not gain a footing until around 1970.

The new concepts were deeply influenced by pedagogical ideas which had developed within humanistic psychology in the USA in the fifties and the sixties, where the key concepts were growth, self-realization, and self-actualization.

I shall emphasize two positions related to this development. One is personified by K. Grue-Sørensen, professor of Pedagogy, who is sceptical towards the new pedagogical ideas, the other representative is Johan Fjord Jensen. Professor of Literature, who welcomes the new ideas in several books and articles.

Only during the last few decades have adults been deeply involved in the pedagogical subject matter. As a consequence it became a question how the new concepts of "adult education" and "lifelong learning" are related to old concepts such as "leisure time education" and "folkeoplysning" (popular-national education). During the 1980s, and especially during the 1990s, adult education and lifelong learning have, to a rising degree, been marked with an economic need for a greater production of human capital. Evidently these concepts reflect the revolutionary changes of the educational system and the working life of our time.

The Danish folk high school: the school for the Youth

It may be elucidating to distinguish between educating adults and adult education. The fact is that from a historical point of view educating adults is an old phenomenon, whereas adult education is a new one.

If we do not distinguish between these concepts, it is easy to have a misconception of history.This appears very often in descriptions of the Danish folk high school (folkehøjskole) which is frequently described as the world's first school for adults. However, this is not correct. Educating adults has taken place a long time before the founding of the first folk high school in 1844. For instance, evening schools were established in 1814 and Sunday schools before that. The new idea, which the folk high schools launched, was a special purpose of the enlightenment and education, viz. a popular (folkelig)national-enlightenment and education[5].

Adults were not even the target group of the traditional folk high school. The target group consisted of the young people. The word adult was so to speak never used about the students, at the most in connection with the word young, as for instance "the adult youth". The folk high school was understood and referred to as a school for young people and this was due to the fact that a considerable part of the students were between 16 and 18 years old during the first decades of the history of the folk high schools. This understanding was supported by the developmental psychological theory that the psychical constitution of the young people made this age group particularly receptive to a popular-national revival.

In 1904, Ludwig Schrøder, the first Principal at Askov Folk High School, wrote an article about "The Years of Youth and the School for the Youth", describing the folk high school as a school for young people and Grundtvig as the ideas man of this type of school. And "just as Rousseau asserted the gospel of childhood Grundtvig asserted the gospel of youth. Just as Rousseau defended childhood against being considered a mer preparation to becoming adult, Grundtvig has defended youth against being considered to be a mere preparation for a future time of deeds". In fact adult life.[6]

It is not until about 1970 - when adult education has become a special field - that youth is replaced with adult age as being the period of life, which is the target of the folk high school.

Adult Education

In English there is a long tradition of using the expression "adult education". However, this does not mean either that adult education was aimed at a specific age group in the Anglo-American tradition. Adult education also aimed at helping people to grow up, to become of age. Thus there was a distinction

---

5 Ove Korsgaard Kampen om lyset, Dansk voksenoplysning gennem 500 år. 1997.

6 Ludvig Schrøder Den nordiske folkehøjskole (The Norse Folk High School) 1904:2.

between becoming of age in the outer sense of the word, viz. the legal sense, and becoming of age in the inner sense of the word, viz. morally. The latter was not automatically the consequence of the former. To become of age was also a learning process, and adult education was meant to contribute to a successful result.

Even though the Anglo-American tradition has not developed a concept of enlightenment which is equivalent to the concept of "folkeoplysning" in Denmark or "folkbildning" in Sweden (popular-national education) the Anglo-American and the Nordic traditions still agree in some essential respects, for instance they both regard themselves as part of the non-formal system, viz. the free non-governmental educational system.

Great Britain was the first country to introduce the concept of lifelong learning. In 1919 a committee appointed by the Department of Education and Science prepared this in a report on adult education.

The report states, "That the necessary conclusion is that adult education must not be regarded as a luxury for a few exceptional persons here and there, nor as a thing which concerns only a short span of early manhood, but that adult education is a permanent national necessity, an inseparable aspect of citizenship, and therefore should be both universal and lifelong".[7]

The report states a national need for lifelong adult education. However, no connection is established between adult education and the formal educational system, adult education is still to be conducted by the non-formal education system.[8]

Even though the concept of lifelong education was already used in connection with the concept of adult education in 1919 it did not spread the following three decades. This did not take place until the concept was re-introduced by UNESCO at the end of the 1950s. Through the 1960s other international institutions also began to emphasize the importance of adult education and lifelong learning. Different linguistic traditions developed; UNESCO used the

---

[7] *A Design for Democracy 1956:55.* (The book is a re-issue of The 1919 Report with an introduction by Professor R. D. Waller).

[8] The Danish folk high school is an ideal-typical example of a non-formal educational institution, and in international literature it is often mentioned as the first school for adults.

concept of "Lifelong Integrated Education", OECD "Recurrent Education", and the Council of Europe, "Permanent Education".[9] Since then the contents of the concepts have gradually developed and are constantly changing.

In Denmark, the concepts of adult education and lifelong learning were not used until the third UNESCO world conference on adult education in Tokyo 1972.

From Pedagogy to Andragogy

The ideological roots of adult pedagogy must be found in the USA where, in 1926, Eduard Lindeman wrote the book *The Meaning of Adult Education* which has the status of being a classic in the history of adult education. In his book he describes a social philosophy with adult education as the life transforming power. He suggests that the word andragogy is better than the word pedagogy as andros in Greek means man, whereas pais means boy, and andogiké means education.[10]

However, Lindeman's student, Malcolm Knowles, was the first to replace the word adult pedagogy with andragogy, a pedagogy for adults. Knowles' ideas of andragogy take their starting point in the humanistic tradition where the main object of pedagogy is to help the individual to fully develop and make the most of his potential. Abraham Maslow, a representative of the humanistic psychology, refers to this development as a movement towards growth, self-realization, and self-actualization, that is to say a striving towards finding the individually specific and valuable.

The humanistic philosophy emphasizes that man ought to be considered as "existing and in continued formation". Development is not considered to be finished with the early youth, but has to be a lifelong process. In the humanistic philosophy "lifelong development" becomes an ideal. Development is not considered to be a process, controlled from the outside, on the contrary, it is primarily a striving, controlled from within, spontaneous , and lifelong towards realizing man's innate possibilities. To a very high degree the humanistic

---

[9] *Social Change and Adult Education Research* 1993:115ff.

[10] Ove Korsgaard: *Kampen om lyset. Dansk voksenoplysning gennem 500 år*, 1997:411f. (It is relevant here that Lindeman was inspired by Grundtvig and the Danish folk high school.)

psychology influenced andragogy/adult pedagogy which really made lifelong education the ideal.

It is a prominent feature of this kind of andragogy/adult pedagogy - whose ideal is self-actualization and self-realization - that it is not much occupied with the adult's learning of skills and knowledge, but is concentrated upon developing the personality. The idea is: If the development of the personality is normal and appropriate there is no need to give much attention to the development of qualifications.

Knowles started his work with andragogy after World War II. He thought that there was such a great qualitative difference between children and adults that adults had to be taught according to different guidelines. In 1970 he published *The Modern Practice of Adult Education: Andragogy versus Pedagogy*. It is a guidebook and reference book for adult educators who needed help to solve their practical problems. In his book Knowles sets up a contrast between andragogy and pedagogy; he argues that pedagogy could not be used as a method in adult education as it deals with transferring well-known knowledge to a dependent student; andragogy, on the other hand, takes its starting point in the adult's greater independence and ability of taking the responsibility of his own learning.

Knowles is of the opinion that andragogy is necessary in a transforming society where knowledge becomes antiquated and has to be revised all the time. The traditional conception of education as being the transfer of and help to understand well-known knowledge is no longer adequate. There is a need to educate people who themselves understand to learn and to transfer their knowledge under rapidly changing conditions.

Knowles distinguishes between a social and a psychological definition of being an adult. Socially a person is an adult when he/she is able to act socially in the roles that are defined as being adult roles in a certain culture. For instance, the role as a parent, a partner, a worker, or a responsible citizen. The psychological definition refers more to the individual's understanding of himself. When the individual on the whole considers himself/herself to be responsible for his/her own life it is time to be considered an adult person. According to Knowles these definitions must be considered when adults want to be educated. In his everyday life an adult is used to make independent decisions and be responsible for his/her actions and life. Consequently the education must leave room for the student both to participate in managing the development of the education and to be responsible for his/her own learning.

However, andragogy did not gain a footing in Danish, on the contrary, adult pedagogy became the predominant term.

From education to development

In 1972, after the Tokyo conference, Professor K. Grue-Sørensen wrote an article on "adult pedagogy and Life-Long Education" pointing out that the object of pedagogy: up-bringing, education, and instruction appear to be highly expanding activities "which engage a larger and larger part of a life time, both regarding the number of people involved and regarding the share of the life time of an individual which is spent upon these activities".[11]

To a rising degree adult life is involved in the subject matter of pedagogy. This can be traced in the use of the new concept: "adult pedagogy" and "lifelong learning" which appear in the language with "a ring of almost being a slogan of both demand and promise".

However, K. Grue-Sørensen questions whether there is a decisive difference between teaching children and adults. "Is there a demand for a special educational textbook, based upon for instance a special learning psychology for adults? Are the rules of learning and intellectual progress others for adults than for children"?[12]

Is there a special pedagogy for children, young people, adults, and old people? Does learning take place according to other rules for adults than for children and adolescents? "This is a question which can no doubt be answered in the negative" says K. Grue-Sørensen. An education must, of course, consider the student's developmental stage and maturity, and age and social background are constituent parts of these factors.

However, all education is based upon a hierarchy: "some people are teachers, others are students; some people teach, others are taught; some people understand and teach, others are taught".

K. Grue-Sørensen - who is deeply rooted in a cognitively oriented pedagogical tradition - is critical to the shift from "education" to "development" which the

---

11 K. Grue-Sørensen: "Refleksioner over voksenpædagogik og Life-Long Education". In : *Pædagogik* 1974.

12 The same.

humanistic inspired adult pedagogy argues in favour of. According to K. Grue-Sørensen, the concept of education cannot be substituted by the concept of development as development as such is not a pedagogical word. "The word only gets a pedagogical meaning if the issue is a guided or in some other way controlled development". Pedagogical work demands a more specific and ideal aim than common development of the personality.

Therefore K. Grue-Sørensen is critical towards the UNESCO publication *Learning to Be* from 1972. In this publication the development of the personality is considered to be the aim of the education. One of the chapters is called, "Towards the complete man". But - asks Grue-Sørensen - what kind of pedagogy is it that is supposed to develop "the complete man"?

The UNESCO-report is deeply influenced by humanistic psychology and pedagogy. The aim of lifelong learning is to awaken man's innate striving towards growth. The report states that lifelong learning is meant to be the leading idea of the educational policy of the coming years. Therefore, a status of secondary importance is no longer enough for adult education, it has to be involved as a vital element of the educational strategy. This implies that the formal and the non-formal educational system must be more closely connected.

The third main part of the UNESCO report is called "Towards a learning society". The characteristic of a learning society is - according to the report - that larger and larger parts of the population become the subject matters of pedagogy.

However, as Grue-Sørensen warns us, when the wish is to change society into being a large educational institution "it will be difficult to make a distinction between a ruling society and education, between pedagogy and politics".

Grue-Sørensen is critical to the shift from "education" to "development" which is taking place, with adult pedagogy as the driving force. However, he cannot prevent that gradually the concept of development of the humanistic psychology - through adult pedagogy - influences a large part of the pedagogical philosophy.

Adult pedagogy and adult age

While K. Grue-Sørensen was critical of the concept of adult pedagogy (and andragogy). Professor Johan Fjord Jensen uses it as a key concept in his description of "the new adult culture". Rousseau asserted "the gospel of childhood", Grundtvig "the gospel of youth", and likewise Johan Fjord Jensen can be said to assert "the gospel of adult age".[13]

According to Fjord Jensen the most important driving force behind the growth of the new adult culture is the demands of modern society for continued renewal of skills and knowledge, resulting in the fact that education can no longer be delimited to childhood and youth.

However, the demand for renewal of skills and knowledge is not only external demands, but it is also determined by a biological fact, in other words, a considerable prolongation of the life time. Almost half of the prolongation has taken place in this century.

According to Fjord Jensen adult life is being considered a special period of life in the same way as childhood was considered to be in last century, and youth in this one. Formerly the education during childhood and youth aimed at the adult age. To be an adult was to be finished and ready in all the meanings of these words. When a person was adult he was ready and able to start working and to support a family. And this ability was continued until 30 or 40 years later when old age began.

This is no longer the case. Now the adults meet with having to change jobs, place of employment, address, partner, friends, etc. To be an adult means to be subject to the same possibilities and demands which young people are subject to.

Among other things the effect of the new demands on the adults is that now the adults are pressed in to adult education. To be an adult is no longer to be completed, on the contrary, an adult is constantly developing. Fjord Jensen is deeply influenced by the humanistic growth psychology which became so important to adult pedagogy in the 1960's. Further, the idea that adults can grow is inspired by different forms of therapy, by Carl Jung's and Erik Eriksson's psychology, and by eastern philosophy and religion.

Thus the development of the adult age is not only initiated by the demands of the knowledge society, but - according to Fjord Jensen – also by various crises in the immanent dynamics of adult life. He describes these existential crises in adult life as crises of the turning points of life, and they take place at the ages of

---

13 First and foremost Johan Fjord Jensen has done so in his book *Livsbuen. Voksenpsykologi og livsaldre.* 1993.

40, 50, and 60. These crises are all related to an increasing consciousness concerning "the finiteness of the life project".

Adult Education and "Folkeoplysning"

Until few decades ago adult education has been considered to be something extra, something supplementing, compensating, etc. The state authorities did not give it much attention. To a large extent it was left to the non-formal system. This system expanded drastically after World War II. A national spirit of community about democracy is an important ideological background for a number of new initiatives.

However, lead by the labour movement, leisure time was becoming a more and more important and decisive legitimating factor. In Denmark in 1965 the report on "leisure time education of adults" was published and under this new name of the evening school the Act of June 6, 1968 on General Leisure Time Education of Adults was passed. This act is an ideal basis for the new ideas concerning adult education, which gained a footing together with the humanistic inspired adult pedagogy.

However, it was not only leisure time which became a new legitimating factor, this also applied to work. The vocational education and courses preparatory for examinations were given a higher priority. The courses preparatory for adult education for examinations were introduced in 1958 when the technical preparatory courses were established. In 1960, special schools were established, giving adults the vocational qualifications that were necessary in the labour market.

Gradually this development resulted in the fact that a proper adult education system was established, however, this system was also divided. One system aimed at leisure life, the other at the labour market. The first was primarily organized by the non-formal system, the other by the formal system.

As a result of the growth of the new subject matter adult education, there was much uncertainty as to how it was related to the old concept: "folkeoplysning". Consequently, for some decades both terms were used. However, the term "folkeoplysning" was not able to hold its ground. It is being replaced by the two concepts of adult education and lifelong learning.

The development is reflected in the implementation of the so-called 10-point program for adult education and "folkeoplysning" which the Danish Parliament passed in 1984. The aim was to improve the terms of developing adult education and "folkeoplysning" and increase the possibilities of adults to participate in these".[14] Later this Parliamentary resolution was followed by a number of political educational initiatives. At the end of the 1980s two initiatives were taken which will be commented on more closely.

In 1990, Parliament passed the "Act on the Allocation of Financial Support to "Folkeoplysning" to replace the Act from 1968 on leisure time education. This might be interpreted as a victory to the concept of "folkeoplysning" in relation to adult education. However, it is rather that the concept of "folkeoplysning" replaces the concept of leisure time. The decisive fact is that for the first time, the term "folkeoplysning" becomes a legal concept in general adult education. But, as the concept has another historical background – as mentioned above - elements from this history are always involved in the present debate concerning adult education which often results in great confusion.

In 1989 Parliament passed the Act on Adult Education Grants, the so-called VUS-Act. This act is a follow-up of point No. 6 in the 10-point programme. According to this point "the Act provides financial basis for employees to participate in general or vocational training during working hours". As a result of the passing of this Act the term of adult education is really capturing the linguistic field.

The VUS-Act demonstrates a new step towards an increased integration between education and work as it gives adults a possibility of grants to be educated during working hours. While both the Act on Leisure-time education and the Act on "Folkeoplysning" are based upon a connection between education and leisure time, working time is now involved in the subject matter of pedagogy. The Act is meant to ensure a sufficient supply of qualified labour and to adjust existing educational differences of society. In the comments on the Bill it is said that "the Bill aims at a more direct occupational qualification of the labour force".[15]

---

14 Parliament Resolution on a 10-Point Programme on Adult Education and "Folkeoplysning". 30th May 1984, No. B. 114.

15 The Act of Adult Education Grants No. 336 of May 1989.

Parallel system of competence for adult education

In 1996 the Ministry of Education published a "Discussion paper concerning a new parallel system of competence for adult education".

The background of the discussion paper is that there is a need for "a complete system of competence for adult educations".[16] The system of competence for adult education must consist of a well-planned number of well-defined job specifications that are meant for adults with some vocational experience.

The Ministry of Education intends to launch four new specifications:

Basic Adult Education (GVU)
Further Adult Education (VVU)
Diploma Education
Master Education

Contrary to the basic educational system, the intention of the new system of competence is not primarily educational progress, but vocational. First and foremost the intention is that, by improving their competence, adults are able to attend to functions with larger responsibility or move into (partly) new subject areas.

The implementation of this system resulted in a great formalization of all adult education which, from a historical point of view, has been influenced by the non-formal system. Now it remains to establish a formal system, to a certain degree involving the non-formal system. According to the proposals a stay at a folk high school is going to give formal competence.[17]

The system of the further education of adults is part of a process of standardization and formalization. Formalized educations is completed with examinations and tests.

---

16 The Ministry of Education Discussion Paper Concerning a New Parallel System of Competence for Adult Education, 1996:7.

17 Because of the discussion about the discussion paper the name "The Parallel System of Competence" was changed to "The Further Educational System for Adults", however, the basic idea is the same.

Without a leaving certificate or diploma it is very difficult to get on in an education-conscious society. To an increasingly greater extent education has become necessary to have a chance of getting a job, especially the well paid ones. Of course, this does not mean that a diploma automatically results in a job, a diploma only shows that a person has the right to compete in the distribution of jobs.

The differentiation - which to a rising degree is characteristic of the labour market - seems to go hand in hand with a more formalized education market.[18]

From development to education

Behind this development Johan Fjord Jensen notes a confrontation with the concept of "folkeoplysning" based upon a Grundtvigian tradition in Danish educational policy. The characteristic feature of this tradition was - according to Fjord Jensen - that the system of adult education was created against the background of a liberal educational philosophy. Even though occupational possibilities gradually permeated the Act on Leisure-time education with qualifying courses, adult education mainly consisted of instruction, training, and "folkeoplysning" and was not a proper education. Thus the many offers of evening classes, in leisure-time education, at the folk high schools, and, for that matter, also in open education were not first and foremost a result of the interests of the labour market, but the specific need for enlightenment of the adult generation.[19] According to Fjord Jensen this widely branching tradition and the instruction method, based upon freedom, has become an outcast of economic calculations.

According to Fjord Jensen there is a decisive difference between educating young people and educating adults. The most important difference is that the first leads towards the labour market whereas the second leads out of the market and towards adult life as such. Fjord Jensen states plainly that regarding adult education "the labour market is quite secondary and the same applies to the dream of getting on in this market."[20] It does not appear from the context whether there is any empirical instance in support of this bold conclusion. Most probably it is Fjord Jensen's fascination for people who have made a radical

---

18 Cf. Ulrich Beck: Risikosamfundet, 1997:241ff.

19 Johan Fjord Jensen Frirum, 1998:97.

20 Johan Fjord Jensen Frirum. 1998:99.

shift in the middle of their lives which makes him consider the drive towards cognition as being the decisive force behind all adult education. It is not convincing to neglect the fact that there may be (sound) economic, occupational, and career considerations behind adult education.

From the periphery to the centre

From a historical point of view, children and later young people at first became the objectives of pedagogy. However, during the latest decades adult education has become an important public matter. To a greater extent, adults have been involved in the pedagogical subject matter. Adult pedagogy, guidance, and instruction of adults, adult education and lifelong learning have become new core concepts of the educational discourse. Adult education is no longer an appendix to educating children and young people. Through the last 30 years adult education has gradually moved from the periphery to the centre of the educational agenda.

This is evidently a consequence of the growth of the so-called knowledge society. All countries seem to be confronted with the fact that knowledge has become an increasingly more important aspect of global competition. These years the message is expressed in almost identical phrases in a series of national and international reports. In many countries, from Japan to Denmark, the same conclusion can be heard: If we want to manage in the global economic competition, education, more education, and even more education is necessary.

Nowhere is this new educational discourse expressed more clearly than within the field of adult education. Yes, in many ways it is the core of the new discourse that adults have seriously become the objectives of pedagogy. To be an adult person is no longer to be a person who has finished school, on the contrary, he or she is subject to the same demands for education and learning as children and young persons.

References

A Design for Democracy. (The book is a re-issue of The 1919 Report with an introduction by Professor R. D. Waller). Published for The Adult.

Education Association in USA, Canada and Great Britain by Max Parish, London, 1956.

Bech, Ulrich (1997. Risikosamfundet (The Risk Society). Hans Reizel.

Grue-Sørensen, K. (1974). "Refleksioner over voksenpædagogik og Life-Long Education". In: *Pædagogik.*

Jensen, Johan Fjord (1993). *Livsbuen. Voksenpsykologi og livsaldre.* Gyldendal.

Jensen, Johan Fjord (1998). *Frirum.* Klim.

Knowles, Malcolm (1970). *The Modern Practice of Adult Education: Andragogy versus Pedagogy.* Association Press.

Korsgaard, Ove (1997). *Kampen om lyset. Dansk voksenoplysning gennem 500 år.* (English Summary: The Struggle for Enlightenment. Danish Adult Education during 500 Years). Gyldendal.

Lindeman, Eduard (1926). *The Meaning of Adult Education.* New Republic.

Resolution on a 10-Point Programme on Adult Education and "Folkeoplysning". 30th May 1984, No. B. 114.

Schrøder, Ludvig (1904). *Den nordiske folkehøjskole* (The Norse Folk High School). Udvalget for Folkeoplysningens Fremme.

The Act of Adult Education Grants No. 336 of May. The Danish Ministry of Education, 1989.

The Ministry of Education Discussion Paper Concerning a New Parallel System of Competence for Adult Educations. The Danish Ministry of Education, 1996.

Tøsse, Sigvart m. fl. (ed.) (1993). *Social Change and Adult Education Research.* Trondheim.

POPULAR ENLIGHTENMENT - PRESERVED IN MUSEUMS OR STILL ON DUTY?

Some perspectives on Popular Enlightenment in a globalized world

Arild Mikkelsen

Abstract

This article will discuss the future of Popular Enlightenment and Folk High Schools, and raise the question: should the movement fight to retain the influence it has had, or should it resign and preserve its traditions in a museum? The problem might seem odd to some, but the present debate in the Nordic countries has convinced me that this is what it is all about.

I will discuss the problem by referring to four different writers. My intention is not to present these writers in depth or go into any detail in their work. I might even have misread some of them, or might use their arguments in an awkward way. However, I aim to focus on the challenges facing the movement of Popular Enlightenment and Folk High Schools in the present situation.

Development of the Modern Project

The national state is under pressure from many angles these days. The national state and its following national identity has been regarded as a construction of the 19th century, with roots in French rationalism and European romanticism in the early years of 1800. The Nordic movement of Popular Enlightenment, or in the Norwegian language, folkeopplysning (the term is almost impossible to translate correctly), was an integrated and vital element in the development of the national state. Development of individual strong feelings of belonging to a nation, and having a national identity were a contribution from the Popular Enlightenment movement.

As a consequence of, or as a fundamental premise for the development of the national state, came the development of capitalism, the process of industrialization and urbanization, the process we today call the Modern Project. The Modern Project was based on an understanding of science as a important premise for truth and solidity. The Modern Project became perceived as an optimistic, progressive and hopeful project, with a strong belief that injustice could be revealed and corrected, and that all mankind would have a prosperous and good future. Both the bourgeois class and the working class shared this optimism, although for slightly different reasons.

Within the Nordic countries this characteristic trait in the development of modernity simultaneously became a development towards democracy. Different factors caused this development: for the new capitalistic industry it was necessary to find a free labour force in accordance with new ways of production. The ties to the old agricultural system, where the agricultural population was bound to the owners of the farms, had to be broken. The individual had to be defined as free in such a way that he or she could be used in a labour force, bought on the labour market and paid through wages.

This is a common European development. Within the Nordic countries the term Popular Enlightenment emerged together with this development as a vital element of different popular and social movements that were in opposition to the authorities. These movements had a common claim that the supremacy of the state should be replaced by the supremacy of the people. Looking back on this period in our history, it is possible to see that the Nordic Popular Enlightenment was an early and important element in establishing what we today call the civil society. This movement indirectly insisted that the implementation of democracy is more than free elections and democratic legislation, it is also necessary to establish a third sector of free organizations and non-governmental institutions that might be responsible for Popular Enlightenment or "folkeopplysning".

Grundtvig and the Folk High School

The first Norwegian Folk High School was established in 1864, and the Folk High School movement became an exponent of this new understanding of democracy. The Folk High School movement became part of both the national movement that wanted political freedom from Sweden, part of the movement for a renaissance of the Norwegian language and culture, and a part of the political opposition that wanted a parliamentary system which gave power to those who had been elected by the people.

In this sense, Popular Enlightenment and the Folk High School movement have been well integrated in the development of Norway as a national state. Within the framework of the Modern Project it simultaneously advocated democracy. In other circumstances the development of democracy and the establishment of nationality could have been two separated processes. One of the reasons for the development of Norwegian nationalism as a democracy was the Popular Enlightenment movement and the already established Folk High Schools.

The founder of ideas leading to the development of the Nordic Popular Enlightenment and the Nordic Folk High School movement was the Danish priest, poet and philosopher Nicolai Fredrik Severin Grundtvig (1783-1872). I will not discuss the historical process that brought Grundtvig's ideas to Norway, but mention that the Norwegian Folk High School was strongly influenced by these ideas, although the process was complicated, involving many factors. Within the church the Grundtvigian influence was heavily rejected, but his thoughts formed the background for many Folk High School teachers from the 1870s. In his work from the 1830s Grundtvig stressed the concept popular (folkelig) as being one of the main characteristics of a Folk High School. This concept occurred to him at the same time as the romantic movement rolled over Europe. In a sense Grundtvig was influenced by romanticism, especially the German philosopher Johan Gottfred Herder. The Folk High School author and philosopher Jørgen Bukdahl defines popular in a Grundtvigian understanding as being national. For Grundtvig, says Bukdahl, this was to be Danish! (Bukdahl,1971). But this nationalism had a strong element of ideas of social equality. Grundtvig said that this fundamental equality also existed between nations. The ideas of Grundtvig came to a strong degree to influence the development of the Danish society in an evidently progressive and democratic direction.

We also find an element of universalism in Grundtvigs viewpoints. The Grundtvigian ladder of awareness for the Nordic nations was popular (folkelig) in a democratic, national and social way, later Nordic, and ultimately universal. The universalism of Grundtvig is easy to trace in his songs, poems and hymns. The main content of this universalism was that each nation had a specific role to play in the great God-created drama. In this world-wide drama, the roles of each nation could be different, but equally important. The aim of each nation was to be conscious of its own role in this drama, and then fulfil the role. Universalism for Grundtvig also had something to do with his analysis of the importance of language. He regarded man's ability to speak as a gift given by God, therefore his understanding of language was linked to Christianity.

This is not a kind of hidden oppressive imperialism or reactionary nationalism. This is more a programme for developing independent, democratic nations with a strong awareness of their own importance, but inevitably linked to the national state. With this ideological background, Popular Enlightenment and Folk High Schools in Norway could be an important part in the building of national identity, based on both a political, cultural and linguistic awakening.

Jürgen Habermas and popular enlightenment

Is it possible to maintain this progressive ideology when the importance of the national state seems to be declining? Will it be possible to preserve Popular Enlightenment in a globalized, post-modern world, where differences between nations increasingly appear to be diminishing and vanishing? I will discuss these problems from different perspectives, and through the work of different writers, focusing on the idea of Popular Enlightenment.

Nordic Folk High School teachers, and leaders within the field of adult education, have for several years used theories of Jürgen Habermas to support their arguments. They regard Popular Enlightenment as being opposed to all instrumental theories of learning, and have consequently giving Popular Enlightenment a strong progressive potentiality. They have focused on Habermas' description of the differences between the world of systems, and people's everyday lifeworlds. Furthermore, they have drawn a parallel between the Grundtvigian term "living exchange" - his term for dialogue, and the term "Kommunikativ Handlung" by Habermas (Habermas 1999). It is tempting to take theories and terms from Habermas, and use them in an attempt to include Grundtvig and ideas of Popular Enlightenment as a part of the contemporary philosophical debate, proving the current interest of the ideas. In addition to Habermas' insistence on rationality, his assumption is that the problems of democracy today might be solved by dialogue between equal partners. He claims that as partners, they will in fact be able to establish free and uncontrolled dialogue.

If we are to define adult education within the framework and ideas of Habermas, we also have to accept that the ideas of Popular Enlightenment still belong to the Modern Project. In his work Habermas delivers a strong defence of the Modern Project, hoping for its future fulfilment. For him, problems of modernity consist of a fragmentation of the totality in different separated fields, each field being taken over by experts. According to the French philosopher Jean Francois Lyotard, Habermas hopes for a solution of the problems of modernity through a new totality or entity in human life (Røsaak 1999).

By accepting this position, and putting Popular Enlightenment into the same concept, the task of Popular Enlightenment is to construct a bridge over the gaps of fragmentation. The Grundtvigian term "enlightenment for life" could perhaps be interpreted in this manner, but not without running into severe difficulties. In his newly published book the Swedish writer Bosse Bergstedt has quite another understanding of Grundtvig (Bergstedt 1998). He purports that Grundtvig accepted the fact that man could never reach a totality. Living exchange, dialogue and enlightenment for life (livsopplysning) should be understood as an attempt to live with a reconciliation of this fact, rather than trying to build a bridge. Popular Enlightenment or enlightenment for life coincides more with the positions of the philosopher Emmanuel Levinas and his renewal of ethics through emphasizing the meeting with the Other, than to a fulfilment of the Modern Project of Habermas.

If we go to Habermas' position in the issues of nation and national identity, we face equal problems. Habermas defines democracy as an overall society of communication. He accepts that such societies today are separated into different nations. But he advocates a supranational Europe, where a European parliament could take purely political decisions, and where ethnic- cultural questions are left for individual nations to solve in such a way that they still may provide a national identity.

In a newly published book Professor Øyvind Østerud discusses this standpoint of Habermas (Østerud 1999). Østerud criticises Habermas for not giving arguments to support his insistence that a purely political culture might be formally maintained, without the cultural contents of a national identity. By excluding national identity from his wish for a supranational political institution Habermas leaves nationality to the ethnic-cultural field. This might again lead to a kind of ethnification of national identity, and furthermore to right-wing, or even fascist-influenced nationalism.

There is a connection between Habermas' analysis of the Modern Project as an unfulfiled project, and his vision of a supranational political institution in Europe, supported by what he calls "Verfassungspatriotismus". In both cases his strong belief in the ratio of mankind, his rationalism, is his foundation. Popular Enlightenment, enlightenment for life, and the ideas of Folk High Schools, should not unhesitatingly regard themselves as part of this Habermasian interpretation of the Modern Project.

The challenge of globalization, the challenge of the crisis in the Modern Project, correctly characterized by Habermas in terms of fragmentation and lack of unifying ideologies, cannot be met by more of the same, more modernity. If we do so, we let Popular Enlightenment and enlightenment for life be a kind of museum within the Modern Project. Just as the national identification process will be left to the nations under the umbrella of a supranational political institution in Europe, Popular Enlightenment will in the same way be given the task of preserving what is left in modernity, except for the rationality, and end up in a museum. It should be possible to make the ideas of Popular Enlightenment more influential and vital by facing the so-called postmodern society with all its problems without slipping into the museum. Popular Enlightenment deserves better. Globalization is a process that calls for twofold action: resistance against the liberal economy that leaves everything to the market, and at the same time, support to those forces that fight globalization. These counteracting forces should not be underestimated, and the ideas of Popular Enlightenment should be an element here.

In continuation I refer to two writers that both accept the fact that globalization is a process that already exists, both have critical arguments, and both point to possible solutions. Neither actually discusses the ideas of Popular Enlightenment directly, but both have points of view that indirectly touch both Popular Enlightenment and enlightenment for life.

Christopher Lasch and communitarism

In his book "The Revolt of the Elites and the Betrayal of Democracy" (Lasch 1995) Christopher Lasch appears as a strong spokesman for revitalization of democracy in the local community. He quotes the philosopher Hannah Arendt who claims that enlightenment has turned the problem of democracy upside down by saying that it is the equality of all individuals that creates the right to citizenship. According to Hannah Arendt, this is quite the contrary. Citizenship creates equality. Democracy, says Lasch, demands more inspirational ethics than tolerance alone. In Lasch's perspective tolerance should include everybody in a community, making everyone heroes within the local democracy, and everybody should be allowed to contribute with the special gifts they might have. The betrayal of the elite came with the student revolt in the late 60s, when the working class was regarded as lost in their bourgeois attitudes, their self satisfaction and dull establishment. The elite left the common people and the working class behind, accusing them of being traditional and reactionary. Such attitudes were especially evident in the works of Herbert Marcuse in the 60s.

The communitarian point of view that Christopher Lasch advocates, turns the local community into the place where everybody is included in a democratic and living dialogue. The elite speaks only with itself, he says, and this elite has gone much too far in their advanced modernity in lifestyle, art, the gender issue, sexuality and in defending rights for different minority groups. Lasch is looking for the place where good, inclusive dialogue or conversation can take place. He finds this possibility in the local communities, in what he calls "third places". He seeks places where dialogue can develop without other limitations. The place for good dialogue is the third place, situated between the working place and the home or the family circle, or as he says, a meeting place between the rat race and the bosom of the home.

By establishing this third place within the local community, Christopher Lasch speaks more or less directly to the hearts of those who identify with the ideas of Popular Enlightenment and Folk High Schools. Both Folk High Schools and different adult study organizations were established as a direct result of initiative from groups of people that saw the need for such institutions in their communities. This was the main characteristic a hundred years ago, and Folk High Schools and study organizations are still situated and active in the more rural districts. Folk high schools had their strongest supporters and their background among people belonging to the different popular movements. All of these movements or organizations were voluntarily, and free from state interference. The concrete and practical expression of the ideas of Popular Enlightenment were what we today call institutions in the third sector, not far from the understanding of the third places of Christopher Lasch. When he underlines the importance of dialogue or good conversations, he is juxtapositioned to the ideology of Popular Enlightenment, very close to what might be understood as the Grundtvigian position of today.

If we look at the present Norwegian debate on new competence, lifelong learning and adult education, we find some interesting parallels. From my point of view, there is an evident connection between competence given by institutions in the field that, in this article, I have called Popular Enlightenment, and the kind of competence different companies and enterprises ask for, although this connection is still not recognized in a broader scale. This coincides with the thinking of Christopher Lasch and his ideas of the local community. The Norwegian government called for a report on the need for new competence, and a governmental committee was appointed (NOU 1997:25). The committee delivered the report in October 1997. One of the conclusions regarding adult education, Popular Enlightenment and Folk High Schools, was a recommendation to use the local community institutions, especially the Folk

High Schools. These were directly addressed, and encouraged to take contact with smaller companies and enterprises within the local community in order to develop new competence.

In a wider perspective one might conclude that the process of globalization is twofold. On the one hand it weakens the national state, on the other it strengthens both regions and local communities. It is hardly correct to make Christopher Lasch a spokesman of globalization, but his communitarian ideas fit very well into the pattern mentioned above.

In this situation Popular Enlightenment and Folk High Schools must engage themselves in the local community, and in so doing grasp the challenge offered by the globalization - localization process, thereby meeting the suggestions made by the government appointed committee.

In my opinion this is an obvious task for Popular Enlightenment and Folk High Schools, but it should be done without swallowing the whole of Christopher Lasch's argumentation. It is easy to follow Lasch in his wish to establish new relations to the "masses" or the common people, but his dream of a universal basis for new democratic ideas in the local community is more difficult to accept.

Popular Enlightenment and Folk High Schools should provide a two-fold response to the challenge of today. They should both develop new contact with the local communities, utilizing both old traditions and new possibilities, and also establish new international or global relations, and in so doing integrate the consequences of globalization. This might be done by creating networks with similar organizations and institutions in other countries, by establishing bilateral contacts, friendship schools, and by entering different European pogrammes and other supranational new institutions.

By enlivening old networks, and by founding new ones that are able to cope with the global challenge, Popular Enlightenment will recover its influential past position. My point is that the special kind of competence Popular Enlightenment embodies is just the kind of competence international and supranational organizations are asking for - both in the EU, and organizations like OECD and UNESCO. By uncritically following the analysis of Christopher Lasch, Popular Enlightenment might be tempted to withdraw to the museum, not a national one this time, but a local one, placed in a pleasant, but slightly remote community.

Anthony Giddens and his third way

The term globalization is not easy to define. The process that goes on is complex and has many contradictory elements. On the one side globalization can be regarded as a harmonious and inevitable process, as a new phase in the development of the Modern Project. In this perspective, it is a double process of social and territorial fragmentation, and a renewal of the local community, but on behalf of the national state, that loses importance and influence.

This might be the position of Anthony Giddens. Giddens analyses the fragmentation very precisely when he talks about the disorientation of the individual, the feeling of being caught in a universe of events out of control, and impossible to understand. To describe this situation Giddens says that it is not sufficient just to invent a new term and call the situation post modernism. In a new book, "The Third way - The Renewal of Social Democracy" he says: "The overall aim of third way politics should be to help citizens pilot their way through the major resolutions of our time: globalization, transformations in personal life and our relation to nature. Third way politics should take a positive attitude towards globalization - but, crucially, only as a phenomenon ranging much more widely than the global marketplace" (Giddens 1999). Giddens advocates an including society. Everybody must be able to participate in society life as participation is one of the most important factors for developing social equality. Therefore Giddens suggests first of all strengthening civil society.

In their different ways both Christopher Lasch and Anthony Giddens speak up for what is called the global village. The question to ask is: could this global village be the new arena for Popular Enlightenment, adult learning and Folk High Schools? Both Christopher Lasch and Anthony Giddens deliver abstract theories, and their references are European or American more than Norwegian. Lasch is defending the local community against a wave of globalization, in a situation where the elite cannot be trusted by the local people. The elite, as an active part in the advanced modernity, is part of globalization that sooner or later will roll over the whole world. It will in some ways make the world more alike, wiping out some traditional lifestyles, and reducing the varieties of cultures. At the same time, this process will meet forces that will struggle against this process, forces that will try to defend traditional lifestyles and try to preserve local varieties in culture and habits. Here the local community, a third place in Lasch's concept, should play an active role, and Popular Enlightenment could fit in with this.

To enable Popular Enlightenment to fight back in a sensitive and reflected way, the movement must be aware of the temptation of making tradition a goal or aim in itself. If this happens Popular Enlightenment may indirectly come to defend reactionary traits in the local community, or even to defend perverted nationalism. None of these elements have yet been seen, and this is of course not what Christopher Lasch defends. But in redefining the position of Popular Enlightenment, this is one of the dangers to be reflected upon in order to avoid this happening. In his work Anthony Giddens is formulating a new position for social democracy, hoping to revitalize this political movement by recommending the combination of individuality and pluralism instead of the old collectivism. At the same time he insists on participation in the civil society, and Popular Enlightenment could play a part here. It is however very important not to be included in the political strategies of the different social democratic parties, but to keep an independent position.

The pessimism of Zygmunt Bauman

I will conclude this article by discussing some of the points made by the Polish philosopher and professor of sociology Zygmunt Bauman in his newest book "Globalization. The Human Consequences" (Bauman 1999). In his book Zygmunt Bauman has a surprisingly pessimistic outlook upon the globalization process as a whole, and in particular on the people and places left in the aftermath of globalization. So pessimistic is his perspective that the Norwegian professor emeritus in literature, Asbjørn Aarnes, has added an epilogue to the Norwegian translation of the book: To the encouragement of the small ones. Bauman says: "As an integral part of the globalization process is progressive spatial segregation, separation and exclusion. Neo-tribal and fundamentalist tendencies, which reflect and articulate the experience of people on the receiving end of globalization, are as much the legitimate offspring of globalizaton as the widely acclaimed "hybridization" of top culture at the globalized top. A particular cause for worry is the progressive breakdown in communication between the increasingly global and extraterritorial elites, and the ever more localized rest. The centres of meaning-and-value production are today extraterritorial, and emancipated from local constants - this does not apply, though, to the human condition which such values and meanings are to inform and make sure of".

Christopher Lasch forsees the future solution in the local community, Anthony Giddens wants to revitalize social democracy by encouraging the individual to be a participant in the civil society, but Bauman talks with sorrow about the localized rest, left behind and being exposed to neo-tribal and fundamentalistic tendecies. Bauman mentions the same dangers that I pointed out above, in connection with the up-grading of the local community by Lasch. Bauman's mission is to ask unpleasant questions, and he shows concern for any civilization that has stopped asking questions about itself. For Bauman, localization is defined as the opposite of globalization, and that means involuntarily being bound to the local community. To be local, or being left at a specific place by a kind of destiny without any possibility to get away, is a sign of deprivation and humiliation in a globalized world, where being on the move is a sign of success.

Zygmunt Bauman maintains that this pessimistic analysis will, be reality for the third world to a dramatic extent. In his analysis he also mentions the northern parts of Norway, and suggests that they may also come to suffer under the same development. For the third world globalization means a new worldwide disorder. I understand that Bauman also suggest that the rest of the world will to some degree suffer from this global freedom to move. He predicts that it will be more and more difficult to melt together social matters and other issues into effective collective activity. It is not easy to find any hope of a good solution, but according to Bauman the first step is to start asking these unpleasant questions, and focus on the human consequences of globalization. Following this, a new consciousness may rise and be, a new kind of universalism that will include the common people. Bauman's only promise is to never forget the small and the poor.

Towards a conclusion

This article has tried to compare Popular Enlightenment and the Folk High School movement with different theoretical perspectives. My aim has been to focus on the globalization process, and to look for possibilities to sustain the ideas of Popular Enlightenment in the future.

In the perspective of Habermas, we will have to exchange the Grundtvigian term "living exchange" with the term "Kommunikativ Handlung". We will have to relinquish the view that human beings are unpredictable, that everyone is a riddle, or an unsolved experiment to use Grundtvigian terms. Instead, we will have to accept the rationality of Habermas. In his world of daily living, the free dialogue is based on the presumption that people are rational, and that rationalism is the guarantee for democracy. It is difficult to see where this free and rationale dialogue can emerge, even more so as the process of globalization continues. To push Popular Enlightenment into this philosophy would be to reduce the foundation for Popular Enlightenment, and the specific outlook upon people that is a basic premise here.

If weinterpret Christopher Lasch, a little provocatively, he wants to relegate Popular Enlightenment to local museums, with the noble task of rescuing the community from reactionary or unpleasantly traditionalistic points of view. The risk of causing quite the opposite is, as I have tried to explain, a real possibility. Popular Enlightenment and Folk High Schools have an important role to play in a local community, but in a much more positive and progressive way.

Anthony Giddens asks Popular Enlightenment to join him in building the new social democracy, and thereby contribut to the further development of society. But his perspective is a little too abstract and too harmonious to be followed without hesitation. Between the harmonious outlook of Giddens, and the pessimism of Bauman, Popular Enlightenment and the Folk High School movement can find interesting and important reflections concerning their possibilities for influencing on future development by taking dual action in this globalization process.

I am convinced that neither Popular Enlightenment nor the Folk High Schools have yet reached a stage where they are candidates for being put into museums. Quite the opposite, Popular Enlightenment and Folk High Schools are more in the wind than ever before, and they should be aware of their potential. A Finnish proverb says: when the wind blows, some build shelters, others build windmills. It is time for Popular Enlightenment to build windmills.

References

Bauman, Z. (1998). Globalization. *The Human Consequences.* Cambridge.

Bergstedt, B. (1998). *Den livsupplysande texten.* Stockholm: Carlssons Bokförlag.

Bukdahl, J. (1971). *Folkelighed og Eksistens.* Gyldendal.

Giddens, A (1990). *The Consequences of Modernity.* Cambridge.

Giddens, A (1998). *The Third Way – The Renewal of Social Democracy.* Cambridge.

Grundtvig, N.F.S. (1832, 1983). *Nordens Mytologi.* Samleren.

Habermas, J. (1993). *Nasjonalisme og nasjonal identitet.* Oslo: Cappelen.

Habermas, J.(1999). *Kraften i de bedre argumenter.* Oslo: Gyldendal.

Korsgaard, O. (1997). Kampen om Lyset. Oslo: Gyldendal.

Lasch, Chr. (1995). *The Revolt of the Elites – and the Betrayal of Democracy.* New York.

Levinas. E (1993). *Den Annens Humanisme.* Aschehoug.

NOU 1997:25 *Ny kompetanse.*

Røsaak, E. (1999). *Det postmoderne og de intellektuelle.* Spartacus.

Østerud, Ø. (1999). *Globaliseringen og nasjonalstaten.* Gyldendal.

THE FOUR MOMENTS OF ADULT EDUCATION: FROM MORAL ECONOMY TO LIFE POLITICS

Petri Salo & Juha Suoranta

Introduction

The formation of adult education in theory and practice can be described in terms of historical changes in the vocabularies used in the various texts of the discipline. Vocabulary refers not only to legitimative text as such but also to discursive practices (Foucault), that is, to the idea that words and deeds (things) are inseparable: words have practical consequences in the real world and diverse practices become legitimate texts of the discipline. When connected to the social climate (or ethos) and the social policies of a given time these discursive practices will become the hegemonic struggles of adult education. In other words, the basic question is: what do we mean when we talk and write about adult education?

In this article, we first divide the history of adult education into four moments[21]. These moments of adult education apply to Scandinavia but in our view are valid to some extent in other parts of the Western world as well. In the second section, we go on to evaluate the current situation of adult education policies from the individual and social points of view. Thereafter, we try to define different forms of communities and explicate the role of the adult educator in these communities. In conclusion, we take a preliminary look at the future of adult education by considering the fourth moment of adult education - the moment of life politics.

---

[21] It goes without saying that it would have been possible to use some other terms, such as 'phase' or 'era', instead of 'moment' in dividing the history of adult education. We believe, however, that the term 'moment' makes our intention more clear than other terms: that the division in question is not meant to be strict historical description, but analytical framework which gives an overview to the changing functions and meanings of adult education over time. The term 'moment', with its own rhetorical power, has applied from Denzin & Lincoln (1994).

At present, there are at least two distinct and opposite vocabularies in the theory of adult education. Firstly, there are vocabularies, which emphasize adult education as a vehicle for economic efficiency and growth. In this vocabulary, adult learning and being are understood in an instrumental and largely asocial sense. As Usher, Bryant and Johnston (1997, xvi) write, in this vocabulary, "to the extent that adult learning has been individualised and privatised, it has become part of the 'culture market' and the 'market culture' which characterises postmodern times, albeit a market which excludes as well as includes." Here, adult education becomes defined as part of the logic of business life, part of consumerism and market effectiveness.

Secondly, there are vocabularies which are in theoretical opposition to the discourse of economics (Welton 1995b, 11). One is critical learning theory, which is based on Habermas' texts. In his introduction to *In Defense of the Lifeworld*, Michael Welton (1995a, 3), known as a critical adult educator, states that "In our dreadful neo-conservative times, the university-based study of adult education is under intense pressure to abandon any kind of critical social theorizing in favour of short-term training programs for whatever "need" panic-stricken governments deem salient."

Another such vocabulary is constructionist adult education theory, which maintains that the restructuring of Western societies presupposes new theoretical thinking and practices in adult education as well. As Jansen & Wildemeersch (1998, 226) claim, in adult education theory it is crucial to ask how one may "enhance people's opportunities to participate in social contexts and be present in social places that enable them to connect personal qualities and desires to their competency to experience responsibility and togetherness with others." Despite their differences in details, both critical and constructionist theories of adult education refuse to accept easy solutions to new societal problems. Business-oriented adult education is seen almost as a cancer in society and a danger to the emancipatory goal of adult education.

This is the theoretical landscape of our text. Our own view can be described as critical-constructionist (postmodern) thinking. We want to keep the idea of hope very much alive in the vocabularies of adult education and hold out the hope that new solidarities will emerge and see "the need to foster hope, to promote radicalism, to hold out the possibility of more radical change, to bring the light of radical critique and politics to the blinding light of the media, to revitalize radical theory and politics, however modestly and tenously" (Kellner 1995, p. 45). Furthermore, we argue, and want to believe that the logic of adult education differs dramatically from the logic of business life and economics.

The four moments of adult education - a historical framework

The starting point for our historical framework is Finland. Then the perspective is widened to comprise the development in Nordic countries. Some overall aspects of the development in Western world is also taken into consideration. The historical framework can be compared with other descriptions of the development of adult education in the Nordic countries (e.g. Abrahamsson 1992; Nordhaug 1986).

Moral economy 1850-1945

There are two main arguments for considering the discourse of moral economy as the first phase of adult education. Firstly, the birth of adult education in Finland is grounded in a great transformation from a pre-modern, agricultural society to a modern, industrial society. Secondly, the mode of capitalistic production partly determines the ideas of moral behaviour and the good life (Alasuutari 1996, 105). *The term 'moral', thus, refers to the process of modernization which, for the large part, was the same as the process of nationalization - at least in the Nordic countries. Nationalization, in turn, was a true moral and pedagogical endeavour in its innermost spirit.* Therefore, the rise of adult education has to be seen as a central part of the modernization process in Western societies. These two tendencies combine in the moral discourse of adult education.

The phase of moral economy was instrumental in that it forced people to adapt to a new notion of linear time, the time of the machine, which differed from pre-modern time. There was also an intensive nationalism which, along with the mode of production, ruled the discursive practices of moral economy. The purpose of the elite was to educate the masses into citizens of a newborn nation. It was argued that education (one's own language, one's own will) was the strength of a nation. In this interpretation, the origin of liberal adult education is part of the dramatic political-economic change in which nation states, industrial capitalism and the proletariat are born. In Finland, the Swedish speaking elite and the Finnish nationalists were at the front line of the nation state ideology. A crystallization of that ideology can be found in Zachris Castrén's (1929) report, which is clearly emphasized people's own free education and cultivation of their own life in their own 'place' and living conditions.

In the other Nordic countries, the moment of moral economy was based more on the social movements (revivalist, temperance and worker's movements) that sprang up from grass-roots level activities and the social orientation and commitment characteristic of these movements. The objective of the folk enlightenment that emerged from social movements was firstly to improve the overall conditions for the common people, who had been socially, economically and politically torn from their agrarian roots and, secondly, to influence the development taking place in society by educating individuals capable of taking care of themselves. The philanthropical and liberal ideals regarding folk enlightenment that were dominant amongst the bourgeoisie and the revivalist and temperance movements (first education, then bread) were to be challenged and replaced by the more radical and socialist ideals and trends within the worker's movements (first bread, then education). These ideals and features brought forward the oppositional dimension of the folk enlightenment, whose aim was to question and change the existing social order (Ambjörnsson 1988; Nordhaug 1986; Olsson 1994).

In the Anglo-American context, the moment of moral economy is characterized by pragmatism. Finger (1990) states that adult education was not developed to promote or oppose modernity; instead, it grew out of everyday life, practices and problems. Adult education dealt mainly with the problems caused by the failures in conventional education and dysfunctions generated by the project of modernity and (the process of) industrialization. Adult education at that time could be seen as a practical "repair-activity" fulfilling its function in a realistic, pragmatic and non-ideological way. It was neither the aim nor the function of liberal adult education to support the development of modern, industrialized society. The aim was simply to produce humanistic, creative and practical solutions to the everyday problems generated by the ongoing processes of modernization and industrialization.

Planning policy 1945-1985

The shift from moral economy to planning policy meant changes in the discourse and practical functions of adult education. The shift took place after the Second World War and was driven by rapid changes in production technologies and economic structures. Economic change forced educational institutions to rethink content and curricula in vocational adult education. Research findings in economics (see, particularly, Niitamo 1958) showed that higher education in particular plays a crucial part in the growth of the gross national product. At the same time, there emerged a consensus that adult education policy should be directed and controlled by central government in the same way as other parts of society. The phases and symbolic universe of planning policy are well documented and stored in diverse committee texts.

From the 1980s the positive correlation between education and economic growth has begun to reach its saturation point.

The moment of planning policy was also characterized by bureaucratization of the activities taking place in the social movements and by the fact that the oppositional dimension of the folk enlightenment which strove to affect the existing order was neutralized by public funding for and steering of folk enlightenment. The grass-root level social commitment typical of early folk enlightenment in Nordic countries was institutionalized. Folk enlightenment as such became detached from the everyday problems and challenges. The overall orientation and focus within the folk enlightenment shifted from certain groups of people and communities to individuals, and the movement gradually became mainly a vehicle for individual development and self-realization. When its original oppositional idealism was replaced by the ideals of growth, efficiency and commercialism, folk enlightenment became closely connected to the overall educational system, within which it gradually took on a complementary role (e.g. Nordhaug 1986; 1991).

In the middle of the moment of planning policy, during the rapid growth in the field of adult education which took place in the late 1960s and early 1970s, industrial development, economic growth and globalization led to the emergence and crystallization of three paradigmatic orientations globally: the first was the concept of lifelong education, which was brought forward by UNESCO and is characterized by the idea of scientific humanism; the second was andragogy, which is based on the idea of adult development and an assumption of self-directedness; and the third was the critical and radical orientation which has its roots mainly in the South American context and in the pursuit of political empowerment (Finger 1995).

The market economy 1985-

Although the moment of market economy can be said to get started in the 1980s, in Finland, the end of planning policy and the start of market economy was marked by the so-called renewal of state funding in liberal adult education in early 1990s. In short, this meant that institutions had to get an increasing part of their funding from open educational markets. They were forced to raise their course fees and, in that respect, indirectly foster educational inequality. Even before that, there were debates concerning the status and functions of liberal adult education, i.e., its role in the era of fast-growing profit-oriented adult training and continuing education. In any case, liberal adult education is now subject to the laws of free enterprise.

The discourse of the market economy embodies the ideas of an innovative society and innovation centres, with innovations usually referring to economic values and technological development. In the market economy phase of adult education, words such as customer, consumer, vocational adult training, competition, consulting and even evaluation refer directly or indirectly to economic efficiency and added value. From the point of view of liberal adult education, however, innovations can also be various and social in nature.

According to Jarvis (1996, 233-234, 240), continuing education was established as a concept and a form of education in order to serve the economic and technological forces behind the market economy and to support the ambition of creating, developing and maintaining an open, globalized market. Continuing education became an important commodity on that market and is about to displace the traditional concepts and forms of adult education, especially the thoughts and activities characteristic of the tradition of liberal adult education. This development is mainly due to the fact that continuing education represents an open and comprehensive perspective on adult education and refers to both vocational and non-vocational education.

Life politics 2000-

The last moment of our classification of adult education - life politics (see Giddens 1991) - is on shaky ground. This uncertainty is due to both the classification itself and the present social situation to which life politics as a concept refers. Firstly, the concept of life politics is an indefinite and vague one. Giddens uses it together with such concepts as identity, identity politics, self, self-reflection, life course, life style and welfare, and tries to fit them all into in the same picture of post-traditional society. Secondly, social reality itself is in constant flux. Interpretations of experiences are almost necessarily uncertain, and uncertainty also characterizes people's biographical consciousness; it has become risk consciousness (Beck 1994).

However, the idea of life politics is of importance in adult education if we think that adult education as practice and theory ought to offer some solution to the experienced feelings of insecurity - or at least act as a negotiator of meanings in an era of unanticipated social and structural changes. These are the reasons why we will save further discussion of life politics in adult education for the last section and move on to interpret two current ideologies in adult education, individualism and market orientation, challenging and counteracting the idea of life politics.

The contemporary framework: individualism and market orientation

The current adult education policies as well as the vocabularies of adult education in most Western countries rest mainly on the ideas and principles developed during the third moment of adult education. Jansen and Wildermeersch (1998) identify two current tendencies in the field of adult education. The first of these tendencies has to do with the individualization and privatization of the sphere of learning and development. The second has to do with the practice of both framing and defining the individualized spheres of learning and development in relation to the labour market and doing so using the terms which dominate the rhetoric of the labour market. The ultimate objective of the individualization in adult education - manifest in the privatized development of personality, identity and morality - is to increase freedom, maximize the range of choices and, guarantee the survival of the individual adult learner. But this also means that risks and problems become individualized and privatized.

The concept of qualification has become one of the most important factors in the effort to couple adult education tightly to the labour market. In a situation where citizens - privatized actors - cannot be ruled and controlled by using moral imperatives (Protestant work ethic during a period of high unemployment) lack of qualifications or competencies is used as a means of social integration and labour market policies. The need for or lack of qualifications is brought forward in a very pragmatic, objective and non-moral way and can therefore be used to control and influence both marginalized groups and citizens who have simply made wrong choices with respect to their education and training.

One of the features of the development which has resulted in individualization and privatization of the sphere of learning and development in adulthood is that professional adult educators are even about to take over even the sphere of everyday learning and the natural development in everyday life. Legitimized by the current rhetoric, in which concepts such as uncertainty and change are the most powerful ones, adults are offered training in coping, living and surviving, in other words, how to live their own lives. This development might lead to a situation in which coping and everyday living are reduced to a certain number and kind of skills and qualifications. These coping skills and qualifications will, in turn, like all other qualifications, be defined beforehand on the system level and mediated only through institutionalized educational activities and by authorized experts (Collins 1991, 6).

The current tendencies in adult education - individualization and market orientation - can be understood as signs of the final phase or crisis of the forms of adult education that made possible the development of the modern, industrial society. But these tendencies can also be understood as signs of the beginning of a new era, as prerequisites of the moment of life politics. According to Finger (1995, 112-117), we have during the 1990s come to meet two fundamental challenges both of which question the objectives and methods of the traditional adult education that aims to promote (the process of) cultural modernization and techno-economic development. The first of these challenges is the growing awareness of the biophysical limits of industrial development and economic growth. The second has to do with an insight into the outcomes of socio-cultural change in the Western world. This insight entails a growing awareness of the shortcomings, or the crisis, of the market economy and the Western way of living and thinking. Neither the process of Westernization nor the extensive development of adult education and dissemination of information has resulted in the rise of enlightened, responsible, emancipated and morally well-behaved citizens capable of developing and sustaining justice in society and an enlightened world culture.

Instead, we have witnessed the spread of social fragmentation as well as a loss of a sense of community and collective projects. We find ourselves in a situation in which, firstly, the idea of lifelong education as a promotor of overall development and well-being has to face the biophysical limits of growth, secondly, the concept of andragogy, based on the idea of self-directedness, is about to strengthen the instrumental "cult of efficiency" (Collins 1991, 1-32) - resulting in élitism, individualism and the survival of the fittest - and finally, critical and radical adult education has lost its field of action, the nation-state, now that all the crucial political decisions are made in either global or local arenas.

One could also claim that the traditional folk enlightenment organizations in the Nordic countries, which Grönholm (1995, 74-75) calls first generation adult education organizations, find themselves in crisis along with the very idea of welfare state. Institutionalization and bureaucratization of the functions of the first generation adult education organizations is reaching its peak. The organizations find themselves in a new situation and a new context, in which they have neither been able to produce new challenges for citizens nor bring new content to concepts such as general education or democracy. They have been powerless in the face of the deep economic recession and the overall social and societal consequences of recession.

This might be due to the fact that the folk enlightenment organizations have been neither problem-oriented nor able to utilize resources originating from everyday life or problems. Instead, we have witnessed the rise of new action-oriented social movements (single-issue movements, gay and lesbian movements, environmental movements) which seem to meet the current challenges by drawing on everyday practices and global moral issues (see also Nordhaug 1991, 88). The shift from a collectively oriented and counteracting role, which evolved in the early moments of folk enlightenment, towards the present, individually oriented and market-based role within which the maintenance of the existing social and societal order is a crucial element, has led to a situation which can be characterized as abandonment of an oppositional role, traditional principles and basic ideas.

From utilitaristic to aesthetic learning communities

The concepts community and community sense are frequently brought forward in current debates concerning the overall cultural, political and economic changes taking place in late modern societies, as well as in debates concerning the connection between adult education and overall change in the society. The concept of community as well the community as a unit of social interaction can be understood in several ways, but it is possible to identify three general perspectives on or forms of community and sense of community in the debates. These three forms of community will be presented briefly and discussed in relation to the challenges for adult education during its fourth moment.

Three forms of learning communities

The traditional communitarians propose a return to the traditional community, a *gemeinschaft*, in which social interaction and joint actions are based on traditions, shared norms, moral obligations, collective virtues and locality. To counter the weakening of social norms and values that has led to the erosion of the individual lifeworld and a strong emphasis on egoistic subjectivism and individualism, communitarians offer solidarity, participation, collaboration, dependency and social control, all of which are based mainly on intensive face-to-face interaction in daily communal life (e.g. Sarmela 1989, 24-25). The main role of adult education in the traditional community is to mediate and strengthen the traditions, moral obligations, social norms and values attached to pursuit of the common good (Jansen & van der Veen 1997, 271). The challenges associated with the concept of a risk society are not confronted actively; rather, one could state that these challenges are "bypassed" by creating alternatives to them within the community. The emphasis in the role of the adult educator is on the moral and social dimension. The adult educator can be seen as a charismatic leader, a master or paternal or maternal figure who creates and mediates the unifying ethos of togetherness (see Suoranta 1998b, 27).

Postmodernists and liberalists put forward an idea or a vision of community which is quite opposite to that of the traditional community. The postmodern community is described as a light or thin one and is mainly based on spontaneous experiences, images and an absolute individual freedom. Individuals should be able, whenever they wish or feel the need to, to "throw themselves" into the community for an evening or weekend and have the possibility to express and actualize their immediate needs and take part in exciting experiences. The sense of community should not be restraining or bind the individuals to any kind of commitments. It is expressed through intensive shared aesthetic or hedonistic experiences, which, instead of solidarity and loyalty, are based on symbolic togetherness (fashion, habits of consumption) and fascinating rituals (Bauman 1996, 38-39). The role of adult education in a postmodern community is to continuously respond to the ever changing needs and wishes of the individuals and to deliver emotionally "wrapped" and "hot" topics in a context that somehow differs from customary, everyday life. The adult educator could be compared with a performance artist who is capable of picking up the most obvious phenomena and aspects of daily life but also capable of renewing the package and the emotional charge attached to those aspects. The adult learner is a hedonistic consumer, and adult education at large could be considered as consumption (Suoranta 1998b, 27).

Besides these two perspectives on communities it is possible to identify a third alternative or perspective, one which is especially interesting from the viewpoint of traditional liberal adult education, or the Nordic folk enlightenment movement. This third perspective on the idea of community will be called reflexive-aesthetic (Jansen & van der Veen 1997, 271; Jansen & Wildermeersch 1998, 223-226; Lash 1995, 215-224). The reflexive dimension implies an ambition to establish a balance between the individual and the community, as well as between the community and the environment. This balance can only be reached through open, respectful and intensive interaction. The reflexive-aesthetic community is founded on everyday reality and daily life and, especially, the shared experiences and practices which evolve from individuals acting together. Shared meanings are created through a continuous dialogue within the community. Individual latitude is accepted; the continuous dialogue guarantees that the individual members of the community become aware of themselves and their relationship to the community as a unit. Self-actualization and the awakening of personhood requires an authentic dialogue within the community. Dialogue functions as a means of mediating fundamental experiences of everyday life and problems, as well as of eliminating alienation from other individuals (Kurki 1996, 178). Reflexivity also implies the will and the ability to confront the world outside the community and is a fundamental aspect of the continuous and conscious interaction which aims to utilize the community's internal diversity and multiplicity as a vehicle for continuing development. Internally good is not encountered apart from the world and daily life; rather, it is constantly included in the sphere of everyday activities, practices and meanings.

The aesthetic dimension of the community sense manifests itself in activities and actions whose purposes and objectives are already and naturally present. Instrumentality, rationality and the remote ideals of democracy or solidarity are replaced by spontaneous and natural forms of activities and togetherness - simply acting and being together without concern about the long-term benefits and profits. The driving force for these activities can be found in everyday life experiences and immediate daily needs. Another aspect of the aesthetic dimension can be found in a shared life style, often expressed by images, symbols or other stylistic devices (Maffesoli 1995, 24-25; Jansen & Wildermeersch 1998, 224).

Problems in community interaction

In the current debate concerning new forms of communities and their role in post-welfare societies, there is a tendency to forget the problems community ideologies entail. Here, it is necessary to bring out two main problems.

The first and largest problem is the interaction and cooperation between diverse communities and the interaction between a particular community and society as an historically coherent political system. On both levels of interaction there is an issue of which Allardt (1991) reminds us when talking about societal circumstances and the conditions for new social movements. Relatively small communities are often quite self-sufficient and closed in that they have their own norms and moral systems. At the extreme this can lead to the rejection and hatred of other people, that is, others who do not share the same ideology or even the same opinions.

The second problem in community ideology concerns the interaction inside one particular community. It is not always certain that people can act together and think of a community as a public sphere where local equality would prevail. It is more likely that in a consumer and predatory culture (McLaren 1995) people are used to acting in an individualistic way. In this respect, we have to remember Erich Fromm's (1970) prophetic words that Western culture has a tendency to transform the human beings into Homo consumens, the perfect consumer, who does not care about anything but his or her own success and capability to earn and spend more than before. It must also be taken into account that everyday life contains many micro-scale problems in interaction which operate in all communities regardless of their other means and ends in furthering their chosen way of life. In such a social situation of structural violence - as Fromm terms it - community ideology can produce illusory closeness and episodes of social life which could be called, following Erikson (1963, 269), little shared moments of disgusts.

The above-mentioned problems certainly do not remove the necessity of discussing and creating new forms of communities and social movements as vital social inventions of the post-welfare world. The problems are like reminders of the fact that we should - to paraphrase Fromm (1970, 46) - distinguish two ideological stands in adult education: that which understands and aims at the well-being of people and that which treats people as objects with the aim of making them useful for the technological society.

Life politics: towards the fourth moment of adult education

In this final section we turn to examine the possible new scheme of adult education practice in the near future, the fourth moment of adult education which focuses in particular on improving people's welfare and empowerment. We believe that the debate concerning life politics in the theory and practice of adult education not only shows the inventiveness of the social scientist but also genuinely represents a substantial step forward.

The need for or the development of the fourth moment of adult education can be considered using the viewpoints brought forward by Finger (1990). In his opinion, the original function of adult education - adaptation to change by creating repair activities - is gradually to be replaced by the production of new meanings and the creation of active, collectively oriented solutions.

The challenge for adult education in late modern or post-modern society is to create a holistic strategy for survival. In order to be successful, this strategy has to be closely related to everyday practice and the natural interaction between individuals and the communities they are part of. The philosophical foundations of this post-modern survival strategy have to be based on the natural and close connections between individual and social learning as well as between learning and transformation.

It might be an exaggeration, though, to suggest that in postmodern societies all solutions must be negotiated as if nothing can be taken for granted. Although constant negotiability, insecurity and risk consciousness are almost like social facts of the present, there are still life areas in which it is possible to live and act like before.

This commonality is precisely what diverse forms of communities strive for. It could be argued, then, that reflexive being, stressed in life politics, is more an option than an necessity; it is consciousness about the choices of life. In this respect, adult education in the moment of life politics can heighten a human being's general reflexive capacity in life. This is not always a good thing. We need only think about our awareness of the connections between happy consuming, cheap commodities and child labour.

It is self-evident that life during a period of life politics is characterized by uncertainty. Life politics refers to the fact that ambivalences and uncertainties must be met eye to eye. The individual has to learn how to function as a planning centre for his or her own actions, and this has to be done in a much stronger sense than ever before.

Nothing can be taken for granted - not one's lifestyle, the skills one has acquired, one's friends, work, or one's family. Everything must be planned just for the time being, and one has to be prepared to plan things over and over again (Jansen & Wildermeersch 1998, 217).

The market economy has left as its legacy at least the following social uncertainties in the life-world which disturb the phase of life politics in adult education. Firstly, there is the correlation between work and education. The changes of getting work other than McJobs after secondary education have decreased dramatically. It is improbable that adult education alone could do much to improve the situation without decent work places. Secondly, from individual's point of view globalization has meant a heightened ecological awareness. On the one hand, it is well known that nature is loaded with waste and toxin of various kinds; on the other, it is equally well known that there is very little that can be done about the situation. Thirdly, the feeling of social security has dropped at the same time as former social ties to family, social class and profession have become looser. The facts described above lead us to a situation in which, according to Beck (1994), ambivalence becomes a basic experience.

What, then, does this all have to do with adult education theory? In conclusion, we want to bring out five issues - differentiation, consumerism, social responsibility, new social movements and community - which, in our view, are of interest and value in sketching the fourth moment of adult education. We are not offering definitions, let alone solutions, but would like to open a forum for further discussion.

Differentiation. The current situation is characterized by the fact that it is no longer possible to find a single source of or reason for social problems. For example, in Finland the mental and social problems can be examined using a fourfold model with two dimensions: big and small welfare and big and small misery (see Karisto 1998, 73). Big welfare refers to a lifestyle which is possible in all situations only for a small minority, whereas small welfare refers to the smooth flow of daily life for the majority of people. On the other hand, we have big misery, which refers to the overwhelming and all-embracing circumstances of life, and small misery, which refers to the necessity of everyday survival and the anxiety springing from confrontation with the omnipotent wealth and the never-ending possibilities of consumption.

Consumerism. Secondly, the entertainment-oriented lifestyle forces adult educators to compete on a consumer market and to do so with all the other providers of entertainment and free-time services. Adult education is just another cultural product, part of the cultural industry, and nowadays there is little or no difference between education, leisure and entertainment (Usher et al. 1997). These recent ideas echo the words of Urpo Harva (1910-1994), the first professor of adult education in Europe. According to Harva (1971, 91), "the use of leisure in adult education will partly be dependent on the supply of other activities and partly on the supply of other pastimes such as clean water, lakes teeming with fish, fresh forest filled with the song of birds, nightclubs, playhouses, brothels, cheap travel around the world, and trips to the moon."

Social responsibility. The issue of new civic duties can be seen as a central component in the debate within the social sciences about the rules of a civil society. Two central aspects have been brought forward in this debate. Firstly, it has been noticed that besides social rights individuals also have a certain number of social responsibilities. Secondly, the role of free non-governmental organizations has been emphasized in reflections on the structure of the civic society. When non-governmental organizations are functioning well, individuals will not be at the mercy of the state, the economy or the family.

New social movements. It is about time in adult education that we took an interest in studying new social movements and diverse forms of community life. There is an array of social movements which work effectively in the informal field of adult education; these include social activism, the animal rights movement, movements for sexual diversity and tolerance, ethnic groups and multiculturalism. Usher and Edwards (1994, 202) argue that "within new social movements and perhaps also in feminism, there is a project of challenge and transformation of self and society where autonomy is created (and re-created) through application (struggle) within specific social formations." More than that, people socially classified as mixed, perverts, oppressed, marginalized, or who must be defined in anti-essentialist terms are those who put new emerging cultural forms into practice (Rose 1998). To put it plainly: "The culture-creating group lives on the fringes" (Fromm 1970, 32).

Community. One of the most important demands of adult education theory during the moment of life politics is that it responds to the current discussion about the new forms of the sense of community sense. If adult education is to support the development of reflexive-aesthetic communities, it must become integrated with the everyday activities in the community and adult educators must deal with everyday life in the community. The sense of community and internal good cannot be reached through formal studies or through study arrangements tightly connected to the prevailing ethos and policies in the traditional educational organizations. Instead, both the sense of community and internal good can be realized by creating and cultivating reciprocal relationships based on being and living, and, above all, sharing the joys and sorrows of everyday life. In this kind of community, the adult educator becomes a co-actor amongst other actors; the main role of the adult educator is to function as an agent of internal change, a reflective partner in discussions and dialogues (Kurki 1996, 178; Suoranta 1998, 28).

In this perspective, at the centre of community action is the reflective and interpretive self as social actor. Social reflexivity and individual sensibility are characteristics which build communities. Grossberg's (1992) concept of a mattering map is of particular interest here. A mattering map refers to a socially constructed affectual (or, to use Barthes' word, pleasurable) state or structure which for its part determines those aspects of life which matter most in certain social situations. The idea of affectual mattering maps connects our discourse to the idea of the politics of singularity. The politics of singularity as part of the ethics of life politics in adult education means that people act together but acting together does not mean utilitarism such as that found in trade union-based cooperation. What it does mean is that people learn to respect otherness as otherness (see Agamben 1995). Future communities are communities without a direct economic profit orientation. Future communities cannot be taken for granted; they are not self-evident, but constructed locally and situationally. In this perspective, communities can be imagined and represented as collectives and areas of becoming and uncertainty (Rose 1998).

References

Abrahamsson, K. (1992). Öppna frågor om vuxenutbildningens nya omvärld. In K. Abrahamsson (ed.) *Hela vuxenutbildningen! En framtidsbild i historiens ljus.* Stockholm: Brevskolan, 10-27. [Questions to be answered considering the new context of adult education]

Agamben, G. (1995). *Tuleva yhteisö.* Tampere: Gaudeamus. [Becoming a community]

Alasuutari, P. (1996). *Toinen tasavalta.* Tampere: Vastapaino. [The second republic]

Allardt, E. (1991). Kestävän kehityksen yhteiskunnallisista edellytyksistä. In I. Massa & R. Saarinen (Eds.) *Ympäristökysymys.* Helsinki: Gaudeamus, 11-23. [About the social conditions of durable development]

Ambjörnsson, R. (1988). *Den skötsamme arbetaren.* Malmö: Gustavssons. [The conscientious worker]

Bauman, Z. (1996). *Postmodernin lumo.* (transl. Jyrki Vainonen) Tampere: Vastapaino. [Fascination of the postmodern]

Beck, U. (1994). Reinvention of Politics. In U. Beck, A. Giddens & S. Lash. *Reflexive modernization. Politics, tradition and aesthetics in the modern social order.* Cambridge: Polity Press.

Castrén, Z. (1929). *Valtio ja vapaa kansansivistystyö.* Helsinki: Kansanvalistusseura. [State and liberal adult education]

Collins, M. (1991). *Adult education as vocation. A critical role for the adult educator.* London: Routledge.

Denzin, N. & Lincoln, Y. (1994). Introduction. Entering the field of qualitative research. In Denzin, N. & Lincoln, Y. (Eds.) *Handbook of qualitative research.* Thousand Oaks: Sage, 1-17.

Erikson, E. (1963). *Childhood and society.* New York: Norton.

Finger, M. (1990). Does adult education need a philosophy? Reflections about the function of adults learning in today's society. *Studies in Continuing Education,* 12 (2), 99-106.

Finger, M. (1995). Adult education and society today. *International Journal of Lifelong education,* 14 (2), 110-119.

Fromm, E. (1970). *The revolution of hope.* New York: Harper & Ro Publishers.

Giddens, A. (1991). *Modernity and self-identity.* Cambridge: Polity Press.

Grossberg, L. (1992). Is there fan in the house? The affective sensibility of fandom. In L. Lewis, (ed.) *The adoring audience. Fan culture and popular media.* London: Routledge, 50-65.

Grossberg, L. (1996). Identity and cultural studies - is that all there is? In S. Hall & P. du Gay (eds.) *Questions of cultural studies.* London: Sage, 87-107.

Grönholm, C. (1995). *Adult education - passionate learning.* Worldview. Anatomy, Scope. Ekenäs: Fonda Publishing.

Harva, U. (1971). *Suomalainen aikuiskasvatus.* Helsinki: Tammi. [The Finnish adult education]

Jansen, T. & van deer Veen, R. (1997). Individualization, the new political spectrum and functions of adult education. *International Journal of Lifelong education,* 16 (4), 264-276.

Jansen, T. & Wildermeersch, D. (1998). Beyond the myth of self-actualization: Reinventing the community perspective on adult education. *Adult Education Quarterly,* 48 (4), 216-226.

Jarvis, P. (1996). Post-modernity, Education and European identities. *Comparative Education,* 32 (2), 171-184.

Jarvis, P. (1997). *Ethics and education for adults.* Leicester: NIACE.

Karisto, A. (1998). Pirstoutuvan elämän politiikka. In J.P. Roos & T. Hoikkala (eds.) *Elämänpolitiikka.* Helsinki: Gaudeamus. [Life politics of fragmented life]

Kellner, D. (1995). *Media culture.* New York & London: Routledge.

Kurki, L. (1996). Kasvatustiede sosiaalipedagogiikan peilissä. In S. Anttonen & V. Huotari, V. (eds.) *Työn alla kasvatustiede.* Tampereen yliopiston kasvatustieteiden laitoksen julkaisuja B:14, 163-185. [Educational science seen from the mirror of social pedagogy]

Lash, S. (1995). Refleksiivisyys ja sen vastinparit. In U. Beck, A. Giddens & S. Lash. *Nykyajan jäljillä.* (transl. Leevi Aho) Tampere: Vastapaino, 153-235. [Reflexive modernization. Politics, tradition and aesthetics in the modern social order]

Maffesoli, M. (1995). *Maailman mieli. Yhteisöllisen tyylin muodoista.* (transl. Mika Määttänen) Tampere: Gaudeamus. [Mind of the world]

McLaren, P. (1995). *Critical pedagogy and predatory culture.* London & New York: Routledge.

Niitamo, O. (1958). *Tuottavuuden kehitys Suomen teollisuudessa vuosina 1925-1952.* Helsinki. [The development of productivity in Finnish industry in 1925-1952].

Nordhaug, O. (1986). Adult education in the welfare state: Institutionalization of social commitment. *International Journal of Lifelong Education,* 5 (1), 45-57.

Nordhaug, O. (1991). Aikuiskasvatuspolitiikka ja vapaan sivistystyön järjestöt Norjassa. *Aikuiskasvatus,* 11 (2), 86-94. [Adult education policy and the organizations of liberal adult education in Norway]

Olsson, B. (1994). *Den bildade borgaren.* Malmö: Gustavssons. [The educated bourgeoisie]

Rose, N. (1998). *Vallan ja vapauden välissä: Hyveen hallinta vapaassa yhteiskunnassa.* Janus. [Between power and freedom]

Sarmela, M. (1989). *Rakennemuutos tulevaisuuteen. Postlokaalinen maailma ja Suomi.* Porvoo: WSOY. [Structural chance to the future]

Suoranta, J. (1998a). Ihmisen yksityisyys ja luova lepo - aikuiskasvatuksen merkityksestä työn jälkeen. In P. Sallila & T. Vaherva (Eds.) *Arkipäivän oppiminen.* Helsinki: BTJ Kirjastopalvelu, 219-263. [Individual's privacy and creative rest]

Suoranta, J. (1998b). Aikuisoppijan merkitys moderneissa ja postmoderneissa teorioissa. *Aikuiskasvatus*, 18 (1), 22-32. [The meaning of a learning subject in modern and postmodern theories]

Usher, R. & Edwards, R. (1994). *Postmodernism and education.* London & New York: Routledge.

Usher, R., Bryant, I. & Johnston, R. (1997). *Adult education and the postmodern challenge.* London & New York: Routledge.

Welton, M. (1995a). Introduction. In M. Welton, (ed.) *In defense of the lifeworld.* Albany: Suny, 1-10.

Welton, M. (1995b). The critical turn in adult education theory. In M. Welton (ed.) *In defense of the lifeworld.* Albany: Suny, 11-38.

THREE FORMS OF KNOWLEDGE

Bernt Gustavsson

Introduction

In our time the question about the meaning and the boundaries of knowledge has come to the fore. According to the standard definition of knowledge that we find in encyclopaedias, knowledge is characterized by emanating from a belief for which one can find good arguments, a belief that can be justified. This definition originates from Plato and is also an expression of the idea of the existence of an absolute form of knowledge, which distinguishes it from belief and opinion (doxa and episteme). Aristotle, already, suggested two other, practical forms of knowledge - techne and phronesis - besides the theoretical form. Episteme has to do with insights into how the world is built up and functions, whereas techne is connected with craft and how to make things. Phronesis, practical wisdom, is about ethical and political knowledge in a wide sense, and connected with social and cultural communions.

These three forms of knowledge exist around us today and are debated and disputed in various ways in philosophical and scientific literature. Episteme is mostly treated within the field of theory of science, During the last ten decades practical professional knowledge has been mentioned under different names, for instance, "tacit knowledge", and has been brought forward as an alternative or a complement to episteme. Practical wisdom as a form of knowledge is debated today both within neo-Aristotelian and hermeneutic schools of thought.

The aim of this article is to describe what characterizes these three forms of knowledge, from what traditions they have sprung, and to compare them with the purpose to demonstrate how they relate to each other. The conception of knowledge as belief-based is thus completed by action-based and ethically-based conceptions. The critical difference, which is made clear in the discussion, is that the theoretical conception of knowledge is supplemented by two practical forms of knowledge. The theoretical knowledge is abstract and universal, whereas the practical is connected with different contexts and situations. Techne is sometimes said to be instrumental, in the sense that it treats knowledge as a means to attain an external purpose, in which the aim has an external relation to the means. In contrast, phronesis is characterized by means and goals being internally related to each other.

In later years the meanings and the boundaries of knowledge have been given more and more attention in educational debate as well as in society as a whole. There is talk about "the knowledge society", i.e., school is obliged to teach more "knowledge", or about "knowledge enterprises", or that an increasing number of jobs are becoming more "knowledge intensive". In short, the concept of knowledge has become something of a *motto*, not least in politics. However, few people explicitly state what they mean by knowledge or what kind of knowledge they think should be taught or awarded. Quite often information and knowledge are confused. In my view, what human beings have learned and internalized constitutes knowledge. Information, on the other hand, is floating around us as detached pieces and becomes knowledge only when we have assimilated it, understood it and placed it in a context.

This article is based on the contents of a forthcoming book about knowledge, with the preliminary title "Three forms of knowledge". My purpose is to discuss different forms of knowledge that we have access to in contemporary debate within the fields of philosophy and science. The three forms are *scientific knowledge, practical professional knowledge*, and *ethical-political knowledge*. This trisection of knowledge originates from Aristotle and is much discussed today.

Episteme, techne and phronesis

The standard definition of knowledge found in every encyclopaedia emanates from Plato. It proceeds from what people *believe* to be true, what they have a general opinion about. However, for this belief to be regarded as knowledge, *good arguments* have to be presented. What one believes has to be justified in some way. Knowledge, thus, becomes equal to *"true, justified belief"*. Concerning what really justifies this true belief, there are different views in various academic traditions. In the very essence of knowledge there is a basic distinction embedded between opinion, belief (doxa), and absolute, true knowledge (episteme). Ever since the scientific revolution in the 17th century and until our time, science has claimed ownership of this secured form of knowledge. The question of truth and secure knowledge is discussed in terms of boundaries for what is science and what is non-science. The variety of conceptions is rich, and, at the same time, the legitimacy in episteme as the only true form of knowledge is increasingly being questioned.

In the trisection of knowledge the *belief-based* conception of knowledge is one. The second form, here named practical professional knowledge, is *action-based* and finds its primary support in modern pragmatism. The third form is ethics-based and has its support in neo-Aristotelian or hermeneutic schools of thought. These three forms are henceforth called episteme, techne, and phronesis.

Techne

Plato's idea of knowledge as one and only one, was criticized already by Aristotle. In his *Ethics* Aristotle asks what use the artisan can make of the form of theoretical knowledge Plato talks about. There is a special form of knowledge we use to make things, both materially and spiritually, which he calls techne, i.e., technical knowledge. This name may lead one's thoughts into technology in the modern sense, but techne has a richer meaning, in that it connotes that knowledge is in human hands. Craftsmanship is the ideal in this form of knowledge. There is no difference between art and craftsmanship in this ideal, it contains everything human beings have created or produced. Techne is of current interest in the field, which has been recently opened up by research on the characteristics of practical professional knowledge.

In this vein the concept of tacit knowledge has been much used, although with two connotations emanating from two different conceptions of knowledge. One conception proceeds from the idea that there are two distinct areas of knowledge, one is tacit, the other one is not. Knowledge is, thus, divided into being either implicit or explicit. The expressions of this view of knowledge abound. One of the most common is to make a distinction between intimate knowledge and declarative knowledge.

The second conception proceeds from the idea that all knowledge has a tacit dimension. A distinction is made between what is in focus and the background inherent in all knowledge. The "focal knowledge" always has a tacit pre-requisite or background. That to which we direct our attention is the centre of knowledge. This is true for all forms of knowledge, whether we strike a nail with a hammer or investigate a scientific problem. The two conceptions have, unfortunately, caused much controversy in epistemological debate in recent years. Two of the most important and influential thinkers here are Ludwig Wittgenstein and Michael Polanyi.

The study of knowledge as it appears in professional life was introduced at the beginning of the 1980s through various channels. Research was carried out in order to investigate what happened when many jobs where computerized. The long-time critique of the dominance of scientific knowledge was also carried into the study of the nature of practical professional knowledge. Thus, the dominance of the Platonic view of knowledge came to explain why this form of knowledge had been suppressed for so long in the ongoing discussions about knowledge. According to the prevailing view, the practice in which knowledge was to be used was expected to receive and apply authorized scientific knowledge. Knowledge was, in this way, transformed into being technical and instrumental in relation to its users. The alternative was for the practitioner to expose knowledge about his/her profession by reflecting on what he/she was engaged in.

From the turning point created by this kind of research, a number of different conceptions of the nature of practical professional knowledge have been presented. One rather common line of research, known as "situated cognition", holds that knowledge and learning are pursued in practice, that is, in the actual situation where the knowledge is used. Such a view can be generalized to all knowledge and all learning. In this way, knowledge becomes strongly connected to its practice, its situation and its context.

The two forms of knowledge, episteme and techne, are defended by different ways of thinking, which means that different philosophical traditions are used to motivate and justify each position and view. Episteme can be justified by means of both a rationalistic and an empirical knowledge tradition. These two traditions have been the cornerstones of all discussions about knowledge. Whether knowledge has its origin and its ground in the senses or in reason has been a seed of dissension ever since the birth of natural sciences in the 17th century. The two lines of thought are used in different varieties also in today's debate about the foundations of knowledge. First and foremost these discussions go on within theories of science in the English speaking, Anglo-American world.

Knowledge and information

These traditions, however, are not sufficient to give practical professional knowledge a firm philosophical ground. Therefore, much research on the nature of practical professional knowledge goes back to the so-called pragmatism. "Pragma" means "action" and pragmatism has, as distinguished from other epistemological schools, an action-oriented view of knowledge. In other words, action is the point of departure, not a belief, as is the case in the ordinary definition of knowledge. Pragmatism has various advocates. The most famous, and the one who has made pragmatism well known in education as well as in political debate, is the American philosopher John Dewey. The idea of using actions as the basis of the study of knowledge is promoted by several important philosophers of our time. The strangest thing about contemporary discussion on knowledge is that it is carried on within widely separated grooves. This phenomenon is partly caused by the specialization of knowledge, but also by restrictions created by different cultures and traditions. There is one debate that concerns knowledge in school and education, there is another that concerns professional knowledge, a third debate is connected to commercial life, and a fourth with technical-economic development.

In the mass media the debate about knowledge has become more and more adapted to the market and a view of knowledge as a competitive commodity. Knowledge in education is presented as complete packages to be sent out into the world on the Internet or by mail. Knowledge then becomes an exchangeable entity, it is given an exchange value as an article that can be bought and sold on the international market. "Knowledge", "knowledge society", and "knowledge enterprise" have become fashion words, which, like some other concepts within education and learning, threaten to superficialize and reduce the very essence of the words and concepts that are used. One of the most common mistakes is to disregard the essential distinction between information and knowledge. "Information" constitutes the "pieces" that can be delivered as parcels. We may look for information on the Internet as well as in the library. But it is transformed into knowledge only when we have made this information our own property. The important difference between information and knowledge is that knowledge is something personal, something internalized, whereas information is the separate pieces that overflow all banks. Knowledge has human beings as its carriers and it becomes human because it is incorporated into our personalities. It is internalized by our interpreting and attempting to understand the complex abundance of information that is forced upon us. In order to make it comprehensible it we need to be place it in a context. In this perspective, there are two characteristics of knowledge: it is interpreted and understood, and thereby personally internalized, and it is placed in a context. There is an essential difference between being well-informed and being knowledgeable.

Phronesis

The difference is striking between the discussions on knowledge that we have access to through research and philosophical development and the discussion on knowledge that are actually carried on within these fields, the difference is striking. No matter how surprising it may seem to someone untainted by philosophical germs, the fact is that most of the expositions about knowledge that are available today are based on the Aristotelian trisection of knowledge. The knowledge Plato had in mind was *episteme*, the Artisan's knowledge was *techne*. There is also a third form, *phronesis*. Phronesis is often translated as "practical wisdom". This form of knowledge is directed towards ethics and politics. To Plato the human being who had true knowledge about the world was a wise man. Insights into the eternal world of ideas made the wise man qualified to make decisions about society and human affairs. He who knows the truth, does what is right, this was a thought he had inherited from Socrates. No, says Aristotle, there is one kind of knowledge that differs from this. It does not belong to what is absolutely true, it is not eternal, and it is not abstract. It has to do with the concrete society in which humans are living, it is built into different communities. Man cannot live a perfect life without being part of a society. Man is a political and social being and can actualize his innate resources only by virtue of belonging to some kind of community. To this end, theoretical and abstract knowledge is not sufficient. Something that might be called sound judgement is needed, i.e., the ability to make proper decisions in concrete situations. This kind of knowledge is therefore both political and ethical.

This form of knowledge, phronesis, exists today in two different lines of thought. One is the neo-Aristotelian, which, based directly on Aristotle's writings, attempts to re-create phronesis as a modern form of knowledge. The other is the interpretative, or hermeneutic, line. Phronesis is often used in connection with a critique of a lack of values, ethics, and meaning in modern society. Advocates of both these lines direct their critique towards the instrumentalization of humans as well as knowledge. By instrumentalization they mean that knowledge is more and more converted into a means of effective development. Thereby the lack of meaning and values has emerged which is said to characterize modern society.

Thus, a gap is created, not only between episteme and phronesis, but also between techne and phronesis. In various contexts, traditional science is blamed for having caused the lack of ethics and values in modern society. "Expert knowledge" is seen as part of the power executed by mechanisms of the market and the state in order to bring about a never-ending increase in productivity and societal effectiveness. The "technical expert" becomes the symbol of goals-means-efficiency, causing increasing alienation and dehumanization. Even if there are varieties in the analyses of modern conditions, the collective critique is directed towards what happens with knowledge and with the our possibilities to understand our world.

This standpoint also includes critique of fundamental parts of the views of the human being and knowledge in Western civilization. Not only has modern science peeled off ethical values from the human beings and the nature, it has also contributed to their destruction by its basically exploitative position. Instrumental knowledge emerged when the pioneers of the natural sciences separated man from nature. This meant that man was seen as separate from nature but also as separate from himself. The world was divided into man and nature, soul and body, spirit and matter, a position usually named dualism. It resulted in a view of knowledge which presupposes that the carrier of knowledge, i.e., the human being, starts from zero at the onset of the process of knowing.

Typical expressions of these ideas can be found in empiricism as well as in rationalism. Both lines of thought presuppose a zero point of knowledge, from which the search for new and absolute knowledge starts. This means coming to terms with traditions and authorities and other things that might keep us away from new knowledge. Advocates of empiricism presume that the human soul is like an empty tablet (tabula rasa) on which reality makes its imprints through the senses. The rationalists assumed that they would arrive at a point where thought is pure and free from all traditions, authorities and prejudice. It is exactly this zero point that several contemporary lines of thought are grappling with and trying to find an alternative to.

The common view is that knowledge has no such zero point, but that we have different vantage points from the beginning, inherent in the culture and the society in which we live. The action-oriented pragmatist presupposes that man existed, from the very beginning, in the world in which he acts. The action itself, the practice, is the starting point of new knowledge. It is by reflecting on our practice and treating it theoretically that we develop our knowledge. The point of departure, then, is not zero, but rather the action, the practice, in which we are already involved.

At about the same time as pragmatism was developed during the last half of the 19th century, another influential line of thought was born. It was phenomenology, whose creator was Edmund Husserl. One of the concepts he created, in order to demonstrate that knowledge has no neutral zero point, was "lifeworld". He opposed the abstractions of modern science, which had made knowledge into something strange and alien to the everyday, concrete world of the human being.

All knowledge has its beginning and its foundation in the human life-world, the world where things seem naturally familiar and in which we carry out our daily chores. The life-world concept has thereafter been in frequent use in the human and social sciences. Thereby phenomenology has become an epistemological alternative to the traditional view of not only knowledge but also science. Husserl thought he would arrive at a form of absolute knowledge different from the one presumed by natural science, also using another route than that of modern science. He is still thinking in terms of episteme.

So far, we have looked at two influential lines of thought about knowledge during the 20th century, i.e., pragmatism and phenomenology. The pragmatist view of knowledge is techne, in the sense that it regards knowledge as practical and as an instrument for action. Phenomenology has developed in many different directions after Husserl, partly in its own furrow, partly within the hermeneutic tradition. They all contribute to connecting knowledge with action, practical activities and our everyday life.

Contextualized knowledge

One of the big dividing lines in today's debate has been whether knowledge is attached to certain contexts, or to what extent it can be regarded as independent of social and cultural situations. From phenomenology a movement has sprung, which claims that all knowledge consists of social constructions, that it is a product of social and cultural power structures. This is a development of the life-world to include human communication and action in a wider sense. Knowledge is studied in its sociological contexts. To assert that knowledge is socially constructed is to refer it entirely to social conditions, in the same way as connecting knowledge to the human life-world is to restrict it to the routines and repetitions of everyday life.

The study of knowledge and research under such pretexts is synonymous with studying other forms of human activities and cultures. The researcher acts as an anthropologist or ethnographer, makes himself or herself part of the situation that is to be studied and, thus, becomes a participant in what happens. Such studies made within the natural sciences often result in critical comments, and create polemics and conflicts between social scientists and the natural scientists, who have been subject to study. A common type of defence is to advertise the repeatable experiment as the secure form of knowledge, which cannot be reduced to its social constructions. An experiment, which is repeated under different conditions, can be proved to generate the same results regardless of the social context.

There are, nevertheless, many alternative ways to describe how knowledge is restricted by context. In general scientific debate there exists a concept that has become commonplace even outside the domains of science. This is "paradigm", which was coined by Thomas Kuhn, active in the field of history of science. He holds that scientific knowledge is the fruit of the internal conceptions of the research society. Advocates of a paradigm, i.e., a specific world-view, will at some point stand against new and different world-views, thus, a conflict emerges which in turn will result in a scientific revolution. Paradigms should be regarded as cohesive gestalts. They are the fruits of styles of thinking or collective thinking. The most intense debate has been about the idea that two paradigms are incomparable. Knowledge, thus, becomes relative, which means that the objective, true knowledge, episteme, is threatened. In a historical perspective, knowledge is relative to time. It is also relative to culture. The Western form of knowledge, then, becomes merely one among many and is no longer generally and universally valid. Episteme is a threatened form of knowledge. It is not difficult to pick out several concepts in modern philosophy and research, which in various ways treat knowledge as contextual, that is, dependent on its social and cultural conditions. Some of these concepts are culture, tradition, life-form, habitus, and communion. This way we are coming back to phronesis, which is proclaimed to be an alternative form of knowledge, both as tradition and as social communion.

A contemporary form of phronesis is maintained by the so-called Communitarian school, which has been part of the discussion concerning society, democracy, and knowledge since the beginning of the 1980s, especially on the American continent. Communitarians represent a line of thought, which favours communion before modern individualism. The question is brought to the fore, e.g., in the discussion of different rights and liberties. If these rights are intended for all mankind, they are also claimed to be universal, that is, they are valid always and everywhere. This is how human rights came to be part of the constitution in many countries and how the UN Declaration of Human Rights was created. Such universalism can conflict with customs and norms of human co-existence in different cultural communions. Contrary to universalism there is specificity, i.e., specific cultural communions and their rights to exist on their own terms. The knowledge embedded in these communions is, in Aristotelian terms, phronesis. Episteme in the form of universal rights will be put up against the norms that are valid in a particular communion, or phronesis. The question is, what is meant by communion and what forms of communion are awarded? Here is a conservative side which prescribes traditional values and norms, in contrast to several modern lines of thought. One can trace a preference for hierarchical and authority-bound communions and traditions. It may be expressed as defence of the values of the Catholic Church. A typical example that demonstrates the problems with this attitude is inhumane acts performed against women in some traditional cultures, such as female circumcision, or the male-dominating polygamy. The kind of questions of knowledge and ethics that such conflicts raise, can produce new ways of thinking and, simultaneously, knowledge about norms, customs, and values.

Transcending our own contexts

The neo-Aristotelian direction in modern thought is not a comprehensive phenomenon. The movement has its various advocates who interpret and present knowledge in connection with ethical and political matters in accordance with their different views and lines of thought. One who has become commonly known in Sweden lately for his contributions to the debate on the meanings of multicultural society, is the Canadian thinker Charles Taylor. He can, in a sense, be characterized as a communitarian, but as such he has a Hegelian and hermeneutic stance rather than a neo-Aristotelian. Hegel's ideas about man as a member of a social communion are analogous to Aristotle's, however. A commonly used concept today is "civil society", an expression of the social communion without which the human being cannot actualize his or her potential. Hegel thus develops the thought of communion to encompass larger social units and not only the traditional units such as family, tribe, or congregation.

One idea that Taylor received from Hegel, among others is that our identity and self-understanding emanate from a social recognition. It is by taking individual differences and a mutual recognition of these differences as a starting point, that the identity of the modern human being is developed. This is also the way that it becomes possible to live in a multicultural society, in people from different cultural communions recognize each other as equal by virtue of their differences. Taylor thinks that even Western liberalism must regard itself as a culture among others, that cannot lay claim to a universal or commonly accepted truth or set of norms. Truth, knowledge, ethics, and norms are created in dialogue between different horizons of interpretation, i.e., between different ways of interpreting and understanding the common world in which we all live.

Owing to Taylor's philosophical contributions the communitarian thought becomes more radical in one step. Values, knowledge, and norms are not invariable, laid down by tradition. They are changed as society changes and as different cultures are given opportunities to meet in dialogue. An American neo-Aristotelian philosopher, who is now reviving the Aristotelian idea of phronesis, is Martha C. Nussbaum. She is a classical scholar and departs directly from classical sources in her writings about ethics, politics, and knowledge. Nussbaum passes severe criticism upon the communitarian school and its one-sided critique of the ideas of Enlightenment. She maintains that neo-Aristotelian insights may very well, in a fruitful way, be combined with ideas of Enlightenment. In one of her latest books she gives an example about the possibilities of renewal in higher education. She proceeds from the tradition called "liberal education" in the English-speaking world, which would correspond to the tradition of "Bildung" on the European continent and in Sweden. In short, Nussbaum holds that modern liberal education goes on in two steps. The first step is to study critically one's own tradition and culture, the other is to study other cultures. The basic idea is that we are both local and global beings. We belong to one or more local communions, and, at the same time we are citizens of the world. This double citizenship renders us the possibility to study both what we are safely anchored in by our traditions, and new things and ideas brought about by other cultures and human beings. As an alternative to the often devotional view of one's own traditions held by communitarians, Nussbaum maintains a more critical attitude. As a thinking human being one should act like "the gadfly on the horse's back". The expression is taken from Socrates who thought that a reflected life had a higher value than life that just goes on. It is necessary for the further existence of democracy that humans are capable of keeping a critical attitude to power and of constantly irritating it, just like the gadfly on the horse's back.

Hermeneutic phronesis

By this way of expressing knowledge in connection to ethics and politics we are getting close to the interpretative or hermeneutic view, the other tradition which carries phronesis as one form of knowledge. Both Taylor and the founder of modern hermeneutics - Hans Georg Gadamer - start from a Hegelian line of thought. It is Gadamer who revives the hermeneutic ideas by proceeding from a classical tradition of Bildung which Hegel, among others, has brought forth.

The basic idea of interpretation and understanding in this sense is that we use what is familiar and close to us when trying to interpret and understand new, alien, and different phenomena that we encounter. Knowledge is created when different interpretations meet. Therefore, the dialogue is central in the process of creating knowledge. Knowledge is, further, always conditioned by the tradition or traditions from which it has sprung, and in which we, ourselves, are placed. The form of knowledge thus produced is fronesis. In this sense, fronesis is characterized by being possible to apply in concrete situations. We interpret and understand according to the horizon that surrounds us in the present time, the familiar, with the help of which we interpret and understand what we perceive. Knowledge in this interpretative sense is so intimately connected with the human creation of values and meaning. Knowledge and ethics can thereby not be distinctly separated. Phronesis includes both knowledge about how the world is constituted and the values and meaning that we grant the world. Knowledge, thus, becomes a genuinely human concern. The knowledge that is interpreted and understood by people is embedded in individuals as well as in human communions.

The difference

The question is, what really constitutes the difference between the three forms of knowledge, episteme, techne, and phronesis? Episteme is knowledge characterized by being theoretical, abstract, universally valid and justified. The common definition of knowledge as emanating from belief, which has been justified by good arguments, episteme contrary to doxa, is an idea inherited from Plato and richly represented in contemporary debate about knowledge. Techne is practical knowledge emanating from craftsmanship and in its classical form devoted to the creative and productive abilities. Aristotle made a distinction between two different kinds of action, one where the end of the action is outside (poeisis) and another where the end is intrinsic, i.e., embedded in the action. Techne is connected to the first kind where the means are central, and is therefore often named instrumental knowledge. The aim, the purpose, is disconnected from the means that are used.

Phronesis is also practical by nature. But the major difference between techne and phronesis is that in phronesis the aim, the meaning, and the purpose, are inherent in the means. Purpose and means have an internal relationship. This is what makes phronesis ethical as well as political knowledge.

Episteme is said to be independent of values or ethical positions. It is "knowledge for its own sake", or "genuine ground-research". The idea is that knowledge, or the search for knowledge, is an end in itself, something that we can neither foresee the results of nor know how to use. Therefore, it is free from values and ethics. This is also said to be a condition for a free and independent search for knowledge. All involvement of ethical or political considerations in the knowledge process is then thought to result in lapses, which are not very difficult to point out throughout the history of science. On the other hand, how knowledge is to be used, is, according to this line of thought, for ethical committees or politicians to decide.

Ethical options

The effect of this line of thought is that ethics and knowledge are seen as separated from one another. When difficult decisions have to be reached, decisions with serious consequences for humans, the moral philosopher is called in as an expert in order to answer for the ethical choices. We get one expert who answers for his specialized knowledge in a certain area, and another who is responsible for ethical and political consequences. If we look at the map that describes different ethical options three different alternatives will emerge.

The most influential alternative is the so-called utilitarianism which today is represented by the majority of ethical experts. It is a consequence-ethical position, which departs from the utility of different alternative solutions. If we ask what utility is, the answer will be "happiness" - "greatest possible happiness to the largest possible amount of people". Increase of happiness and decrease of suffering is a good intention, which few could reject. According to many utilitarians of today this principle should be valid not only for humans but also for animals and nature. What happiness is, becomes the difficult question, which remains unanswered. One answer to the question what happiness is, was already given during the Classical time, though. Happiness is pleasure (hedone). The idea that pleasure is the highest value of all, a Hedonist thought, is cherished by many even in our time. Aristotle's statement that, living for the sake of pleasure is to live "like cattle", has thereafter become a classical motto.

An alternative often placed in opposition to utilitarianism is a so-called duty-ethical or rule-based position. According to this position there are certain moral rules and laws that it is man's duty to follow. The origin is Kant's idea about ethics as a special area outside both scientific and æsthetic knowledge. In Kant's world morality is constituted by the idea of man as a being free to decide over himself. "The practical reason" and "the moral law" within us are carried by man alone. Here a borderline is drawn which is humanistic. Man is the only creature who cannot be made into mere means, because he is in himself an end. The idea that the human being is something special in nature by virtue of being the only creature who can make his own decisions, is something that Kant has in common with an Aristotelian view of ethics. But Kant has moved so far away in his thoughts from the idea that there are inherent aims and purposes in the world, that to him there is no room for the form of knowledge we call phronesis. Those acts that require some kind of insight, in the Aristotelian sense, he simply calls "technical-practical". The practical becomes equal to the technical. Thus, ethics is placed outside knowledge but also becomes episteme. Moral law is eternal and universal. What is right is right to all people always and everywhere. This is Kant's alternative to utilitarianism. On this point, the different positions of today deviate, both in political and ethical debate. Those who maintain the ideas of universal rights and norms and those who claim that these are to be referred to specific communions, constitute two diametrically opposite positions, which have influenced the debate during the last decades. It is in this tension we may find many interesting attempts to solve political as well as ethical problems.

The good life

Aristotelian ethics is a third alternative. When we talk about phronesis, ethics and knowledge cannot be separated. Because purpose and means are intimately connected, knowledge is in itself ethical. Even to an Aristotelian happiness is essential, but in a sense quite different from that of the utilitarians. The Aristotelian concept of happiness, eudaimonia, is strongly connected to how man can actualize his possibilities as a human being in the communion in which he lives. This does not refer to man the way he seems to be here and now, but rather to how he could be like, were he able to actualize his possible resources.

The basic question for the Aristotelian is what can be said to constitute a good life for a human being. The good life first and foremost means being able to actualize our dormant possibilities. The purpose of ethics is to show and give arguments for ways how to actualize our human possibilities. The Greek concept of areté (virtue) means that ability which shows us the way from how man actually is to how he could be were he allowed to realize his inherent possibilities. Virtue is, thus, something quite different from what this word may be associated with in modern language. Virtue is a trait which cannot be read into general rules, because what is good for man varies from one situation to another. To decide what is good and what is the right thing to do, is part of man's capability to act. It has to be constantly practised and applied. This capability includes making decisions about what is good and right in one case and not in another. Thus, virtue is something that is involved in many human activities. Different activities carry different kinds of virtues, since the decisions that are to be made vary between situations. The virtues connected with different forms of knowledge are, by Aristotle, called intellectual virtues. One virtue is about establishing how things are (episteme). Another virtue is connected to the craft and the ability to make things (techne). A third virtue has to do with being able to decide what is a good life for the human being (phronesis). Because the matter of a good life is linked with the activities we engage in, phronesis becomes a superior virtue. In its contemporary, neo-Aristotelian and hermeneutic versions it also becomes the superior form of knowledge. Phronesis, in short, means having the quality of a sound judgement.

This knowledge includes being able to make good decisions in concrete situations, to know what is right to do at the right time and in the right way.

References

Aristoteles, Den Nikomachiska etiken. *Daidalos*.

Chaiklin, S., Lave, J. (1996). *Understanding practice: Perspectives on activity and context.* Cambridge University Press.

Dewey, J. (1916,1966). *Democracy and education.* Free Press, Prometheus books.

Dewey, J. (1910,1991). *How we think,* Free Press. Prometheus books.

Gadamer, H. G. (1960,1975). *Truth and Method.* Daidalos.

Gadamer, H. G. (1997). *Sanning och metod i urval av Arne Melberg*, Daidalos.

Gordon, C. (1980). *Michel Foucault, Powerknowledge: selected interviews and other writings 1972-1977.* Harvester Press.

Klein, G. (1998). *Korpens blick: Essäer om vetenskap och moral*, Bonniers.

Lave, J. (1991). *Situated learning: Legitimate peripheral participation.* Cambridge University Press.

Lyotard, J.F. (1979). *The postmodern condition: A report on knowledge.* Manchester University Press.

Macintyre, A. (1981,1985). *After Virtue: A study in moral theory.* Duckworth.

Molander, B. (1993). *Kunskap i handling.* Daidalos.

Nussbaum, M.C. (1989, 1997). *The fragility of goodness: Luck and ethics in Greek tragedy and philosophy.* Cambridge University Press.

Nussbaum, M.C. (1990,1992) *Känsland skärpa tankens inlevelse: Essäer om etik och politik.* Symposion.

Nussbaum, M.C. (1995). *Poetic Justice: The Literary imagination and Public Life.* Beacon Press.

Nussbaum, M.C. (1997). *Cultivating Humanity: A classical defense of reform in liberal education.* Harvard University Press.

Platon (1996 nytryck). *Teaitetos.* Nya doxa.

Polanyi, M. (1983). *Tacit knowledge.* Peter Smith, (1958, 1998) Personal knowledge: towards a postcritical philosophy, Routledge.

Rolf, B. (1991). *Profession, tradition och tyst kunskap: En studie i Michael Polanyis teori om den professionella kunskapens tysta dimension.* Nya Doxa.

Ryle, G. (1949,1990). *The concept of mind.* Penguin.

Schön, D. (1983,1991). *The reflective practiotioner: How professionals think in action.* Ashgate.

/

POLITICAL EDUCATION: A CONCEPTUAL APPROACH

Sigvart Tøsse

Abstract

The basic question of this article is: What is political education and how should a political educational practice be analyzed? Has political education specific aims, content, or methods, or should it be measured by its effects? The discussion in this paper shows that there is no general agreement on what is meant by political education in terms of aims, content or method, and also shows different views on which learning arena is most preferable. Adult educators have even disagreed as to whether political education should aim for everyone or whether it needs to be conveyed through mediators. A discussion on political education in terms of aims, content, method, arenas, clientele, and effects will be useful - even necessary - in any analysis of educational efforts and practice of this kind. The literature shows, however, a vast array of possible approaches to mapping political education. The concept will have several and interrelated dimensions which provide us with the additional approach of analyzing the value dimension, information dimension, inquiry dimension and participation dimension in political education. I conclude by arguing for political education as a broad and overall concept which out of necessity aims for neither citizenship nor democracy in the liberal sense. Civic education, education for citizenship, education for democracy, and political literacy are all kinds of political education with more specific meanings and connotations.

Historical background

Political education, civic education, education for citizenship, education for democracy, political literacy and other related concepts have always been of vital interest in adult education. (I here use political education as a common concept, but I will discuss some differences later in the article.) In Norway this issue was put on the public agenda when local community self-rule was introduced in 1837. The Act stipulated that the entire population was to be schooled, as one of the parliament members declared, which was, of course, an impossible demand, but this extension of democracy was later followed up with funding for adult high schools and public subsidies for evening classes (Tøsse,

1997). Throughout the 19th century it was felt that providing the populace with more education was a prerequisite for the enfranchisement of the people. Education for everyone had to precede democracy. In the 1920s and 30s, when democracy was under threat from fascism and other right or left wing attacks on the parliamentary system, private and public educational bodies intensified their efforts to secure democracy through education. After the Second World War, Germany especially placed strong emphasis on political education ("Politische Bildung" and "Politische Erziehung") as a means of rebuilding democracy (Brennan, 1981:5). In fact modern adult education was related to a high degree "to the post-war consensus trying to create a more educated and enlightened citizenship, avoiding the pitfalls in the socialization of citizen and the nurturing of a political culture which led to fascism and totalitarianism in Europe" (Torres, 1996). A revival of the interest in political education emerged in the late 1960s and a new concept, political literacy, emerged (Porter, 1981:188). Political education had by then garnered world-wide interest at all levels of school and adult education, not least in post-colony countries, with Tanzania serving as an outstanding example. Finally, after the breakdown of communism, democratic political education has attracted renewed attention (Vain, 1992). Education for democratic citizenship has become of vital interest for the Council of Europe, which has arranged several seminars on the topic, and it continues to attract a great number of researchers. Since 1994 a research network on active democratic citizenship has existed within the European Society for Research on the Education of Adults (ESREA), and the Danish government, for example, appropriates a great deal of money for projects examining the relation between education and democracy. Political education has also expanded from a nation-building aim to the aim of global citizenship (Korsgaard, 1997:21).

Foundations of political education

Political education has been propagated for many reasons when considering particular social situations and historical contexts. I will discuss here the arguments derived from the obligations of democracy, pedagogical imperatives, and the Marxist theory of society and human emancipation.

The obligations of democracy

The main arguments for political and general adult education are grounded in democracy itself as something which must be preserved, strengthened and further developed, as stated by D. L. Boggs (1991):

> "Since democracy is the context and the condition for everything else that is valued – work, family life, religion, politics, recreation, and leisure – preserving its vitality and integrity must be a central objective of adult education".

Two important requirements of democracy to be discussed here are participation and commitment. Participation involves different political arenas, standard governmental arenas as well as non-governmental economic and social arenas which will not only include political parties and government agencies, but also schools, families and the workplace. A common definition of what makes these arenas political is that values, or valuable things, are distributed unequally or unjustly as a result of group activity (Gillespie, 1981:5). To live in a democracy means that adults have to make up their minds about social and political matters, and participation is a prerequisite if they want to influence decisions.

The obligations of commitment derive in part from the problems of democracy. As already emphasized by Rousseau (in The Social Contract, 1762) the human being has a dual role in society. On the one hand he or she is a bourgeois and a private individual, on the other hand a citizen. Man has an obligation both to himself and society, but these dual obligations clash when the interests of the private individual meet the interests of the citizen (Rosenhow, 1992). Democracy has to be learned, as propagated by Dewey (1916), and problems derived from the contrary interests of the individual bourgeois and the citizen must be solved by a stronger commitment to democracy.

Democracy, however, will never be perfect so the continual improvement of education is required. Liberal democracy is especially criticized from the Marxist point of view as limited and illusory and for not having fundamentally changed the economic system. It is hardly controversial to state in general terms that "an appropriate political education or life in a democracy ... will have to encompass some preparation for workplace democracy" (White, 1979). The benefit for society of workplace democracy has also been recognized by the classical liberal John Stuart Mill (The Principles of Political Economy, 1871). Since this time, the labour movements in all countries have been fighting employers and capitalists fiercely for industrial democracy, and whether it is possible or even preferable to extend democracy far into the workplace is still a contentious issue. The socialist demand for economic democracy in the Nordic and Western countries has, however, disappeared from the political agenda and since the 90s, the focus has exclusively been on political democracy.

Educational imperatives

Bearing the requirements of democracy in mind, the educational imperative is to equip the individual with political competence or literacy. Political literacy is defined as a compound of knowledge, skills and attitudes which are politically relevant and will enable an individual to be politically effective (Brennan, 1981:7, 135). This means:

- A critical awareness and understanding of the political system
- Knowledge of the important issues of the day
- Ability of individuals to participate in the political process
- Ability to benefit from one's rights and privileges as a citizen
- Acceptance and tolerance of different political views
- Recognition of problem solving by rational debates within the framework of law

The concept of political literacy may be seen along similar lines as the emphasis of Freire upon language. Being politically literate means to have knowledge of concepts necessary to construct simple conceptual and analytical frameworks. Such concepts may be drawn from everyday life, yet employed more systematically and precisely than usual (Entwistle, 1981:241).

The Marxist view on democracy and social emancipation

The young Marx opposed the idea that the emerging democracies in North America and Western Europe represented the perfect political state. Contrary to the liberal view of the emancipatory effects of a democracy that granted men the rights of liberty, equality, security, and property, man was not free. This restraint was the result of man's dual position within the state as a member of both the civil society and the political state, a distinction that Marx inherited from Hegel. The civil society – family, social classes, associations and so on – was the totality of divergent particular interest, individual and collective, the forum in which every individual carried on his day-to-day existence. The individual was at the same time a citizen and participant in the organization of the state. In the view of Hegel the state was independent of particular interest. Marx, however, did not believe in the state as a mediator between particular interests, but rather saw the state as a tool of social classes (Kolakowski, 1981:125). The state and its bureaucracy represented alienated forces that made men unfree. The state had the same function as religion, i.e. it mystified and alienated men. The state did not abolish the egoistic character of private life but merely provided it with a legal framework. Due to this split existence, democracy disintegrated and alienated men (Rosenow, 1992). Marx hence rejected liberal democracy and its organizations of state ruled by social classes. Democracy had to start from man himself as its aim was to make the state an instrument of man, i.e. dealienate political institutions (Kolakowski, 1981:124 – 126). A political emancipation - encompassing the separation of state from religion, introduction of civil rights and so on - was valuable and important but insufficient and would not free man from his split and self-contradictory mode of existence. Marx argued for a human emancipation "in which man rediscovers and returns into himself" (Kolakowski, 1981:127). This did not mean, however, that Marx, in the same vein as the liberals, encouraged man to be himself, rather liberation meant overcoming man's selfishness and the acknowledgment of man as a social being. This could only be accomplished by means of a "radical revolution". This revolution had to be a total one which took place simultaneously in man's mind and in empirical reality (Rosenow, 1992). The aim of human emancipation was to free man from alienated forces and restore to man his social nature. An integrated man was one who had overcome his own division between private interest and the community, i. e. an individual who accepted the community as its own interiorized nature. The total revolution should bring man to the realization that the collective, generic character of human life is real life, so that society itself takes on a collective character and coincides with the life of the state (Kolakowski, 1981:126). The essence of this "primitive utopian communism" (Kolakowski, 1981:162) is that man has to be changed and reshaped into a new socialist personality endowed with a socialist consciousness whose personal and social interests are fused together to constitute an organic unity (Rosenow, 1992:44).

Characterization of political education

An empirical analysis of political education, I will argue, has to discuss those obligations and imperatives, which will inspire different educational practices. The obligations of democracy may pull in opposite directions; for instance leading to a focus on commitment and learning by participation, a focus on basic skills or on how to influence human consciousness. These practices will usually coincide with different ideological positions and I will discuss some of these later. First; a conceptual approach to political education also has to examine the aims of education, the arenas of education, what special content and which methods are needed, who political education is intended for, and what effect or result political education may have.

Aims

Political education may be understood as teaching or education with certain aims of creating democratically committed individuals and politically competent citizens.

- An aim expressed in general terms which applies to almost all education is to act on the human being to increase the capacities of thinking and acting, i.e. create rational individuals.
- A second aim is to raise the consciousness of humans, or expressed in Marxist terms, to change the consciousness of the oppressed masses who are the victims of false consciousness. This aim is usually implied when talking about empowerment, emancipation, liberation, or development of critical individuals.
- A third aim is the transmission of knowledge, information and facts required to participate in political life, i.e. provide for informed and knowable individuals.
- Political education has further been propagated as a means of nation and state building, especially in new societies, in order to produce patriotic individuals. This aim has sometimes confused political education with indoctrination and ideologically biased education.
- Political education may even be propagated in order to counteract state power and hegemonic forces. Thomas Jefferson, the celebrated president and pioneer of American democracy, stressed for instance the importance of an educated citizenry in order to prevent the abuses of government (Elias & Merriam, 1984:18). We may also regard counter-cultural and counter-hegemonic activities of some subcultures, social movements, and voluntary associations as political education with oppositional aims.

Content

While the necessity and legitimacy of giving some kind of civic education is relatively non-controversial, its content is much disputed. A much-discussed question is whether political education is content specific. For many educators this means teaching a specific curriculum, mainly social and political studies, which serves to promote liberal and democratic virtues. Nevertheless, some would deny that a special political content is needed, rather they argue for a good general education. The answer to the question of what kind of content is most preferable depends on the aims of the education; information and knowledge, attitudes, action, or participation. Preferences according to different views will broadly go in the direction of a general and liberal content, a practical and technical syllabus, or an ideological and value-based content.

Methods and arenas

An important question for educators is which methods and ways of learning will most effectively promote the aims of education. The methods and arenas of learning[22] will also be influenced by whether one prefers a theoretical or practical way of learning or whether the education aims at understanding or action (Entwistle, 1981:235). The school is an important arena. Founders of participatory or progressive schools, such as Heinrich Pestalozzi, Robert Owen (in New Harmony), John Dewey, and Myles Horton (Highlander Folk Schools) have regarded schools as laboratories for experiential learning of democracy (Elias & Merriam, 1984, ch. III; Levin, 1990:170).

Other spokesmen for a participatory way of learning have valued the community as a laboratory for political education, arguing that empowerment and political education will be acquired through participation and actions (Courtney, 1994:473). This view places minor importance on schools as mediators of political literacy, and an informal way of learning is emphasized. Citizenship consists of an informal component, claims Ichilov (1990:13), being shaped rather than intentionally transmitted and learned. Other important arenas for political education are voluntary associations, trade unions, factory councils, cooperatives, and political parties. These arenas are especially efficient in the transmission of ideologically biased or partisan political education. In many countries partisan education is a domain of voluntary associations per se, and most educators will probably agree with Entwistle that such education should not be supported by public finance. Marx himself took the voluntary participation of adults in controversial topics to be axiomatic and assumed that partisan truths should not be taught in schools. Lenin reached a similar conclusion about the inappropriateness of using schools for political indoctrination (Entwistle, 1981:250).[23]

Even the workplace has been regarded as an important arena for political education. The Italian communist Antonio Gramsci maintained for instance that adult education should take place within the industrial context itself (Entwistle,

---

[22] Arenas in this context are learning environments or "social fields", a concept prefered by the German pedagogue, Hermann Giesecke, in his *Didaktik* from 1968 (Tønnessen, 1992:257).

[23] A dissident Marxist and social radical was George Counts who during the depression in the USA in the 30s proposed the use of schools as a means of indoctrination about the evils of capitalism, and believed that school education could lead the nation to socialism (Elias & Merriam, 1984:142).

1981:250; Armstrong, 1988:257). Contemporary adult educators have favoured the possibilities of building political efficacy through workplace democracy (Levin, 1990:164). Pat White frankly states that: "Political education will have to encompass some preparation for workplace democracy". Her statement is founded on a moral reasoning: "political education in a democracy must flow from and be interconnected with moral education", she says, "and it must question the economic system and even educate "against industry in its present form" (White, 1979).[24] Arguments for extended workplace democracy will find empirical support for the proposition that worker participation is associated with a higher level of political participation (Levin, 1990: 164 – 65). Extension of workplace democracy – understood as workers' influence or even workers' management - may accordingly have positive effects on citizenship and political democracy.

Clientele

The obligations of democracy are that political education should be for everyone. It may be argued that everyone has an ability to learn some kind of political literacy if the teaching is adjusted to the level of the learner. Adult education has especially been committed to the disadvantaged and underprivileged, hence political education should be directed at these groups. It is a fact, however, that the participation in adult education of underprivileged groups and the politically ignorant has been relatively low. Provisions in adult education have mostly attracted the middle classes, the 'socially effective' or the 'earnest minority'.[25] Political educators have therefore argued in favour of educating political leaders who under certain circumstances can lead the masses forward (Entwistle, 1996:185). Gramsci meant that innovation had to go "through the mediation of an elite" (Gramsci, 1971:334) and saw the main purpose of workers' education to be educating what he called "organic intellectuals". This socialist view may interestingly be compared to the philanthropic belief that educating the masses from above will most effectively be conveyed through mediators. Henceforth education should foremost address teachers or other trusted persons from the lower classes who are able to spread knowledge, values, and enlightenment to the populace (Tøsse, 1997:63 – 65).

---

[24] In the beginning of the 60s some German educators equated political education with moral education (Tønnessen, 1992:52).

[25] The "socially effective" was used by G. Thompson in 1945, the "earnest minority" by R. Hoggart in 1957. See Steele, 1997:18.

Most educators (and I think Gramsci would have been among them) will probably agree with Entwistle (1996:186) when he says that:

> "if there must be adult education for political leadership, this requires that there must be political education for those who are followers – the 'ordinary' citizens to whom politics is not a major interest or preoccupation. The conclusion is that political education ought to include everyone in a democracy".

Effects

The effects or results of education will have to be related to aims. Desired effects of political education are increased participation, commitment, and engagement. Education may affect both the individual and the whole society and be measured as greater social harmony or radical social change. It is important, however, to be aware of the fact that intentions and effects of education may be contradictory – as demonstrated by the breakdown of communist education. Education may be neutral in intention and non-neutral in effects and vice versa.

Positions and approaches

In the theory and practice of political education we may distinguish different positions and approaches. Four of them will be focused on here.

The liberal position

Liberal education holds a dominant position in schooling as well as in adult education. Strong advocates of the liberal tradition often give the impression that liberal education is the only way to true education: "liberal adult education is not a species of education, it is education", says R. W. K. Paterson (1979:38). Civic education is for many synonymous with teaching which is intended to promote liberal values. The liberal position, dating back to Plato (Entwistle, 1989:116), is to seek knowledge for its own sake and always be committed to the truth. Liberal education is determined in scope and content by knowledge itself and concerned with the development of mind, i.e. to increase the ability to think effectively, to communicate thought, to make relevant judgements, and to discriminate among values (Hirst, 1973:91, 99). These aims require a general content and the liberal educator consequently refuses any specific political education and defends non-political study and liberal education as the best political schooling. He or she will only be committed to knowledge, understanding, and insights in whatever social direction these may happen to point (Paterson, 1979:258). Liberal education then believes in the neutrality of aims and effects which is claimed in theories of liberalism. The latter form of neutrality is perhaps impracticable, as Rawls argue (Rawls, 1993:190ff), but liberal educators will emphatically maintain that civic education must have a neutral aim and just be concerned with producing competent citizens (Coleman, 1998). In a multicultural and multireligious society, devoted liberals may even question whether the state is justified in teaching certain political values or world views if these conflict with other belief systems (Brighouse, 1998).

The community approach

Liberal education is primarily concerned with individual self-empowerment. The community educational approach, on the other hand, aims at empowering the collective (community, class, people or "folk"). More specifically, community education is understood as education of adults in disadvantaged communities and attempts to enrich community life through joint attacks on economic and social problems within the community itself (Entwistle, 1989). Community education includes the non-formal and informal way of learning and intends to make the experiences and problems of the human being as the basis of the educational content. In this way, it may be said to act on the micro level, focusing on learning democracy through participation in the local community arena.

The radical and Marxist criticism

Even if liberal education "reflects a hegemonic cognition" (Courtney, 1994) it has been attacked because of its aims, content, and methods. The main objection of radical critics is that the aim of traditional political education is to integrate and dominate people into one solidified cultural movement, and to preserve the consensus in society. It coincides with social control education (Cowburn, 1986) and the concept of political socialization. In terms of aims, liberal education is stripped of the aim of social change; in terms of content and effects, liberal education is seen to ill serve the worker by making him or her passive (Courtney, 1994).

From a Marxist perspective, ideas, beliefs, and practices serve the interests of the ruling class, "education simply produces a particular consciousness, one suited to the capitalist mode of production" (Harris, 1979:144). Marxists will then dismiss the school curriculum as ideological in consisting of a partial, distorted, or even a false account of reality (Entwistle, 1996:182), i.e. it injects false consciousness. "It is much like living under the influence of a perception-altering drug", says Harris (1979:109) and he goes on to claim that "education is the manipulation of consciousness" (p. 141). If indeed this is true, the mind may also be swayed in a socialist direction by education. Although this notion of the omnipotence of education is criticized as non-Marxist – and in fact opposed by Marx himself (Small, 1983) – it has notwithstanding motivated the rejection of the liberal humanistic tradition and legitimized political education as the indoctrination of certain values and doctrines.

Some of the most prominent socialists have, however, argued that liberal education also has a potential for radical social change. Lenin, who was a strong advocate for political education and propaganda in order to gain support for communist policy, did not demand a radical new education, rather he urged young communists to master the vast store of human knowledge (Lilge, 1977). The Italian communist Antonio Gramsci also favoured a disinterested humanistic education, at least for children, and subscribed to the liberal belief that academic knowledge and the study of liberal culture was the best political education (Entwistle, 1996:184). The achievement of working-class hegemony required not only industrial militancy and political agitation, he said, but political education of a broadly intellectual and cultural character (Partington, 1981). This does not mean that Gramsci dissociated himself from propaganda and indoctrination, and there is no doubt he wished to infuse education with a revolutionary purpose. It was precisely for this reason that he made it an imperative for the working class to produce 'organic' intellectuals and leaders capable of leading the workers; hence they needed the very best in thinking and ideas (Courtney, 1994:471).

The position of Freire

The influential Brazilian educator Paulo Freire is close to the Marxist view, claiming that the most important aim of education is to develop critical consciousness of the oppressed masses as capitalism has victimized them by leading them to acquire false consciousness (Freire, 1973). But he did not believe that this could be counteracted by ideologically biased education from above. Working in poor countries Freire saw literacy as an underpinning of emancipation and empowerment, an avenue towards "conscientization" (Entwistle, 1989). His educational program has five main features:

- A change of content towards a culturally realistic vocabulary, in other words a fundamental emphasis on language. The same applies to the political literacy approach. Entwistle has also compared Freire's attempt to cultivate cultural and political awareness through literacy education with Grundtvigs's notion of the educational potency of the "living word" (Entwistle, 1981:241).
- A change of methods; dialogue as opposed to the traditional "banking pedagogy" (Freire, 1972).
- Acting on the micro and community level. The community is the source of knowledge (Hamilton, 1992:19).
- The seminal potential of learners' experiences. The daily empirical experiences are the point of departure for the awakening of political consciousness (Entwistle, 1981).
- The importance of participation. Freire maintained that an authentic education for democracy could take place only through participation in democratic activities. The Brazilian people, he wrote, "could be helped to learn democracy through the exercise of democracy; for that knowledge, above all others, can only be assimilated experientially" (Freire, 1972).

Freire maintained that all education is political and the goal of the popular education he undertook in Latin America in the 60s was to transform society by starting with the individual (Hamilton, 1992:19). In accordance with this program, educators have to organize their education in a democratic way, only using methods which correspond with their aims and emphasize learning through participation.

Dimensions

An attempt to clarify the concept of political education in terms of aims, content, methods, arenas, clientele, and effects seems hardly to converge into a single definition. There is no consensus of what content most effectively will promote this education or what effect is most desirable. There is disagreement as to whether the aim is to increase the general capacities of thinking and acting of individuals or whether the emphasis should be on developing critical consciousness. The first will point in the direction of a general content, the second to an ideological and a more value-based content. Within the political literacy approach knowledge has a value as a tool or instrument for acting on political arenas. The emphasis here is on a practical and technical content. Political education may take place on almost every educational arena or social field, the workplace included, and in a formal, non-formal and informal way.

Although a definition in terms of aims, content, effects, or methods seems futile, any empirical analysis of political education cannot avoid discussing these aspects of educational practice. They will not, however, suffice separately for an understanding of the concept of political education; it might be argued that they are strongly interrelated. Neither do I think an analysis of political education within the perspective of clarifying aims, content and so on will be quite exhaustive. More conceptual tools may be necessary and an additional approach will be to look at different dimensions and corresponding forms of education. According to Judith Gillespie (1981) four dimensions are distinguished:

Value dimension

Political education has a value dimension which corresponds with indoctrination of a value-based and ideological content. It is concerned with commitment, loyalty, nation building, and national as well as transnational understanding and responsibilities.

Indoctrination is, however, a horrifying concept to educators. Defined as "a systematic attempt to persuade learners of the validity of a belief system or position" (Boggs, 1991:53), its practice should be scrupulously avoided. Nevertheless, indoctrination is not easily separated from either educational practice nor from its normative use. Analyzed as a method, content, aim, or result, Neiman (1989) has questioned the possibility of finding a criterion of indoctrination since a definition presupposes that education entirely produces rational autonomy and has no hidden, biased, or contradictory effects. The practice of indoctrination has rather to be analyzed contextually, and must be understood and clarified in its historical context.

Information dimension

Political education has an information dimension which corresponds to an emphasis on the transmission of basic skills, knowledge, information, and facts required for participating in political life. The focus will be on a practical and technical content and factual knowledge that is necessary for being politically literate, i. e. this dimension implies an instrumental attitude to political education.

Inquiry dimension

Political education has an inquiry dimension that corresponds with a development of intellectual skills and public judgement. Political and social decisions virtually always involve two kinds of judgement; value judgement and technical judgement (Paterson, 1979:262). This dimension is the most important one for the liberal position and puts the focus of education on conceptual and theoretical understanding rather than mere transmission and absorption of factual knowledge or development of technical skills (Elias & Merriam, 1984:27).

Participation dimension

Finally, political education also implies a participation dimension, which corresponds with an emphasis on civic obligations and community responsibility. A participatory educational approach often involves students and adults in social actions in the community and requires action knowledge.[26] It coincides with the community approach and will be found in political-literacy programs with the intention of creating the possibility to learn from experiences. The participatory dimension is also often stressed in radical and ideological political education.

A conclusion so far is that there "is a diverse and vast array of possible approaches to mapping political education" (Gillespie, 1981:8). The concept seems to have no common core and it is obviously used in different ways by researchers, educators and authorities. The reason is clear: The concept of political education and other related teachings are themselves value-based and ideological, and imply moral assumptions. Hence, they are not politically, neutral and the different aims and ideologies of the implementers will determine educational practice. Underlying every program of increasing political or civic competence is a political ideology (Weissberg, 1981:129). From a liberal and Western perspective these concepts derive especially from a commitment to democracy. In this sense we have to agree with Freire that all education is political. But to acknowledge an ideological underpinning, a hidden message in education, and a political aspect of all institutions, is not the same as surrendering the liberal ideals of personal and scientific independence and autonomy. As Dearden (1980) points out; scientific thinking is by nature governed by autonomous criteria (truth and so on) derived from the nature of

---

[26] "Action knowledge" is used by Giesecke as one of the required forms of knowledge in political education (Tønnessen, 1992).

the subject matter and not from any political authority. Truth, says Dearden, is independent of will.

Is there any difference between political and civic/citizenship education?

The last question to be discussed is whether there is any difference of meaning between all the concepts in use; political education, education for citizenship, civic education and so on. As some of those concepts also add democracy to their meaning – for instance 'education democratic citizenship' - the first condition of any attempt to clarify these distinctions will be to clarify what we mean by democracy. Broadly speaking there are two models of democracy. In its first set of meaning, democracy may be understood as a political system focusing on rules in political life, procedural values and what is right. In the second set of meaning, democracy is also conceived as a form of life. In this meaning the terms 'education for democratic citizenship', 'civic education' and so on focus on personal and cultural identity and involve the promotion of what is good rather than what is right. For this second and broader meaning of democracy we should rather use the term 'cultural education', only in its first meaning 'education for democratic citizenship' will it be very close in its concerns and reference points to the term 'political education' (Richardson, 1992).

But how close? How do researchers and educators perceive these concepts? In his book *Education for Citizen Action* (1975) Fred M. Newman defines 'political competence' as the ability to exert influence in public affairs (Weissberg, 1981:130). Remy and Turner use the term 'citizenship competence' with an identical meaning but specifically mention the ability to communicate "effectively with group leaders" (1979, quoted in Weissberg, 1981:131). Barber (1984) defines 'civic education' as the education of judgment, which leads to rational choice. In his definition of 'adult civic education' Boggs (1991:51) also includes value judgments and communicative competence:

> "...the purposeful and systematic effort to develop in adults the skills and dispositions to function effectively as citizens in their communities as well as in the larger world. The purpose is to both develop understanding and judgment about public issues and to contribute to guided and informed decisions and actions through deliberation, public talk, and dialogue".

These purposes, especially the development of critical judgment, are also strongly emphasized in the Nordic tradition of democratic education.[27]

The Council of Europe defines 'citizenship education' as:

> "all the educational practices and courses whose purpose is the passing on and assimilation of the rules of individual and social life ... and the reflection on the role of these rules for school life" (quoted by Tibbits, 1997:313).

When extended to adult education or outside school education, the definitions often add the aim of empowerment, as for example Gus John in the definition he gave at a seminar on Citizenship Participation, arranged by the Council of Europe in Norway, 1998. He attached the aim of empowerment to the development of social skills and reciprocal respect of democratic rights:

> "Education for democratic citizenship presupposes the empowerment of people through the development of the social skills and competence to take control of their own lives and to function as responsible social citizens, demanding and safeguarding their own rights and having due regard to and respect for the rights of others" (John, 1998).

Other definitions of 'political education' and related concepts (White, 1979; Gillespie, 1981) add little to the ones cited above. The literature on the subject matter reveals virtually no differences between civic, citizenship, and political education, which appear to be used interchangeably. All this education appears to comprise a value, information and inquiry dimension and presupposes some kind of content, aim and effect. Some educators also emphasize the importance of free public talk and transmission of values, social skills and political competence through dialogue as an educational method. No one suggests limiting political education to special arenas and clientele. But in the broader meaning of democracy prevailing in the Nordic countries, many claim that democratic and political competence is learned through experience, i.e. by living and participating in democratic organized activities.

---

[27] See for instance working papers from the ongoing Danish research project Adult education, popular enlightenment and democracy (Voksenuddannelse, folkeoplysning og demokrati) published by Forskningscenter for Voksenuddannelse, Danmarks lærerhøjskole.

These concepts nevertheless appear to convey different connotations and particular emphasis and focus when it comes to the aim and content of education. In a narrow meaning political education has been interpreted as the teaching of politics. The political education movement was itself to some extent a product of dissatisfaction with political teaching (Porter, 1981:183). Entwistle (1989:117) claims that the conception of education for citizenship is associated with the liberal position and adds: "Citizenship implies a satisfaction with the political and social status quo". And it is probably an empirical fact that education for citizenship and political literacy has focused primarily on how the existing political system works, not on social change. Does civic education have no aim of social change while political education strives to make the individual an agent of political and social change? I think this demarcation is a bit difficult to defend. Even if liberal education spokesmen such as R. W. K. Paterson will "repudiate social change as an educational aim" (1973), other educational philosophers such as Dewey and Lindeman strongly advocate that a democratic society is committed to change (Elias & Merriam, 1984:50). Recommendations for educational programs in England for instance have also encouraged considerations of alternative political systems and the possibilities of political change. The emphasis in studies, the programs say, should be on issues and problems rather than institutions or procedures (Brennan, 1981:56). It may even be argued that education and change are dynamically interrelated, "without education there can be no change and without change there can be no education" (Korsgaard, 1997:22). Or as Gus John (1998) put it: "Education for democratic citizenship is fundamentally a dialectical process ... that places individuals in a new relationship with themselves as actors, agents in the struggle for change."

The argument will, however, hinge on what we mean by change. By change Dewey obviously meant growth and development which he stated as the aim of all education. If the educational aim on the contrary is revolutionary change - to implement a new economic and social system and extirpate the ruling powers - it would seem rather odd to put such efforts under the heading of civic or citizenship education. They obviously might be called political education, which then encompasses counter cultural and educational work in whatever direction this may happen to point (to rephrase Paterson, 1979:258). Hence we have introduced a difference. The concept of political education does not need to be committed to democracy, as citizenship education usually is understood. Political education may have the aim of promoting any kind of ideology or value and may be applied for instance to historical analysis of nazi education, workers' education as well as to the educational efforts of the Communist Party in pre-communist China (Foley, 1993). A corollary will be that all 'civic education', 'education for citizenship' and so on may be called political education while not every kind of political education aims at citizenship. In our Western societies citizenship is committed to the ideal of democracy – which also has a cultural dimension focusing on personal and cultural identities and these aspects are not always and in every sense political.

References

Armstrong, P. F. (1988). L'ordine Nuovo: The legacy of Antonio Gramsci and the education of adults. *International Journal of Lifelong Education*, vol. 7, no. 4.

Barber, B. (1979). *Strong Democracy*. Berkely: University of California Press.

Boggs, D. L. (1991). Civic education: An adult education imperative. *Adult Education Quarterly,* vol 42, no. 1.

Brennan, T. (1981). *Political Education and Democracy.* Cambridge University Press.

Brighouse, H. (1998). Civic Education and Liberal Legitimacy. *Ethics,* vol. 108, no. 4.

Coleman, J. (1998). Civic Pedagogies and Liberal-Democratic Curricula. *Ethics* vol. 108, no. 4.

Courtney, S. (1994). Adult education and the modern nation-state: Reflections on "Social Commitment and Adult Education". *International Journal of Lifelong Education,* vol. 13, no. 6.

Cowburn, W. (1986). *Class, Ideology and Community Education.* London: Croom Helm.

Dearden, R. F. (1980). Education and Politics. *Journal of Philosophy of Education,* vol. 14, no 2.

Dewey, J. (1916). *Democracy and Education*. New York: Macmillian.

Elias, J. L. & Merriam, S. (1984*). Philosophical Foundations of Adult Education.* Malabar: Krieger Publishing Company.

Entwistle, H. (1981). The Political Education of Adults. I D. Heater and J. A. Gillespie (ed). *Political Education in Flux*. London: SAGE Publications.

Entwistle, H. Political education (1989). In C. J. Titmus (ed*.) Lifelong Education for Adults. An International Handbook.* Pergamon Press.

Foley, G. (1993). A 'democratic moment': Political education in the Chinese liberation struggle. *International Journal of Lifelong Education*, vol. 12, no 4.

Freire, P. (1972). *Pedagogy of the Oppressed*. Penguin Books.

Freire, P. (1973). *Education for Critical Consciousness*. New York: The Seabury Press.

Freire, P. (1974). Education: Domestication or liberation. In Lister, J. (ed*.) Deschooling*. Cambridge: University Press.

Gillespie, J. A. (1981). Introduction. In D. Heater and J. A. Gillespie. *Political Education in Flux*. London: SAGE Publications.

Gramsci, A. (1971). *Selections from the Prison Books*. London: Lawrence and Wishart.

Hamilton. E. (1992). *Adult Education for Community Development*. New York: Greenwood Press.

Harris, K. (1979). *Education and Knowledge: The Structural Misrepresentation of Reality*. London: Routledge and Kegan Paul.

Hirst, P. (1973). Liberal education and the nature of knowledge. In R. S. Peters. *The Philosophy of Education*. Oxford University Press.

Hoggart, R. (1958). *The Uses of Literacy*. Harmondsworth: Penguin Books.

Ichilov, O. (1990). *Political Socialization, Citizenship Education, and Democracy*. Teachers College, Columbia University.

John, Gus (1998). *Citizenship Participation: New Skills and Capacities*. Paper presented at Council of Europe seminar on Citizenship Participation, 22. – 24. October in Lillehammer, Norway.

Kolakowski, L. (1982). *Main Currents of Marxism*. Oxford University Press.

Korsgaard, Ove (1997). Internationalization and Globalization. *Adult Education and Development,* no. 49.

Levin, H. M. (1990). Political Socialization for Workplace Democracy. In O. Ichilov. *Political Socialization, Citizenship Education, and Democracy.* New York and London: Teachers College Press, Columbia University.

Lilge, F. (1977). Lenin and the Politics of Education. In J. Karabel and A. H. Halsey. *Power and Ideology in Education.* New York: Oxford University Press.

Neiman, A. M. (1989). Indoctrination: A contextualist approach. *Educational Philosophy and Theory,* vol. 21, no 1.

Partington, G. (1981) Gramsci and Education. *Educational Philosophy & Theory,* no 1.

Paterson, R. W. K. (1979). *Values, Education and the Adult.* London: Routledge & Kegan Paul.

Porter, A. (1981). Political Literacy. In D. Heater and J. A. Gillespie. *Political Education in Flux.* London: SAGE Publications.

Rawls, J. (1993). *Political Liberalism.* New York: Columbia University Press.

Richardson, R. (1992). Identities and Justice: Themes and concerns in education for citizenship. *Journal of Moral Education,* vol. 21, no. 3.

Rosenhow, E. (1992) Bourgeois or Citoyen? The Democratic Concept of Man. *Educational Philosophy & Theory,* vol. 24, no. 1.

Simon, B. (1985). *Does Education Matter?* London: Lawrence and Wishart.

Steele, T. (1997). *Cultural Studies 1945 – 65. Cultural Politics, Adult Education and the English Question.* London;: Lawrence & Wishart.

Torres, C. A. (1996). Adult education for Development. In A. C. Tuijnman (ed). *International Encyclopedia of Adult Education and Training.* Pergamon.

Tønnessen, Rolf Th. (1992). *Demokratisk dannelse i tysk perspektiv. 20 års diskusjon om Hermann Gieseckes syn på den politiske oppdragelsen.* (Democratic education in a German perspective. Twenty years of discussion on Hermann Gieseckes' view on political education.) Oslo: Universitetsforlaget.

Tøsse, S. (1997). *Kunnskap, danning og opplysning.* (Knowledge, education and enlightenment.) Trondheim: NVI.

Vain, K. (1992). Human Rights, Political Education and Democratic Values. *Educational Philosophy and Theory,* vol. 24, no. 1.

Weinstein, M. (1991). Critical Thinking and Education for Democracy. *Educational Philosophy and Theory,* vol. 23, no 2.

Weissberg, R. (1981). The Politics of Political Competence Education. In D. Heater and J. A. Gillespie. *Political Education in Flux.* London: SAGE Publications.

White, Pat (1979). Workplace Democracy and Political Education. *Journal of Philosophy of Education,* vol. 13.

Contributors

Per-Erik Ellström
PhD, professor in education at the Departement of Education and Psychology (IPP), chairman and director at the Centre for Studies of Humans, Technology and Organization (CMTO), University of Linköping, S-581 83 Linköping, Sweden.
Main field of research: Qualification requirements and work-based learning, HRD and learning organizations, problem solving and learning in work groups, strategies and processes of organizational change and development. Ongoing Research Projects: Long-term effects of work-based education and training in SME's, Occupational Identities, Work and Learning in the Health Care Services, Change Processes and Strategies in the Implementation of Process Oriented Production in Industrial Settings, Continuous Improvements and Process Innovation.
Phone: +46 13 28 44 31; Fax: + 46 13 28 44 35; E-mail: perel@ipp.liu.se

Bernt Gustavsson
PhD, Docent in education at the Departement of Education and Psychology (IPP), University of Linköping, S-581 83 Linköping, Sweden, professor II at Lillehammer College (Høgskolen i Lillehammer), Norway. Address: Högbygatan 18, 60380, Norrköping, Sweden.
Main field of research: The history of ideas, lifelong learning, history of education and popular education in Sweden and South Africa.
Phone: 013-282136; Fax: 013-282145; E-mail: bergu@ipp.liu.se

Steen Høyrup
Master in Psychology, Associate Professor at the Royal Danish School of Educational Studies, Emdrupvej 101, DK-2400 Copenhagen NV.
Main field of research: Learning and Organizational Development.
Phone: +45 39 69 66 33; Fax: +45 39 69 74 74; E-mail: Steen_H@dlh.dk

Ove Korsgaard
PhD, Associate Professor at the Royal Danish School of Educational Studies, Emdrupvej 101, DK-2400 Copenhagen NV, Denmark.
Main field of research: Adult Education, Democracy, Globalization
Phone: +45 39 69 66 33; Fax: +45 39 36 74 74; E-mail: ove@dlh.dk

Paula Kyrö
PhD (Educ) and PhD (econ), Docent in entrepreneurship education, Jyväskylä University and the faculty of education, Helsinki Universities, Professor in entrepreneurship, the faculty of economics, Jyväskylä University, Kirkkotie 37, FIN-04310 Tuusula, Finland.
Main field of research: Entrepreneurship, postmodern transition, entrepreneurship education, entrepreneurship and sustainable development, women entrepreneurship and professions and professional services.
Phone: 358-9-2733551; Fax: 358-9-2757897; E-mail: paula.kyro@dlc.fi

Erika Löfström
M.Ed., PhD student, researcher at the University of Helsinki, Vantaa Institute for continuing Education, Helsinki, Finland.
Main field of research: Human resources management, apprenticeship training, cognitive style.
Löfström is autumn 1999 working full time in the United States with her PhD.
Address in USA: 1280 South Alhambra Cr. 2305, Coral Gables, FI 33146.
Phone: 1-786-268 1258; E-mail: tlofstro@students.miami.edu

Arild Mikkelsen
Project manager in the Norwegian Adult Education Association (VOFO) and working with a project in connection with the adult learning reform in Norway. He is former head of the Norwegian Folk High School Association and member of the Nordic Folk High School council. His educational background is music, philosophy and Nordic literature.
Address: Stevning 20, 3320 Vestfossen, Norway.

Maarit Pitkänen
Master of Social Science, Service Manager, Electronic Business Services, Harmajankatu 3 B 29, 00180 Helsinki, Finland.
Main field of research: Organizational (culture) studies.
Phone: + 358 9 567 3318; Fax: +358 9 567 3145;
E-mail: maarit.pitkanen@icl.fi

Petri Salo
LicEd, Assistant in Adult Education, Åbo Akademi University, Finland
Main field of research: Liberal adult education in Finland and Nordic countries, organizational learning and schools as organizations.
Phone: +358-6-32 47 412; Fax: +358-6-32 47 403; E-mail: psalo@abo.fi

Juha Suoranta
PhD, Professor of Education at the University of Lapland, Finland.
Main field of research: Methodology of human sciences and theoretical questions of adult education.
Phone: +358-3-2660266; Fax: +358-3-2660266;
E-mail: juha.suoranta@urova.fi

Jukka Tuomisto
PhD, professor in adult education at University of Tampere, P.O. Box 607, FIN-33101 Tampere, Finland. He is member of the steering group of ESREA, the Finnish Adult Education Research Society and involved in the national development project of Finnish liberal adult education.
Main field of research: Adult education in working life, adult students in higher education and theory and history of adult education.
Phone: 358-03-2156095; Fax: 358-03-2157502; E-mail: anjutu@uta.fi

Sigvart Tøsse
Cand. phil. (history), associate professor at Norwegian Institute of Adult Education, Nedre Bakklandet 60, N-71014, Trondheim, Norway.
Main field of research: History of adult and popular education, workers' education and adult education policy.
Phone: +47 73 99 08 53; Fax: + 47 73 99 08 50; E-mail: sigvart.tosse@nvi.no